LIFE OF GOETHE.

LIFE

OF

JOHANN WOLFGANG GOETHE

BY

JAMES SIME

KENNIKAT PRESS
Port Washington, N. Y./London

LIFE OF JOHANN WOLFGANG GOETHE

First published in 1883
Reissued in 1972 by Kennikat Press
Library of Congress Catalog Card No: 77-160782
ISBN 0-8046-1614-0

Manufactured by Taylor Publishing Company   Dallas, Texas

CONTENTS.

———◆◆———

CHAPTER I.

CHAPTER II.

CHAPTER III.

CHAPTER IV.

CHAPTER V.

CHAPTER VI.

CHAPTER VII.

CHAPTER VIII.

CHAPTER IX.

CHAPTER X.

NOTE.

—◆—

THE best sources of information about Goethe are his own works and letters. It would be ungrateful, however, not to acknowledge the service which has been rendered to students of his character and genius by various German scholars. Among the writers whose researches I myself have found helpful, I may name Heinrich Düntzer, Herman Grimm, Karl Biedermann, and Erich Schmidt.

J. S.

LIFE OF GOETHE.

CHAPTER I.

JOHANN WOLFGANG GOETHE was born at Frankfort-on-the-Main on the 28th of August, 1749.

His grandfather, Frederick George Goethe, who sprang from a family belonging to the working class, and was himself a tailor, made his way, in the latter part of the seventeenth century, from Artern on the Unstrut to Frankfort. Here he settled, and, early in the eighteenth century, took as his second wife a handsome widow of thirty-seven, Cornelia Schelhorn, the owner of the inn, "Zum Weidenhof." Frederick George is said to have been a man of pleasant manners and a skilful musician. His second wife was in every way worthy of him, an energetic and kindly woman, with all the gracious qualities evoked in generous natures by prosperous circumstances. They had three children, of whom Johann Kaspar, Goethe's father, born on the 27th of July, 1710, was the youngest.

Johann Kaspar Goethe was sent to school at Coburg, where he heard of the death of his father and only brother. Afterwards he studied law at the Universities of Leipsic and Giessen, and took the degree of Doctor of Jurisprudence. He practised for some time at the imperial chamber at Wetzlar, and then travelled in Italy. Finally he returned for life to Frankfort, where he lived with his mother in a house she had bought in a street called the Hirschgraben. His mother's fortune made it unnecessary for him to accept any fixed appointment, and during the reign of the Emperor Charles VII. he attained a position of considerable dignity by securing the title of an imperial councillor (Rath). He was somewhat pedantic, capable of vehement outbursts of anger, but honest to the core ; and he combined with a sound knowledge of law, a real love for art and literature. He had given much attention to Italian, and was an ardent student of Tasso, his favourite author.

On the 20th of July, 1748, when he had reached the mature age of thirty-eight, he married Catharine Elizabeth, the daughter of Johann Wolfgang Textor, the chief magistrate of Frankfort, grandson of an eminent jurist of the same name who received the office of first syndic of Frankfort in 1690. Catharine Elizabeth was only seventeen years old at the time of her marriage. She was bright and pretty, fond of music and poetry, and remarkable for her power of inventing the kind of tales that fascinate children. Her new home was in the house of her mother-in-law, with whom she was able to live on the most friendly terms. Her husband loved her warmly, and, although she made no profession of romantic attachment to him, she responded to his feeling with sincere affection and respect.

Goethe was their first-born child, and after him came his sister Cornelia, who was fifteen months younger than he. There were several other children, but none of them lived long enough to influence Goethe. To his sister he was devoted, and, as years passed on, there were few things in the world so precious to him as her love and sympathy. She was of a thoughtful temper, loyal and affectionate, and in her brother's youth no one had half so much control over his restless and fiery spirit.

Like his mother, Goethe had brown hair and dark, lustrous eyes, the penetrating glance of which, from childhood to old age, never failed to impress those who met him. He was a vigorous and active child, and at an early age gave evidence of a highly imaginative temperament. His grandmother's house consisted of two old houses joined in one, and the thought of its dark passages and corners often filled him with dismay in the night-time, and made sleep impossible. From a room in the back part of the house, where the children were allowed to play in the summer, there was a charming view, with wide gardens in the foreground, and, beyond the city walls, a fertile valley stretching towards Höchst. Goethe himself has described how he used to sit at the window of this room and watch thunderstorms and sunsets, and how the spectacle of nature, combined with the sight of children playing in the gardens and the sound of balls rolling and ninepins falling, often filled him with a feeling of solitude and a vague sense of longing.

The children spent much time with their old grandmother, who loved them dearly. On the Christmas before her death she delighted them by providing a puppet-show setting forth the story of David and Goliath. This puppet-show made a great impression on Goethe, and afterwards he was permitted to find out the secret of its working and to dress up the figures for new representations.

When Goethe was in his sixth year, his grandmother died; and soon afterwards his father carried out a plan he had long cherished, that of rebuilding the house to suit the wants of his family. The work was carefully superintended by the elder Goethe himself, and the house was transformed to a handsome, convenient dwelling, with well-lighted rooms tastefully decorated. He had an excellent collection of books, and they were now properly arranged in his study. His pictures, most of which were by Frankfort artists, were also brought together in a room fitted up for their reception, and the walls of the passages were adorned with maps and engravings. He had brought back with him from Italy many fine specimens of Venetian glass, bronzes, ancient weapons, and other artistic objects. In the new house these treasures were put in cabinets, and no pains were spared to secure that they should be effectively displayed. A room on the top floor, looking out upon the street, was set apart for Goethe.

During the latter part of the time when the house was being rebuilt, Goethe and his sister were sent to live with relatives, and it was during this period that he began to have some knowledge of his native place. As the town in which the Emperors were elected and crowned, Frank-

fort held a position of high honour among the free
imperial cities of Germany. Within its old walls and
gates it still retained, in its architecture and customs,
many traces of the troubled, picturesque life of the
Middle Ages. Even in childhood Goethe delighted to
walk about its quaint streets, and afterwards he made
himself familiar with every link that was known to con-
nect the town with the events of past times. He liked
to see the gilt weathercock on the bridge of the Main
gleam in the sunshine, and to watch the arrival of boats
laden with goods for the market. On market-days there
was always a bustling, lively crowd on the space around
St. Bartholomew's church, and Goethe found it a source
of endless amusement to push his way among the throng
and to note the odd humours of buyers and sellers. In
later years he had an especially vivid recollection of the
spring and autumn fairs, when the town was full of
visitors, and serious business was associated with all sorts
of noisy popular entertainments.

The council-house, then, as now, called the Römer,
had a strong fascination for Goethe. He never forgot
his first visit to the imperial hall in this famous building,
where the emperors dined on the occasion of the coronation festival. Here he saw half-length portraits of
many of the old emperors, and what he heard about
them set his imagination at work to call up graphic pictures of the great events of Germany's stirring, splendid
history. He examined with keen interest the Golden
Bull of Charles IV., and this naturally led to his visiting
the grave of Günther of Schwarzburg, Charles's rival, in
St. Bartholomew's church. Growing up amid such

scenes and associations, Goethe naturally acquired a decided taste for the study of history and antiquities.

Much thought and care were devoted by the elder Goethe to the education of his children. He himself took the work in hand, but for special subjects he called in the aid of private tutors, from whom Goethe and his sister received lessons in association with the children of some neighbouring families. Goethe's father and tutors were astonished at the ease and rapidity with which he mastered the most difficult tasks. Nothing seemed to be too hard for him. It was often, however, in childhood, a relief to escape from his father's rigid discipline, and to enjoy a little talk with his mother, who was always ready to feed his imagination with tales of adventure in fairyland. He contrived, too, to read a good many books —among others, German translations of "Robinson Crusoe," and Lord Anson's "Voyage Round the World." Among his father's books were the works of Fleming, Canitz, Haller, Hagedorn, Gellert, and other German poets, and he found much in them to awaken and foster his love of poetry. Klopstock's "Messiah," the first three cantos of which had been published the year before Goethe's birth, was not thought to be good enough for a place in a select library, for Goethe's father, like many another critic of the eighteenth century, held that rhyme was essential to poetry. Goethe and his sister were delighted to receive secretly the loan of a copy from an old friend of the family who regularly read it, as a pious exercise, once a year in Passion Week. They learned by heart some of the most striking passages, which they often recited to one another. One Saturday evening, when their father was being shaved, they sat behind the stove, and repeated in whispers a wild dialogue between Satan and Adramelech. Cornelia became more and more excited as the dialogue went on, and at last, forgetting her father's presence, she uttered in a loud voice the words, "How am I crushed!" The barber was so startled that the contents of the lather-basin were dashed on the Herr Rath's breast. Strict inquiry was made, and Klopstock's epic was at once ignominiously banished from the house.

Of greater influence on Goethe than any of the more formal works he read at this early stage, were the badly-printed folk-books, which he bought in great numbers. They suggested to him many a strange and romantic tale, and it may have been one of them that introduced him for the first time to the story of Faust.

About the time of his seventh birthday, the civilized world was stirred to its depths by the outbreak of the Seven Years' War. Goethe's maternal grandfather, Textor, sided with the Austrians. His father, on the contrary, was an enthusiastic adherent of Frederick the Great, and would not listen to a word against his hero. This difference of opinion led to serious family quarrels, and Goethe, who, of course, took his father's view, was astonished to hear the language used about the great Prussian king by his grandfather, for whose sayings he had always had unbounded reverence. Rather more than two years after the beginning of the struggle, the people of Frankfort were made to realize with painful vividness some of the more disagreeable aspects of war, for by an act of treachery on the part of the civic authorities, the French, the allies of Austria, were allowed

to station a body of troops in the city. To the horror of
Goethe's father, he was told that he would have to receive
into his house a French officer called Thorane, for whom
it was necessary to provide good quarters. In vain the
indignant councillor protested against this arrangement.
The decision was final, and he had nothing for it but to
give up to the intruder the rooms on his first floor, which
he had decorated and furnished at so great a cost, and
with so much care. Count Thorane was a cultivated
gentleman, with all the courtesy of his class; and he was
anxious to cause as little annoyance as possible to his
host. He could not, however, prevent the coming and
going of many persons who had to see him on military
business, and the result was that the most orderly household in Frankfort was thrown into dire confusion. This
was aggravated by the fact that Thorane, who was much
pleased with some of Dr. Goethe's pictures, invited various
artists to the house to execute a large number of commissions for him, and Goethe's room had to be given up
to them as a studio. Frau Goethe, whose cheerfulness
was not easily quenched, made the best of unpleasant
circumstances, and tried to mitigate some of the incon-
veniences of her position by learning French; but her
husband was irreconcilable, and became more and more
embittered against the French in general, and against
Count Thorane in particular.

Goethe, although sorry for his father, was delighted
on his own account by the new turn of affairs. The
monotony of life was broken by a great excitement, and
every day brought with it some fresh and unexpected
pleasure. His frankness, brightness, and geniality won

Thorane's heart, and they became excellent friends.
Goethe was especially interested in the proceedings of
the artists who had taken possession of his room, and
with their aid he began with zeal to practise drawing, in
which he acquired considerable skill. He learned to
speak French fluently, and was charmed to have an
opportunity of hearing French plays, many of which
were now acted in Frankfort. Thus, at a most impression-
able age, he passed under a wholly new and stimulating
set of influences, and it was the recollection of these
influences that made it impossible for him, long afterwards, to join the majority of his countrymen in vague
and indiscriminate abuse of the great French people, to
whose civilization he owed some of the best impulses
of his life.

In 1761, after more than two years of almost constant
irritation, Goethe's father got rid of his troublesome
guest, but the French did not quit Frankfort until the
end of the following year, when the Seven Years' War
was about to close. Goethe's father celebrated the conclusion of the Treaty of Hubertusburg by presenting his
wife with a gold snuff-box, on the lid of which, set with
diamonds, was an allegorical picture of Peace. Goethe
had often to go to the goldsmith to urge him to make
progress with this piece of work, and he took full advantage of the chance of having long talks with a craftsman
who had much to tell him that was full of interest.
This was thoroughly characteristic of Goethe, who found
almost any subject attractive when he could get information about it from some one practically familiar with its
details.

Lessons had been sadly interrupted during Thorane's stay in the house. After his departure they were resumed with double vigour. Goethe had already a good knowledge of Latin, Italian, and French, and some knowledge of Greek. To these languages he now added English, and he also made considerable progress in Hebrew. For the exercises he had to write for his father he often chose the form of dialogue; and one elaborate exercise he designed as a series of letters, the various correspondents writing from different parts of the world and in different languages. It was in connection with these letters that he began the study of Hebrew, as one of the correspondents wrote in Jew-German, for a thorough mastery of which a knowledge of Hebrew seemed to be necessary.

In his twelfth year Goethe was confirmed. Even before this time he had had, in a childlike way, many a serious reflection about the supreme subjects of human thought and interest. The earthquake at Lisbon in 1755 had led him, child as he was, to ask how such disasters were to be reconciled with God's infinite love. Shortly afterwards he took to his room a red lacquered music-stand, which he used as an altar, piling on it various objects representative of nature, and placing on the top a fine porcelain dish, in which were some pastiles that emitted, in burning, a sweet fragrance. These pastiles he lighted by means of a burning-glass which caught the rays of the rising sun; and so he sought to express reverence for aspects of the Divine essence which, he thought, were not sufficiently recognized in the ordinary religious services. He was a great reader of the Bible, and was especially attracted by the early chapters of the Book of Genesis, which transported him into an ideal world full of grave and strangely picturesque figures. The tales of this part of the Bible acquired for him, of course, fresh significance and beauty, when he was able to read them in the original Hebrew.

In 1764, when Joseph II. was elected and crowned King of the Romans, Goethe had an opportunity of seeing, at Frankfort, some of the splendid ceremonies connected with a coronation. He was then in his fifteenth year, and already he was passing through an experience which had opened a new world of joy and longing. He had fallen violently in love with a pretty girl called Gretchen, who was two or three years older than himself, and did not belong to his own class of society. On the evening of coronation-day, when the town was brilliantly illuminated, they strolled through the streets together, and on parting from him at the door of her mother's house she honoured him for the first and last time by kissing his forehead.

Goethe had made the acquaintance of Gretchen through some comrades of his, with whom he would certainly not have been allowed to consort had his father known of his association with them. One of them, with Goethe's aid, secured employment in a public office ; and in this position he was guilty of some offence which exposed him to severe penalties. When the affair came to be investigated, Goethe's name was mentioned in connection with it, and to his dismay, on the morning after the coronation, he had to make a clean breast of all that had been going on, including the story of his love for Gretchen. This put an end to his first romance, and for days he remained in his room, overwhelmed with grief and shame.

His, however, was too elastic a spirit to be long incapable of rebound. A friend in whom he had confidence came to his help, and with this wise counsellor he turned from thoughts of love to the study of ancient philosophy. The two together took long walks in the surrounding country, where Goethe drew sketches of scenery, which had the good fortune to please his father. And so his wounded pride and affection were quickly healed, although the incident had made so deep an impression upon him that half a century afterwards, when he wrote his autobiography, he could not recall it without a certain bitterness.

By this time Goethe's father had decided that he was to enter the legal profession, and had begun to prepare him for future work by reading with him various law books. Goethe offered no objection, but he was already dimly conscious of some of the impulses which were to bring him to the front rank among the great names of the world ; and he resolved that during his university career his energies should be devoted not to law, but to literature. In 1765, shortly after his sixteenth birthday, he said farewell to his family, and started for Leipsic, where he was to study.

He was now a handsome and vigorous youth, with comparatively wide intellectual interests ; and his good looks, high spirits, and lively talk made him a universal favourite. His childhood and boyhood had been as happy as those of any great poet have ever been, and all the circumstances of his life had been favourable to natural mental growth. He had given ample evidence of quick perception, eager curiosity, and a remarkable power of penetrating to the secrets of subjects that interested him ; and his great creative faculty had at least made preliminary efforts to reveal itself. Even in early boyhood he had so large a share of his mother's gift of story-telling that groups of companions delighted to gather around him to hear his entrancing tales. He had also written many verses, the themes chosen for two of his more ambitious productions being Christ's descent into hell and the story of Joseph and his brethren. Just before he quitted Frankfort he almost completed " Belshazzar," a tragedy written in imitation of Klopstock's "Solomon." In composing this tragedy he was stimulated by a wish for the approval of some unknown beauty, whose sway over him had succeeded that of Gretchen. Never, perhaps, was there a poet more susceptible than Goethe to feminine influence, and the thorough comprehension of this deeply significant fact is essential to any true appreciation of his genius and character.

CHAPTER II.

AT Leipsic Goethe settled in two pleasant rooms in a house near the university, overlooking a court through which people were constantly passing to and fro. He happened to arrive at the time of the autumn fair, and he had an opportunity of seeing many foreigners whose appearance interested him. Leipsic, which, as the centre of the book trade, was relatively more important then than it is now, made a most agreeable impression on him, and he looked forward with delight to the years he was to spend there. He was especially charmed with the free and pleasant manners of the people, which presented a striking contrast to the somewhat formal and rigid rules of social intercourse at Frankfort.

A few days after his arrival he was admitted a student at the university. He was obliged to join some law classes, but he also heard lectures by Ernesti on Cicero's "De Oratore," and by Gellert on rhetoric and German literature. At first he attended his classes with exemplary diligence, but he soon made up his mind that they could not be of much service to him. The professors of law had little to say that he had not already learned at Frankfort, or that he could not readily master without

their aid.   Gellert's lectures seemed to him pedantic and
commonplace, and even Ernesti, a scholar of high distinction, did not help him to penetrate to the spirit, or to
feel more deeply the charm, of Latin literature.   During
the whole time of his residence at Leipsic he continued,
of course, to attend the university, but his relation to it
was more nominal than real, and exercised little influence
on his intellectual development.

He was received in a friendly way by Böhme, the professor of history, whose wife, a cultivated and pleasant
woman, liked to talk with him.   She offended him a
little, however, by laughing rather too freely at some of
his Frankfort modes of expression, and by disparaging
the writings of his favourite poets.   Every day he dined
at the house of one of the medical professors, where he
met chiefly students of medicine and natural science.
When the novelty of his position at Leipsic wore off, he
began to miss the pleasures to which he had been accustomed at home, and, above all, he longed for some
friend to whom he might confide his inmost thoughts and
aspirations.   Gradually he fell into a dejected and for-
lorn state of mind, and so keenly did he suffer that in the
spring of 1766 one of his Frankfort friends, Horn, who
came to study law at Leipsic, could not find in him
a trace of his old liveliness and good humour.   The
presence of Horn, who remained for some years one
of his most intimate comrades, did much to revive
Goethe ; and soon afterwards the process was completed by another friend, Schlosser, who took Leipsic
on his way from Frankfort to Treptow, where he was
to act as private secretary to Duke Frederick Eugene of

Würtemberg. Schlosser, who ultimately married Goethe's
sister, was a man of vigorous and independent character,
somewhat stern in manner, but essentially kind and sym-
pathetic, and he quickly succeeded in restoring Goethe
to all his former cheerfulness and self-confidence.

Schlosser put up at the house of a vintner called
Schönkopf, who, his wife having come from Frankfort,
always welcomed visitors from her native place.   Goethe
was so much pleased with the company at Schönkopf's
table that he determined to dine and sup there daily, and
this resolution he acted upon during the remainder of his
time at Leipsic.   Schönkopf had a pretty, coquettish
daughter, Anne Catharine, and, needless to say, she no
sooner saw the susceptible Goethe than she made a
conquest of him.   Like Gretchen, she was his senior by
two or three years, but that, he felt, only made her the
more worthy to be loved.   Annette, as he usually called
her, accepted his devotion with pleasure, and was sincerely fond of him; but, having a shrewd suspicion
that she could never be his wife, she gave him no
marks of favour that she was not equally ready to give
to other admirers.   Many a time Goethe was thrown into
a fever of jealousy by her kindness to his rivals, but she
had only to smile on him to exalt him to a heaven of
enchantment and delight.   Upon the whole, his relation
to Annette, which went on for years, seems to have
brought him more misery than happiness.   It was impossible for him to claim her love as exclusively his
own, yet he could not bear to think of it as a treasure
that might pass into the possession of some one else.

He had not the good fortune to meet at Schönkopf's

any one who could be of vital intellectual service to him, but he enjoyed familiar intercourse there with many agreeable people—among others, Behrisch, a scholar who acted as tutor to a young Count. Goethe liked him as a loyal friend and intelligent critic. Gradually Goethe extended the circle of his acquaintance, until he had almost as many friends in Leipsic as in Frankfort. It was especially pleasant for him to visit at the house of Breitkopf, a printer, who had two sons about Goethe's own age, one of them an admirable pianist and clever composer. Goethe was often present at musical parties in this hospitable house, and he himself took part in them, for he could not only sing, but play the flute. Afterwards he acquired some skill as a player on the cello.

By far the most eminent man with whom Goethe came into direct contact at Leipsic was Oeser, the director of the academy of drawing, painting, and architecture. Oeser was a native of Presburg, in Hungary, and had all the energy and enthusiasm so often possessed by his countrymen. His own artistic achievements were not of permanent importance, but he had an extraordinary power of exciting interest in art, and of stimulating to high effort all who came within the range of his influence. Long before this time, at Dresden, he had been intimate with Winckelmann, who had learned from him the doctrine that the qualities which give enduring charm to works of art are simplicity and calm. Goethe, who had a longing to master artistic methods, became his pupil, and he never forgot that he owed to this wise and genial teacher the germs of his most fertile ideas about art, and the first effective encouragement he had

ever received to do full justice to his own powers. At
Oeser's home in Leipsic, and at his house in the
country, he was always a welcome guest. Oeser
had two daughters, one of whom was married. The
other, Frederika, about Goethe's age, lived with her
father. Handsome, sprightly, and clever, she became
one of Goethe's best friends.

Oeser was not his only instructor in art. Stock, the
engraver, lived with his wife and two young daughters
(afterwards the wives of intimate friends of Schiller), at
the top of the house in which was the home of the
Breitkopfs. From him Goethe took lessons in etching, at
which he worked with great enthusiasm and perseverance.
He also amused himself by carving boards for book-
binding. There seemed to be hardly any limit to
Goethe's activity. Even he could not hope to excel in
all his many undertakings, but in everything he tried he
gained enough of insight to enable him to distinguish
sharply between good products and bad, and to appre-
ciate and enjoy those wrought on true and enduring
principles.

All good pictures accessible at Leipsic he made himself
familiar with, and in 1767 he took a short holiday
for the purpose of studying the picture gallery at
Dresden. He stayed at the house of a worthy,
humorous shoemaker, with whom he had much friendly
talk. At the gallery the pictures of all the great schools
interested him, but those of the Dutch school, from their
fidelity to fact, appealed to him most strongly. Day after
day he resumed his study of the masterpieces he loved,
and so deeply did they influence his mind that, when he

returned to the actual world, he could not help seeing things as if they formed part of a picture. His friend, the shoemaker, seemed to him like a figure that had stepped out of a canvas by Ostade.

Powerfully as Goethe was fascinated by art, literature remained the real mistress of his affections. The Latin classics he read with growing pleasure, but he also constantly felt around him for new impressions and impulses, and by a kind of happy instinct he was led to the writers who were best fitted to nourish his genius. At Frankfort he had read Wieland's translation of Shakespeare, and now Dodd's "Beauties of Shakespeare" came in his way. His study of this selection did not yet disclose to him Shakespeare's real significance, but it prepared him for deeper comprehension at a later stage. Wieland, having left far behind him the Pietistic fervour with which he began his career, was now tricking out in all sorts of forms, both of verse and prose, his easy Epicurean philosophy. Goethe read eagerly every one of his later writings ; and, so far as style was concerned, he learned much from Wieland, who, with all his faults, knew how to present his ideas, such as they were, with lightness, delicacy, and grace. In 1766 Lessing's "Laocoon" was published, and Goethe has described with what delight he and all the younger men of his day received this masterpiece of a great and serious spirit. As if by a flash of lightning, it revealed the broad lines of distinction that separate the arts from one another. It showed, too, that it is only by keeping strictly within its natural limits that each art can attain its highest objects, and that of all the arts poetry is necessarily the deepest, the

most far-reaching, and the grandest. All this was new
to Goethe, and spurred him to think out for himself the
fundamental problems of critical thought. Not less
enthusiastically did he welcome Lessing's " Minna von
Barnhelm," which still remains the most exquisitely
finished play of its kind in the German language. It
impressed Goethe, because Lessing, unlike other German
dramatists, had selected his motives directly from the
life of his own time, but had conceived them with an
imaginative force and subtlety that made them perennially
interesting. In the spring of 1768 Lessing spent a
month at Leipsic, but unfortunately Goethe did not see
him. About the same time Goethe was shocked by the
tidings of the murder of Winckelmann, for whom he had
the deepest reverence, and whose writings on ancient art
must be counted among the most potent of the influences
that enriched and developed his intellectual life.

From the beginning of his residence at Leipsic Goethe
was a constant attendant at the play, and he sometimes
acted—always with considerable success in comic parts—
in private theatricals at Schönkopf's house. Thinking so
much as he did about the drama, he could not but try
his hand at dramatic composition ; and in the winter of
1767-68 he produced two plays—" Die Laune des Ver-
liebten" (" The Lover's Humour ") and " Die Mitschuldigen" (" The Accomplices "). The former is essentially
a presentation of his own experiences in his relation to
Annette Schönkopf. The latter contains an unpleasant
picture of facts akin to those which were forced on
his attention at Frankfort in connection with the incident that led to his separation from Gretchen. Both

are written in rhymed alexandrines, and show that Goethe, like most of his contemporaries, still looked for his models to the French classic drama.

At Leipsic Goethe was known as a young poet much given to biting satire. In his autobiography he gives an account of a visit he paid to Gottsched, who had at one time been in some sort the literary dictator of Germany ; and from this amusing narrative we can see with what mocking humour he waited on the old pedant, who found it so hard to realize that his day was past. Clodius, who prided himself on his dignified style, Goethe enraged by producing parodies of his pompous verses. At heart, however, Goethe was too generous to care a great deal about work of this sort ; what he liked infinitely better was to give direct poetical expression to his own thoughts and feelings. This he did at Leipsic in a considerable number of lyrics, some of which were set to music by the elder of the two brothers Breitkopf. These lyrics lack the perfect rhythm, the indefinable charm of his later work in this kind, but they have vigour and a certain grace, and show at least something of what ultimately became his astonishing mastery of apt and picturesque diction.

In 1767 Goethe introduced to the Schönkopfs a friend of his, Kanne, a Saxon advocate. Kanne was charmed with Annette, and Goethe was thrown into the depths of despair by seeing that she was not disinclined to respond to his advances. In vain he tried to still his agitation by flying to nature for consolation, and by writing satirical verses on the untrustworthiness of young maidens. He became thoroughly wretched, and his unhappiness, associated with various other causes, among which he himself afterwards included some irregularities in his mode of living, made him seriously ill. At last, one night in July, 1768, he had a severe attack of hemorrhage, and a doctor had to be hastily summoned. For some time it was feared that he might be suffering from disease of the lungs During his illness he was tenderly cared for by his friends, and when convalescent he was cheered by the bright, wholesome talk of his friend Frederika Oeser, who, when he visited her in the country, laughed at the ridiculous notion of a young fellow thinking of dying of consumption. The process of recovery, however, was slow, and finally he decided to return to Frankfort, and to set off on his birthday, a day which he regarded as a lucky one for the beginning of important undertakings. On the 26th of August he called at the Schönkopfs, and bade adieu to Annette, who agreed to let him write to her once a month. It filled him with sadness to think that this might be their last parting, and on the following evening—he was to leave next day—he could not resist the impulse to go once more to her home. He saw the lamps burning, and hovered about the door-steps, but had not courage to enter.

At Frankfort the invalid was received with infinite sympathy by his mother and sister; and his father, seeing him pale and thin, concealed the bitterness he felt at the disappointment of the hopes that had been so warmly cherished. Goethe was happy to be at home again, amused himself by drawing and etching, sent little gifts to Annette, and wrote in good spirits to Oeser and some of his other Leipsic friends. But before the end of the year he was again prostrated, suffering this time from a different malady. His agonies were frightful, and his mother, driven to despair, took the Bible, and resolved to be guided by the first words on which her eyes should happen to light. Fortunately she came upon the words of Jeremiah, "Thou shalt yet plant vines upon the mountains of Samaria." She was at once relieved, and ever afterwards this was her favourite "promise." Goethe quickly recovered, but early in 1769 he had another illness, by which he was confined to his room for a month. It became evident that his constitution had been rudely shaken, and that only time and vigilance could restore him to full strength.

Among his mother's most intimate friends was a certain Fräulein von Klettenberg, who belonged to the church of the Moravian Brethren. With a noble purity and dignity of character she combined a deep mystic piety. During Goethe's illness Fräulein von Klettenberg, who showed him great kindness, gained a strong influence over his mind; and there are many indications that at this time he thought often and most earnestly on the profoundest questions relating to human life and destiny. He even worked out for himself an elaborate theological system, in which a place was found for the Trinity, Lucifer, the Elohim, Man, and for the Fall and Redemption. These speculations were connected with the study of alchemy, to which he was led by his doctor, who, like Fräulein von Klettenberg, was one of the Moravian Brethren. Goethe not only made many experiments in accordance with the rules of alchemy, but read all the old books on this subject on which he could lay his hands.

In the autumn of 1769 he received from Leipsic a

volume consisting of some of his lyrics, with the melodies to which they had been set by Breitkopf. The volume gave him little pleasure, for he was now occupied with other interests. He was more deeply stirred by a glimpse he had of General Paoli, who passed through Frankfort on his way to England. Paoli's noble and romantic career had kindled Goethe's enthusiasm, as it had kindled that of Boswell, and, mainly through Boswell, that of Johnson and all the other members of the brilliant literary set with whom the Corsican hero was soon to be on pleasant terms in London.

Meanwhile, Goethe had learned that Annette had been betrothed to his friend Kanne. He was struck with dismay by this intelligence, and could not help hoping that something might at the last moment prevent their union, and that he himself might be able to take his friend's place. Annette, however, did not share his wishes, and by and by both the joy and the torment that had so often been evoked by his love for her were for ever dispelled by her marriage.

Goethe's father was most anxious that his study of law should as soon as possible be resumed. Accordingly, in April, 1770, having spent about a year and a half at home, he started for Strasburg, where, for various reasons, it had been decided that he should take his degree. He was now in his twenty-first year. He had not been restored to perfect health, but he was strong enough for the work that lay before him, and he had no longer any fear that he had been stricken by a mortal malady.

Alsace, although a province of the French monarchy,

was still essentially German. Not until the time of the Revolution did the people cease to think of themselves as Germans, and begin to be proud of their connection with France. In entering Strasburg, therefore, Goethe had no feeling that he had come to a foreign town. It contained, indeed, a strong French element, but the mass of the inhabitants spoke his own language, and retained the manners and customs of their Teutonic forefathers. As in Frankfort, so in Strasburg, there were many survivals of former ages, and these at once attracted Goethe's attention. He was of course especially impressed by the minster, by far the most splendid building he had yet seen. He studied it closely within and without, and became an enthusiastic admirer of Gothic architecture, which he had always heard decried. Often, especially at sunset, be mounted the tower to enjoy the wide and varied prospect visible from the top.

He had pleasant rooms in the old Fish-market, and dined at a table where he met many students whom he liked. At the head of this table sat Salzmann, a middle-aged actuary, a man of fine taste and cultivated intellect. He took to Goethe at once, discussed philosophy with him, and was able to give him useful hints as to the studies for his degree. Among the men whose acquaintance Goethe made at this table was Jung Stilling, who, at the age of thirty, trusting in Providence for the means of living, came to Strasburg to study medicine. Stilling always retained a vivid recollection of the first occasion on which he saw Goethe. He and his friend, Herr Troost, took their seats at the table before any one else had arrived. By and by the guests came in, and among them one who entered briskly, a young man "with large bright eyes, splendid forehead, and handsome figure." This was Goethe. "'That must be an excellent man," whispered Stilling's companion. Stilling was of the same opinion, but thought he might give them some trouble, as he seemed "a wild young fellow"—an impression which was afterwards found to be mistaken. On a later occasion one of the guests tried to raise a laugh at Stilling's expense. He was sternly rebuked by Goethe, who now sought Stilling's friendship, and became warmly attached to him.

Introduced by Salzmann, Goethe was welcomed at many houses in Strasburg. He was still to some extent under the influence of the mystical ideas which had taken so strong a hold of him during his illness, but they did not prevent him from enjoying to the full the social pleasures within his reach. Of dancing he never could have enough, for it had all the charm of novelty, dancing-parties being at that time unknown in Frankfort and Leipsic.

He had the pleasure of seeing the young princess, Marie Antoinette, as she passed through Strasburg on her way to Paris; and in June he enjoyed with a fellow-student, Weyland, a ride across the Vosges mountains to Saarbrück. On the way back, at Niederbronn, he was surprised and delighted to find fragments of ancient pillars, sculptured altars with inscriptions, and other Roman remains. These objects, lying about in farm-yards, called up before his active imagination a vivid picture of the widespread civilization of Rome.

Goethe had not forgotten that he had come to Strasburg to take a degree, and soon after his twenty-first birthday, having attended the proper courses of lectures at the university, he passed the necessary examinations. He then began to prepare his dissertation, choosing as his subject the doctrine that it is the duty of the State to establish a form of religion to which all citizens shall be obliged to conform. During the remainder of his stay he gave attention at the university chiefly to chemistry, anatomy, and other sciences. He also devoted a good deal of time to the study of the antiquities of Alsace, his interest in which had been thoroughly aroused by the treasures at Niederbronn.

One day in September, 1770, Goethe accidentally met a young clergyman on the steps at the entrance to the inn, " Zum Geist." He knew that Herder had just arrived at Strasburg, and could not doubt that this was he. Goethe greeted him respectfully, and Herder, attracted, like every one else, by the young student's manly bearing and frank expression, responded pleasantly, and entered into conversation with him. This led to an intimate friendship, and the consequences were of the highest importance for Goethe. Herder was at this time only twenty-six years of age—that is, five years older than Goethe—but his character had been matured by hard discipline, and he had already made a good reputation as the author of two collections of essays full of energy and fresh thought. He was not one of the great creative spirits of the world, but he had an intellect of restless activity, endowed with an extraordinary faculty for the apprehension of far-reaching ideas. He had enthusiasm, too, and a noble, inspiring conception of the part that properly belongs to the individual mind in its relations to the world at large.

Having given up his work as preacher and school-master at Riga, he had spent some time in France; and he had lately accepted the office of tutor to the young Prince of Holstein-Eutin, whom he had accompanied to Strasburg. This appointment he now resigned, having received a promise (which was soon fulfilled) of the chief pastorate at Bückeburg, where he proposed to marry Caroline Flachsland, to whom he had become engaged at Darmstadt. He remained, however, rather more than six months at Strasburg, mainly that he might be cured of an affection of the eyes, by which he was much troubled. A painful operation was performed, and recovery was less rapid than he expected. Goethe was one of his most constant visitors, and missed no opportunity of serving him. Even when his health was good, it was rather difficult for Herder's friends to hit it off with him, for with all his excellent qualities he was irritable, and apt to be somewhat arrogant; and his temper was not improved by his sufferings. But Goethe, who recognized the essential greatness of his character, was not discouraged by his occasional rudeness, and was well rewarded for the fidelity with which he waited upon his new friend.

At this time the serious thought of Europe was passing through one of the most momentous revolutions the world has ever seen. Beyond all question the foremost figure in the movement was Rousseau. As a man of letters Rousseau was far inferior to Voltaire, and his knowledge was neither so wide nor so exact as that of Diderot. But his ideas corresponded to the deepest needs of the age, and he had the enthusiasm, the pro-

phetic ardour that commanded for them the attention
of mankind. The civilization of France he had shaken
to its centre, and in Germany the impression he had
produced had been hardly less profound. Everywhere
generous minds were filled with discontent with the
world as it actually existed. Everywhere they were re-
volting against forms and conventions, and crying out for
a return to " nature," for the free growth and expression
of the innate qualities of humanity—qualities which,
when not corrupted by unjust institutions, were, according to Rousseau, always pure and noble.

Herder, who had studied Rousseau closely, had appro-
priated all that was most vital in his teaching, and had
applied his doctrines, not only in the criticism of life, but
in his judgments of literature ; and now he made Goethe
a sharer of the intellectual wealth he had himself acquired. Goethe had already been a reader of Rousseau,
but from this time, as we know from the characteristics
of his early writings, his mind was deeply penetrated by
the spirit of " La Nouvelle Héloïse " and " Émile." Of
still greater importance was the help he obtained in the
comprehension of the full splendour of Shakespeare's
genius. Of all poets, Shakespeare, as Herder taught,
was the one in whom nature had found her truest in-
terpreter; and, returning in earnest to the study of his
dramas, Goethe was impressed, as he had never been
impressed before, by their power and beauty, and felt
more and more strongly that it would be impossible
for him ever to exhaust their meaning. Herder had
also much to say about Swift, Richardson, Fielding,
Sterne, and Goldsmith ; and to a circle of friends, of

whom Goethe was one, he read "The Vicar of Wake-field," the humour, pathos, and idyllic charm of which filled them with delight. Through Herder's influence Goethe began the serious study of Homer; and even from "Hamlet" he did not receive a deeper inspiration than from the "Iliad" and the "Odyssey." Macpher-son's rendering of Ossian had touched the imagination of Herder, and he communicated his enthusiasm for it to Goethe, who perceived in "Fingal" and "The Songs of Selma" many a trace of a great and entrancing primitive literature. From Herder, too, who was familiar with Percy's "Reliques," Goethe first learned that some of the finest manifestations of the poetic impulse are to be found in popular songs and ballads. This revelation gave him exquisite pleasure, and it led to his collecting folk-songs, the directness, freshness, and simplicity of which, but with a new and subtle delicacy, were repro-duced in his own lyrics.

Thanks to the influences under which he was brought by Herder, Goethe, during his residence at Strasburg, experienced a great intellectual awakening. He did not accept any body of doctrines as a complete and final ex-pression of truth. On the contrary, the supreme service done to him by Herder was that in regard to things of the mind he was delivered from subservience to external authority. He now began to look out upon the world with his own eyes, and to test opinions by the free exer-cise of his own judgment. He had met Herder at the very moment when he needed, and was capable of responding to, the stimulus of an original mind at a stage of development more advanced than his own

When he parted from his teacher, it was no longer necessary for him to sit at the feet of a master. He had learned that great achievements were possible only if, like the poets into whose secrets he was penetrating, he brought himself into direct contact with the facts of the world, and trusted absolutely to the inherent impulses and laws of his own intellectual and imaginative powers.

During the period in which he was deriving fresh ideal impulses from Herder, Goethe was drinking deep draughts of the sweetest joys of the actual world. In the autumn of 1770 he rode with his friend Weyland to the pretty Alsatian village, Sesenheim, where Weyland wished to visit Pastor Brion, whose wife was related by marriage to one of his half-sisters. As they approached the quaint old parsonage, standing with its quiet garden in a well-wooded country, Goethe's restless spirit could not but feel the soothing influence of a scene at once so beautiful and so peaceful. Pastor Brion, a most amiable and hospitable clergyman, had four daughters, one of whom was married, while three lived with their parents. There was also a son about eight years old. A simpler, happier family did not exist, and we cannot wonder that Goethe (not, as he afterwards thought, on his first visit, for he then knew nothing of Goldsmith) sometimes compared it to the family of the Vicar of Wakefield. Some whim made him present himself in disguise, but he soon appeared in his real character; and as he was pleasantly received, he at once felt at home. The youngest daughter was not old enough to interest Goethe. The others were Salomea, who was about his own age, and

Frederika, who was in her nineteenth or twentieth year. Frederika had a slender, graceful figure, with rich masses of fair hair, dark-blue eyes, and finely modelled features. She was rather delicate, but had a fresh appearance, due to the sweet, wholesome air of the country. Behind her coy and maidenly manner were hidden possibilities of deep and passionate devotion, and her charm was made all the more alluring by the contrast she presented to her robust and outspoken elder sister.

In his autobiography Goethe gives a matchless description of his relation to this lovely girl. It is impossible to trust the details of the picture, some of which are known to be inaccurate; but there is no reason to doubt that in its main outlines it reproduces faithfully what actually happened. At any rate it is certain that he loved Frederika with all his heart; not as he had loved Gretchen and Annette, for their influence had never gone far below the surface; but with a love full of romance, with a passion that glowed and flamed with ever-increasing intensity. And Frederika—how was it possible for her to resist the young poet's wooing? He had come to her suddenly, like some radiant being out of an unknown world, and in response to his fervour her heart throbbed with love, and pride, and joy.

Immediately after his first visit he wrote to her to say that never had Strasburg seemed to him so empty. Many other letters followed, but unfortunately they were afterwards burned by Frederika's sister. He repeatedly visited Sesenheim, and shortly after Easter, 1771, Frederika came to Strasburg with her mother and sister. While she remained, Goethe and she had some happy hours together; yet somehow she did not seem quite herself in a town; he felt that they were in perfect sympathy only in the country, where they could be all in all to one another, with nature around them reflecting their happiness.

At Whitsuntide he went again to her home, intending to return to his studies after a short visit. But she was not very well, and day after day, week after week passed, and he was still at Sesenheim. During this visit he made himself highly popular in the village, and occupied himself in all sorts of ways, learning how to make basket work, painting the pastor's carriage, and planning the reconstruction of the parsonage. He went on, too, with his study of Homer, and read to Frederika a translation he had made of "The Songs of Selma." And all the time the passion of the lovers grew and struck its roots deeper in their hearts.

At last, when June was far advanced, he was forced to drag himself away, for it was time that he should proceed to his degree, the taking of which had been too long delayed. The university authorities were scandalized by some of the opinions advanced in his dissertation, but admitted his ability, and directed him to take part in a public disputation. The order was obeyed, and he afterwards received a licentiate's degree.

In company with some friends, Goethe now enjoyed a short tour in Upper Alsace. On his return he paid a farewell visit to Sesenheim, and in August he was once more at home in Frankfort.

In the last interview with Frederika nothing was said to indicate that the parting was final. Nevertheless,

Goethe knew that it was so ; and eight years passed before they saw one another again, and then they met simply as old friends. Frederika had never doubted that he proposed to make her his wife, and this had also been assumed by her family. At first the idea of marriage did not occur to Goethe. He thought only of the rapture he felt in her presence, of her sweetness, her grace, and her beauty. When at last he could not avoid reflecting on the consequences of having won a maiden's affections, a prolonged and bitter struggle went on in his mind. That Frederika, if he had been prepared to marry, would have made him truly happy, he loved her too well to question ; and he can hardly have supposed that it would have been very difficult to induce his father to welcome her as a daughter-in-law. But the thought of marriage was repugnant to him. What ! bind himself for life at the very time when he was becoming conscious of his destiny—when it was essential to the unfolding of his genius that his individuality should have free play ! Deeply as he loved Frederika, strongly as he felt the duty he owed her, this consideration gained the day. He must have freedom, let it cost what it might.

Goethe never sought to justify his treatment of Frederika. For many a day he suffered the pang of a wounded conscience. His ultimate decision was right, for he had not reached a stage at which a happy marriage would have been possible ; but he well knew that in a matter of such vast importance he ought not to have created an expectation that, from the nature of the case, was doomed to be disappointed. It can only be said that to a poet of his ardent temperament the power which had cast its spell over him was all but irresistible. Frederika herself, although she seemed to lose all in losing her lover, did not permanently resent the severance of the bond that connected them. She seems to have felt that deep causes had led to their separation. All her life she had a vivid remembrance of the beautiful romantic world in which they had for a while wandered together; and when attempts were made by new wooers to win her hand, her answer is said to have been, "The heart that Goethe has loved cannot belong to another."

His love for Frederika exercised as powerful an influence over him in one direction as contact with Herder had exercised in another. In his meeting with her, and in his parting from her, he had sounded some of the profoundest depths of joy and suffering; and he had passed through a conflict in which his strongest feelings had been arrayed against one another. And in response to the touch of love his genius had sprung into free activity. He had written various lyrics giving utterance to his passion, and to this period also belongs "Heiden-röslein," in which he presented in a new form an old popular song. These perfect lyrics, slight as they are, are the earliest of his achievements in which we find the really characteristic qualities of his poetry. They do not, like his first efforts, bear the stamp of traditional rules, but are the direct expression of his own inward life. For five centuries—from the time when, at mediæval courts, Walther von der Vogelweide had sung his splendid verses—no poetic note of such mingled power and sweetness had been struck in Germany. In these early poems we feel the stirring of the forces of a new spring-time.

They are full of a passionate delight in the beauty of the earth and the sky ; in every line breathing of love they have the accent of sincerity ; and they produce the impression of having flowed without effort from a mind which found the most natural outlet for its feelings in stanzas of noble and flawless melody.

CHAPTER III.

ON his twenty-second birthday (August 28, 1771), the day after his arrival at home, Goethe applied to be admitted as one of the advocates of Frankfort. A few days afterwards he took the oath as an advocate and citizen; and he soon received his first case—an extraordinary one, in which he had to defend a son against a father. Judgment was given in favour of Goethe's client, but both he and the advocate on the other side were rebuked for the bitterness with which they had presented their arguments. In the course of the winter Goethe had only one other case. Law had little interest for him, and he accepted professional work merely to please his father, who was bent on seeing him an eminent pleader.

Of all the studies carried on at this time the one that moved him most profoundly was the study of Shakespeare, and at last he felt that he must find some means of expressing the thoughts and feelings kindled within him by the poet whom he adored. Accordingly he decided that on the 14th of October a Shakespeare festival should be held in his father's house; and it was arranged that there should be a like festival at the same time in Strasburg. The plan was carried out, and Goethe, in language of glowing enthusiasm, poured forth his admiration of the dramas in which, as he said, "the history of the world sweeps on before our eyes on the invisible thread of time."

At Strasburg he had lighted upon the autobiography of Goetz von Berlichingen, the knight with the iron hand, who had played so great a part in the Peasants' War in the sixteenth century. Goetz (born in 1480) was one of the manliest of the warriors who, in the age which formed the border-line between the mediæval and the modern world, fought valiantly for the causes they conceived to be those of justice and freedom. His autobiography is a frank and simple record of his adventures, written with a view to prevent his descendants from misunderstanding him. As Goethe read it, it seems to have flashed upon him that, notwithstanding external differences, there was much inward resemblance between the influences with which Goetz contended and those which in his own day choked up the springs of thought and natural feeling. Goetz had not allowed his spirit to be broken by the tyrannical forces of his period; he had asserted his individuality, and had been loyal to his own loftiest aims. Here, then, was a figure which might be made the medium for the expression of Goethe's own aspirations ; and he forthwith decided that Goetz should be the hero of his first drama.

The execution of the scheme was somewhat delayed ; but, stimulated by his sister Cornelia, to whom all his thoughts and wishes were confided, he set to work early in the winter of 1771, and before the end of the year the

drama in its original form was completed. Its title in this
form was " Geschichte Gottfriedens von Berlichingen mit
der eisernen Hand, dramatisirt " ("History of Gottfried of
Berlichingen with the iron hand, dramatised"). While it
was being written, he read in the evening to his sister the
work done during the day, and he was greatly encouraged
by her warm sympathy. Copies of the play, in manuscript, were despatched to Salzmann and Herder. Salzmann lost no time in congratulating his friend, but Herder's response, to which Goethe looked forward anxiously,
was long postponed.

About this time Goethe made the acquaintance of a
man by whose friendship he laid great store. This was
Merck, paymaster of the forces of Darmstadt, who was
about eight years older than Goethe. He was a tall,
meagre, rather awkward-looking man, somewhat cynical,
but an ardent student of literature, and thoroughly loyal
to his friends. Towards the close of 1771, a bookseller
at Frankfort, asked Merck to edit the " Frankfurter
Gelehrten Anzeigen" (" The Frankfort Learned Notices,"
or "The Frankfort Review," as we might say), a new
literary periodical which was to appear at the beginning
of 1772. Merck accepted the offer, and went to Frankfort to make arrangements with contributors. During
this visit Goethe met him, and they at once became
friends. Goethe joined the staff of the " Gelehrten
Anzeigen," and during the next two years wrote for it a
good many reviews of all kinds of books. The opinions
expressed in these reviews give evidence of a free and
vigorous judgment, and they are set forth in a fresh,
incisive, and picturesque style. It may be safely said

that all great poets are great critics, and in his first efforts at criticism Goethe gave sufficiently clear indications that in the maturity of his powers he would be no exception to the general rule.

He visited Merck several times at Darmstadt, where he became an intimate friend of Herder's betrothed, who often wrote about him to her lover at Bückeburg. On one occasion, when walking to Darmstadt from Frankfort, he was overtaken by a tempest, and had to take refuge in a hut. Here he recited aloud, exactly as the words occurred to him, the " Wanderers Sturmlied " (the "Wanderer's Storm-song "), a series of wild, irregular verses, in which he celebrates the power of Jupiter Pluvius, and apostrophises the Genius that makes the poet's spirit independent of the accidents of time and place. To this period, also, belongs " The Wanderer," a fine poem—suggested, no doubt, by his experiences at Niederbronn—in which a poet converses with a simple young mother in a hut built of stones taken from the ruins of an ancient temple.

It had always been intended that Goethe, as his father had done before him, and as it was the custom of many young advocates still to do, should perfect himself in his profession by practising for some time in connection with the imperial chamber at Wetzlar. Accordingly, he took rooms at Wetzlar, in May, 1772. The work of each advocate at the imperial chamber was exactly what the advocate himself chose to make it, and Goethe chose to make his a mere form. Wetzlar, a little town on the left bank of the Lahn, is situated in a charming country, and he did not feel disposed to burrow among musty law-books when, in bright summer weather, he had a chance of wandering in secluded valleys, and filling his sketch-book with studies of landscape. He also spent a good deal of time in reading Greek poets, taking especial delight in Pindar.

But even the pleasure he found in Pindar and in nature was by and by thrust into the background by a more absorbing passion. The thought of Frederika had often troubled him, but he had so far recovered from the shock of his separation from her that it had become possible for him to be subdued by a new fascination. And the pos-sibility was soon transformed into reality. He had rela-tives at Wetzlar, and having started with some of them one evening for a ball which was to come off at a neigh-bouring village, he stopped the carriage to take up a friend of theirs who was to accompany them. This friend was Charlotte Buff, the daughter of a public official at Wetzlar. She was the second of a family of twelve children, and on her, after the recent death of her mother, had devolved the principal duties of the household. She was nineteen years of age, a beautiful girl with fair hair and blue eyes, remarkable for quick intelligence, and always bright and cheerful in the performance of the most troublesome tasks. Goethe loved her at once, and, with his usual impetuosity, could not help showing how passionately he was devoted to her. Every day he visited her in the afternoon, and delighted to lie at her feet on the grass while the children played around them; and in the evening he was often at the house again, drawn thither by an attraction he was powerless to resist. Charlotte—or Lotte, as she was called—was,

of course, interested in a man who was so different
from all the men she had ever met, and she gave him as
warm and true an affection as a woman càn give to one
who is no more than a friend.   Love she could not
give him, nor did he ask for it, for she had already
virtually pledged her troth.   Her lover was Kestner, the
secretary of the Brunswick Legation.   Kestner, who was
about eight years older than Goethe, was a man of solid
qualities, able and steadfast, devoted to his professional
duties, but with a keen and intelligent interest in literature.   Goethe, before his first meeting with Lotte, had
known him slightly, and soon became sincerely attached
to him, thoroughly appreciating his manly and generous
character.   Kestner saw, of course, the tumult that had
been excited in Goethe's breast, but never either by word
or by look gave the faintest sign of jealousy or of a wish
to hamper Lotte's freedom.

The relation was a most difficult one, and made Goethe
restless and unhappy.   At last the strain became
intolerable, and he resolved to save himself by flight.
On the 10th of September, having dined with Kestner in a
public garden, Goethe spent the evening with the lovers
in Lotte's home ; and, as it happened, the talk became
unusually sombre, Lotte herself giving it a serious turn
by a reference to the invisible world.   On returning to
his rooms he wrote farewell letters, adding next morning
a line for Lotte alone.   " Be ever of cheerful mood, dear
Lotte," he wrote,—"you are happier than a hundred—
only not indifferent !   And I, dear Lotte, am happy that
I read in your eyes that you believe I shall never
change.   Adieu, a thousand times adieu ! "

On the same morning he quitted Wetzlar, haunted by the thought of her, but with the feeling that he was escaping from a grave and imminent peril. At Darm-stadt Goethe had met Frau von Laroche, who had made some reputation as the author of a recently-published romance, " Die Geschichte des Fräulein von Sternheim." She was the wife of a high official at the Electoral Court of Trier, and her home was on the outskirts of a beauti-ful village that nestled at the foot of Ehrenbreitstein. In response, no doubt, to an invitation to visit her, Goethe now made his way slowly down the Lahn towards the Rhine, finding in communion with nature some relief from the depression that had succeeded the excitement of the previous weeks.

During his stay at the house of Frau von Laroche several guests arrived—among them, Merck with his wife and little boy. Goethe thoroughly enjoyed his visit, opening his heart and imagination to all the impressions produced on him by free, joyous intercourse with friends, and by the lovely scenery of the Rhine country. Frau von Laroche, by whom he had not been strongly attracted at Darmstadt, won his confidence and affection ; and he had many a pleasant talk with the eldest of her two daughters, Maximiliane, a girl of about seventeen, whose fine dark eyes and frank, pretty ways might have created for him a new danger but for the power that had so completely subdued him at Wetzlar.

Before the end of September he was back at Frank-fort, and in the course of a few weeks he was again engaged in professional business, to which he continued to give some attention during the whole of the remaining time spent in his father's house. But he was firmly resolved that his real work should be literature, and now so much had happened to deepen his feeling and quicken his imagination that the difficulty was, not how to find something to say, but how to give expression to even a small proportion of the thoughts that pressed upon him for utterance.

At Wetzlar Goethe had received Herder's anxiously expected reply with regard to the "Geschichte Gottfriedens von Berlichingen." It was anything but flattering to the young writer's vanity. Herder had hardly a good word to say for the play, and expressed the opinion that it had been spoiled by his slavish adherence to the manner of Shakespeare. In his answer Goethe acknowledged the justice of the strictures of his extremely candid friend, and announced his intention of completely recasting the work. At Wetzlar, however, he was in no mood to undertake so strenuous a labour, and after his return to Frankfort he was for some time too much occupied otherwise to think of carrying out his purpose. But Merck, who heartily admired the play, urged him to give it its final form ; and early in 1773 Goethe at last took the task in hand. Shutting himself up in his room at the top of the house, he worked at it day after day, becoming more and more absorbed in it as he went on ; and before the winter was fairly over, he finished it. In its new shape the play received the title, "Goetz von Berlichingen mit der eisernen Hand. Ein Schauspiel." ("Goetz von Berlichingen with the Iron Hand. A drama.") It is impossible to compare it with the work as originally written without admiring the high conception of art by which Goethe was controlled in transforming what he had done. In the minutest details he sought for perfection, and entire scenes, in themselves powerful and interesting, were struck out because they did not seem to accord with the scheme as a whole. Long afterwards he taught that it is in "limitation" (*Beschränkung*) that the master reveals himself; and already he had some perception of the vital importance of this great truth.

In working out his conception Goethe did not consider it necessary to adhere strictly to the facts of history. He makes Goetz die immediately after the Peasants' War, whereas in reality he lived nearly forty years afterwards, and distinguished himself in Charles V.'s wars with the French and the Turks. This, however, need not disturb any one in the enjoyment of the play, which is to be judged as a work of art without reference to the actual events which it in part reproduces.

"Goetz" is as far as possible from being a faultless play. Goethe tried to conceive it in the spirit of Shakespeare's historical dramas, but at this early period he had not sufficient mastery of his intellectual resources to be able to give, as Shakespeare gives, unity of design to the representation of a complicated series of incidents. The forces called into exercise have in some instances only an accidental connection with one another; they are not combined so as to produce the impression of a complete and harmonious process of development. Nevertheless, the work is unmistakably a creation of genius. It brings before us in grandly sweeping outlines, and in bold, vivid colours all the leading elements of the national life of Germany in the early part of the sixteenth century. The

characters live and breathe, and their language—fresh,
vigorous, and animated—is that which we should expect to
hear from them in real life. Goetz himself is an admirable
type of a just and fearless warrior. He has not, indeed,
any large conception of the issues towards which his age
is moving, but in the midst of debasing influences he
knows how to maintain the purity of his own impulses,
and how to strike boldly and strongly in defence of ideas
of which he makes himself a champion. Rough in
manner, and a lover of plain speech, he is at heart tender
and humane; and in the most difficult circumstances,
when a character less simple and direct might be liable
to gross misconstruction, there can be no doubt as to the
honesty and dignity of his motives. Men of this noble
mould—frank, unconventional, and true—were never
more needed than in Goethe's own day, and one of the
objects of the play was to suggest that if they were
possible in the sixteenth, they could not be impossible in
the eighteenth century.

A love-story is interwoven with the presentation of
Goetz's activity; and from the point of view of art this
is perhaps the best part of the drama. Weislingen, a
young and brilliant statesman at the corrupt court of
the Bishop of Bamberg, is taken prisoner by Goetz. He
falls in love with the knight's sister, Maria, and his love
is returned. When, however, he goes back to the
Bishop's court, pledged to support no undertaking
against Goetz or his friends, he is overcome by the wiles
of Adelheid, a subtle, cruel, and fascinating woman, who
understands thoroughly the essential weakness of his
character. She professes to love him, and becomes his

wife, and in the end he is poisoned by his servant, who acts as her agent. Weislingen and Adelheid are genuinely dramatic figures, and the character of Maria, simple, affectionate, and loyal, is not less finely conceived. It was Frederika Brion he was thinking of when he depicted Weislingen's love for, and desertion of, Maria. When the play was published, he sent a copy to Salzmann, with a request that it should be forwarded to Sesenheim. "Poor Frederika," he wrote, "will be to some extent consoled when the unfaithful one is poisoned."

The play was printed by Merck, who had started a printing establishment of his own ; and in the summer of 1773 it was published. The enthusiasm it awakened far surpassed Goethe's anticipations. Hitherto the unities of the French classic drama had been rigidly respected in the drama of Germany. Lessing had fought hard to show that they are not essential to a great work of art, but in his own plays he had not cared to violate them. The author of "Goetz" had wholly ignored them, daring to think rather of the vitality of his characters than of the conditions of a well-rounded scheme. To some critics of the older generation the play seemed almost grotesquely extravagant, but the younger men hailed it as a glorious symptom of the uprising of a new and adventurous spirit of liberty. A man of genius, putting aside conventions and artificialities, had gone straight to reality for inspiration, and had uttered a word that delivered them, as they thought, from the necessity of submitting not only to the unities, but to any kind of artistic law. A school of writers

was formed, all of whom looked to Goethe as their chief
Prominent among them was Klinger, a native of Frankfort, the title of one of whose plays, " Sturm und Drang,"
was afterwards accepted as the name of the period in
which it was produced.   Lenz, whom Goethe had known
at Strasburg, and who, after Goethe's departure, had tried
to win the affections of Frederika Brion, was another
member of the group.   These young writers had plenty
of ambition and vigour, but they mistook eccentricity
for originality, sentimentalism for passion, noisy decla-
mation for poetry, and not a shred of interest now
attaches to their productions, except as documents which
throw light on a curious phase of literary history.

After the publication of his play, Goethe became one
of the " lions " of Frankfort, and had to endure the
visits of innumerable strangers who wished to make his
acquaintance.   He acquired confidence in his own
genius, and did not doubt that he would be able to
justify the highest expectations formed as to his future
work.   He was universally liked, for he had all the good
qualities with which he had endowed Goetz, and his
friends found that there was always something exhila-
rating in his frank and brilliant talk.   Yet at this time he
was passing through a period of deep depression.   It
was not connected with any particular misfortune, nor
was it due to love for Lotte, for Kestner and she were
now husband and wife, and Goethe thought of her only
as a friend.   His unhappiness sprang wholly from
spiritual causes.   He had longings which the actual world
seemed to be incapable of satisfying, and the more he
reflected on life, and sought to comprehend its meaning,

the more he was oppressed by the old, old mysteries that have baffled and saddened so many a noble mind. Sometimes the idea of suicide suggested itself, and in his autobiography he has described how he laid a dagger by his bed-side, and before putting out the light tried whether he could not pierce his breast.

In the autumn of 1773, the marriage of Cornelia and Schlosser took place, and they quitted Frankfort, ultimately settling in Emmendingen. This was a severe blow to Goethe, for communion with his sister had been to him a constant source of consolation, and in her absence he was driven in, more than ever, upon himself. A little later in the year he heard with pleasure that he would soon have frequent opportunities of seeing Maximiliane Laroche, who, although still only a young girl, was about to be married to a Frankfort merchant, an Italian called Brentano. The marriage was not a happy one, and proved to be for Goethe a new cause of trouble. Feeling for Maximiliane, both for her own sake and for her mother's (whom he always addressed as " Mamma "), a sincere brotherly affection, he often called upon her, and did what he could to make her life in Frankfort tolerable. Brentano was of a furiously jealous disposition, and, misunderstanding these visits, one day grossly insulted Goethe. Violently agitated, Goethe declined to enter the house again, and, for a long time, saw Maximiliane only when he met her at the play or elsewhere accidentally.

It was always Goethe's habit, when burdened by any feeling, to liberate himself by means of some imaginative effort; and now he felt that the time had come for this mode of relief. He had not to choose a subject, for the plan of a romance had already taken firm possession of his mind. Towards the end of 1772 he had heard of the suicide of Jerusalem, a young secretary of legation at Wetzlar, with whom he had had a slight acquaintance both there and at Leipsic. Jerusalem had loved a married woman, and in a moment of despair had shot himself with a pistol borrowed from Kestner. Goethe, after the first shock of the tidings. was past, decided to give an imaginative presentation of the tale, but in the early part to substitute for Jerusalem's experiences, about which he had only general information, the story of his own love for Lotte. From time to time the execution of the scheme was put off, but when driven by an imperious impulse to give form to the conceptions by which he was haunted, he accomplished his task with almost feverish haste. The work was ended about the beginning of March, 1774, and the greater part of it was written during the preceding month. The figures of the romance stood out before him in sharply-cut outlines, and their story flowed freely from his pen, because in reality it was the story of his own inmost life. He called it "Die Leiden des jungen Werthers" ("The Sufferings of Young Werther").

The work consists of a series of letters written by Werther, and some explanatory statements made by the editor. In his conception of the tale, and in his choice of form, Goethe was deeply indebted both to Richardson and to Rousseau, but especially to Rousseau, the spirit of whose " La Nouvelle Héloïse" breathes in every line of "Werther." " La Nouvelle Héloïse," however, is a book of the past, interesting only to students of literature and of the history of ideas, whereas "Werther" is still alive, and can never wholly lose its freshness.

Werther has many qualities that excite interest and sympathy. He has a deep vein of poetry; Nature appeals to him strongly; he is an enthusiast for the best literature; and he is always generous to the poor and the distressed. But he is incapable of manly decision, and on the slightest provocation he sheds floods of tears, secretly proud of his sensibility as a mark of a superior type of character. When the story opens, he is in a little provincial town, whither he has gone to see about a legacy left to his mother. He is not discontented, for in Homer and Ossian he has the kind of companionship he loves, and in the surrounding country there are exquisite views which he is never tired of admiring and sketching. Suddenly he meets Lotte, and his whole being is transformed. In her are realized all the dreams he has ever had of womanly loveliness and charm. She does not glide into his affections; the moment he sees her—with the children, for whom she cuts the "Abendbrod," clamouring around her—she becomes the supreme object of his devotion. To be in her presence is ecstasy. It is of her that all things in Nature speak to him, and he has no thought, no wish but to serve her. She is already betrothed, but her lover is from home, and as long as he is absent Werther thinks little about him, and lives in a world all glowing with the light reflected from his own happiness.

By and by Albert, the accepted lover, returns, and now for the first time Werther realizes that Lotte is beyond

his reach.   He suffers unspeakable tortures, and knows
not where to turn for relief.   Deep in his heart, before
he ever saw Lotte, the seeds of morbid growths had been
implanted, and in his wretchedness they spring up in
rank luxuriance.   All life becomes hateful to him.   Nowhere can he find anything that does not seem to bear
the mark of some primæval curse.   Even Nature, in
communion with which he has so often felt bounding delight, takes on the aspect of a devouring monster.   Her
forces are pitiless ; and he himself, full of tender com-
passion, cannot move without crushing some helpless
creature under his feet.   Against the very essence of
things he rises in revolt.   Thinking of what life may
mean, he feels that he is standing on the edge of an
abyss, and he looks with horror into its black depths.

At last, yielding to the entreaties of the friend to
whom his letters are addressed, he flies from the scene of
his misery, and, accepting a diplomatic appointment at a
German court, hopes to regain peace of mind by taking
part in the world's work.   But he is slighted in an
assembly of people with whom, as a man of the
middle class, he is not thought fit to associate ; and the
insult so rankles in his mind that he sends in his resignation, and after some months of brooding he cannot
resist the temptation to go back to Lotte.   By this time
she is married; nevertheless, his passion burns more
fiercely than ever, and anguish rends his heart when he
sees her in Albert's possession.   She has always had a
warm regard for Werther.   Now his sufferings arouse her
pity, and in the end she cannot conceal from herself that
she loves him.   But she expostulates with him, and begs

him to leave her, to marry some one who can honourably give herself to him, and to return as a friend. Albert becomes jealous and watchful, and utter shipwreck seems to be the destiny of the newly-formed household. Werther, sick at heart, loathing existence, resolves to bring his agony to a violent end, and after a wild scene, in which Lotte almost loses control of herself, the tragedy closes with his death. The pistol with which he shoots himself he borrows from Albert on the plea that he is about to start on a journey. Lotte takes it from its place, and, having wiped the dust from it, hands it to the messenger with a sad foreboding that some terrible disaster is at hand.

"Werther" is a story of a "mind diseased"; and, judged from this point of view, it stands supreme among the prose writings of the eighteenth century. Goethe himself never wrote, in prose, anything more powerful. Werther's malady was not the malady of an individual only, but of an age. Thoughtful men had outlived their beliefs, their institutions, their customs; all around them was a world touched by the finger of decay. They sought to shake themselves free from the intolerable yoke of the past, but as yet nothing had appeared that could take the place of the old ideas; there was no influence to awaken disinterested enthusiasm, to lead to combined and settled effort for worthy ends. So even the best minds—and perhaps they more than others—felt themselves isolated, and, in the absence of nobler interests, were forced to think much about their own moods, about the ebb and flow of the tides of purely personal feeling. Hence a morbid sensitiveness, an extravagant sentimentalism ; hence, too, a disposition to read the facts of existence in the light of individual experience—a tendency to conclude that, because the hungry " I " was unhappy, therefore the universe was a gigantic blunder and imposture.   In " Werther " Goethe probes this disease to its roots.   It is a profound error to suppose that he intended the hero of the tale to be taken as a complete representation of his own character.   Werther wholly lacked many of the qualities that made Goethe great—his original impulse, his creative energy, his strength of will. But Werther's mood had for a while been Goethe's mood, and it is for this reason that as we read the solitary sentimentalist's letters he seems to start into life, and we learn to know him, back into the inmost recesses of his spirit, more intimately than if he stood before us in actual flesh and blood.   It was a phase—a passing but most striking phase—of his own many-sided nature that Goethe was disclosing, and he could not but write of it in words of searching power.   And yet all was not put down exactly as it came into his mind.   With fine, instinctive art he selected those elements of the tale, and those only, that were fitted to reveal his essential purpose, and to prepare the way for the ultimate issue. When we close the book, and look back, we feel that no other issue was possible.   Were Werther a man of good sense and resolute will, he could easily, no doubt, disentangle himself, but with his character, and in his circumstances, ruin is inevitable.

Lotte, as she is presented in the first part of "Werther," is one of the most exquisite of Goethe's creations.   Her youth and beauty, the frankness of her manner, the joyous spirit in which she devotes herself to others, and the warm poetic feeling combined in her nature with a sound and ready judgment, are brought out with so delicate a grace, yet in such clear outlines, that we do not wonder at the influence she exerts over all who know her, and especially over a sensitive mind like Werther's. It is hard to realize that the Lotte of the second part is also the Lotte of the first, and it may be that here there is a flaw in Goethe's idea of the character. The maelstrom of passion within whose sweep she is caught is so powerfully depicted that at the moment of reading we are not permitted to raise any question as to the consistency of the conception ; but when all is over, we cannot help suspecting that we have been introduced to two Lottes rather than to one. The Lotte who afterwards lives in the imagination is certainly the Lotte of the first part, a sane and wholesome figure, contrasting strongly with the shrill and despairing Werther. Albert stands out less prominently than Werther and Lotte, but he also has living qualities, and if anything could make the final scenes, so far as Lotte is concerned, intelligible, it would be his pompous self-esteem and exasperating respectability.

One of the secrets of the charm of "Werther" lies in its style. It is a style peculiar to Goethe himself, yet without a trace of eccentricity. Strong, lucid, and picturesque, it adapts itself with perfect suppleness to every mood the writer wishes to express ; and it is so absolutely unaffected that, as we read, we think of what is said rather than of the artist's way of saying it. "Werther" is also remarkable as the first modern German book in which we find descriptions of nature that are still full of charm.   It was Rousseau who had opened men's eyes to the splendour and loveliness of the outward world. Goethe had learned all that Rousseau could teach as to the art of suggesting natural scenery to the imagination through written speech, and in " Werther " he went far beyond the highest achievements of his instructor.   His descriptions are often merely rapid sketches, but they are sketches drawn with so sure a touch that they never fail to call up a vision having all the freshness of reality. And they intensify interest in the tale, for nature is brought in less for its own sake than for the sake of its relation to feeling.   It is with Werther's eyes that we see the scenes he reproduces, and he finds in them always a power that responds to his own happiness or gloom.

Few books have ever produced so strong a sensation. Almost everywhere in Germany " Werther " was received with mingled astonishment and delight.   It had come straight from the writer's heart, and went as straight to the hearts of those who read it.   They found in the tale a voice that gave utterance to much that they themselves had been feeling, and many of them not only shed hot tears for Werther's fate, but affected his modes of expression, and even dressed as he had dressed—in blue coat, yellow vest, yellow hose, and top-boots.   By and by the book was translated into almost every European language, and in far Cathay Werther and Lotte were painted on glass by native artists.

At first there was one discordant note in the general chorus of praise.   Kestner was gravely offended by what he took to be a misrepresentation of the relations between Goethe, Lotte, and himself.   In reality there was no misrepresentation, for Goethe had dealt freely with the experiences through which he had passed, using only those of them that were adapted to his scheme, and adding scenes in which there was no element of fact. The Lotte of the first part, notwithstanding her black eyes, is Charlotte Buff, perhaps slightly idealized; but in the second part she is wholly a figure of the imagination. As for Albert, Goethe, if he thought of any one in particular in conceiving the character, thought of Brentano, not of Kestner. In the end Kestner had a better understanding of what had been intended, and was not a little proud of the part his wife had unconsciously played in the creation of so famous a romance.

Goethe himself says that when he finished "Werther" he felt as one feels after a general confession. The load that had weighed so heavily on his spirit was for the moment removed, and, once more free and happy, he looked forward hopefully to new activity. By and by he could even jest about the characters whose woes had moved him so deeply. Nicolai, the Berlin bookseller and man of letters, who had done better work in his time, wrote a parody of the book, showing how in reality Werther and Lotte became husband and wife, and lived happily ever after; the pistol with which Werther had tried to shoot himself having been loaded with chicken's blood. Some verses written by Goethe show that he took offence at this indignity; but afterwards he wrote an amusing little dialogue, in which Werther and Lotte complain of Nicolai's misconceptions. The chicken's blood has blinded Werther, and Lotte, while pitying him, is anything but enchanted by the change this has made in his

appearance. His eyebrows, she says, will never be so
beautiful as they were before. In " Dichtung und
Wahrheit " Goethe speaks of this dialogue with some
pride, and it certainly shows how completely, at the time
when he wrote it, he felt himself emancipated from the
influences from which " Werther " had sprung.

He had not yet, however, brought his powers under
strict control. Many conflicting ideas struggled in his
mind for mastery, and his moods varied from day to day,
one giving way to· another without any apparent reason
and with startling rapidity. Goethe's nature was too
complicated, touched to too many fine issues, to attain
suddenly, or soon, to inward repose.

Two complete prose dramas were written in Frankfort
after he finished " Werther "—" Clavigo " and " Stella."
" Clavigo " is a dramatic rendering of incidents recorded
in the " Memoirs " of Beaumarchais. These " Memoirs "
appeared in Paris in the spring of 1774, and in the
summer of the same year Goethe's play was published.
In imaginative energy, and in range and depth of feeling,
"Clavigo" is far inferior to "Goetz," but it displays a striking
advance in the power of construction. The formerly
despised unities are here observed, and the interest, such
as it is, steadily grows until it culminates in the catas-
trophe. The chief defect of the play ·is that Clavigo, on
whose action everything depends, is too feeble a character
to excite much interest. His cynical friend, Don Carlos,
has, however, marked individuality, and the part played
by him is still found by German actors to repay careful
study. Maria, the heroine, dies of a broken heart, and
in describing Clavigo's desertion of her, as in describing

Weislingen's desertion of the Maria of "Goetz," Goethe did a kind of penance for his treatment of Frederika Brion.

"Stella," which was written in 1775, seems to have been suggested by Swift's relations to Stella and Vanessa. In this play also Goethe respects the unities, and much technical skill is shown in the development of the story. The play in its original form, however, could not now be acted without exciting ridicule. The hero, Ferdinand, having married Cecilia, whom he loves, feels after a while that his freedom is unduly limited by a wife and daughter; and accordingly he leaves them. Then he falls in love with Stella, but her also he ultimately deserts. When the play opens, he has returned in the hope of being re-united to Stella. He finds her, but at the same time finds his wife and daughter, the latter having become Stella's companion. There is now a vehement conflict of motives. Which of the two women shall he select? Cecilia suggests that it may be possible for him to live with both, and this solution, with Stella's hearty consent, he joyfully accepts. Such was the passion for "nature" at the time that the public do not seem to have been in any way offended or perplexed by this strange conclusion; but thirty years afterwards Goethe changed the last act, bringing the play to an end with the suicide of Ferdinand and Stella. A tragic issue, however, could not be made to appear the natural result of conditions which were in the first instance planned for a wholly different scheme.

To this period belong two short plays with songs— "Erwin and Elmire," and "Claudine von Villa Bella." Both are brightly written, but—except in the charm of their songs—they have no qualities that mark them off sharply from work of a like kind done by other dramatists of the time. The idea of the first of these two plays is the idea of Goldsmith's ballad, "Edwin and Angelina."

At this time Goethe sometimes amused himself by writing humorous and satirical sketches, in all of which there is a free and lively play of fancy. The most famous of them is "Götter, Helden, und Wieland" ("Gods, Heroes, and Wieland"), which Goethe (with a bottle of Burgundy on the table) dashed off one Sunday afternoon. Lenz, to whom it was sent, printed it without having received Goethe's permission. In this prose "farce" Goethe very wittily makes fun of Wieland's misrepresentations of Greek mythology.

So many ideas crowded into Goethe's mind that it was impossible for him to realize all his plans. For some time he thought of taking the career of Mahomet as the subject of a poetical drama, and if we may judge from the beginning he actually made, the theme as he conceived it would have given full scope to his highest creative faculties. He also intended to write a poem on the Wandering Jew, bringing out the contrast between the loftiest idealism, as represented in Christ, and vulgar worldly intelligence, as represented in Ahasuerus, who was to have expostulated with Christ for uselessly exposing Himself to danger by the proclamation of unpopular truths. Of this poem he completed only a few passages, written in couplets like those of Hans Sachs— a poet whom Goethe warmly admired. Another of his poetical fragments is "Prometheus," one of the finest of his early writings. The Moravian Brethren, with whom he still occasionally associated, impressed upon him that man, of himself, can do nothing well, and that his aim should be to wait passively for supernatural influences. This doctrine was ill fitted for a young poet who by a law of his nature was impelled to ceaseless effort; and in " Prometheus " he proposed to develop an exalted conception of the power of the free individual mind. The defiant address of Prometheus to Zeus, with which the fragment closes, ranks among the most splendid of his shorter poems.

CHAPTER IV.

YET another great conception stirred Goethe's imagination at Frankfort—the conception of " Faust." With the Faust legend he had long been familiar, and in " Die Mitschuldigen " he had made one of the characters compare himself with Dr. Faust. During his residence at Leipsic, however, he was too inexperienced to have even a faint conception of the deep meanings that lay hid beneath the surface of the story. It was at Strasburg that he began to realize the vast possibilities of the subject. There he thought of it often and profoundly, and it continued to fascinate him after his return to Frankfort. In 1774—or perhaps 1773—he began to write the drama with which, of all his works, his name is most intimately associated. He worked at it, at intervals, until he quitted Frankfort ; he made several references to it in his letters; and to some of his friends he read passages in which he thought they might be interested.

The original " Faust "—the " Faust " written at Frankfort—contains all that is most essential in the First Part as ultimately published.[1] The Faust legend served only

[1] A lady at the court of Weimar—Fräulein von Göchhausen—wrote for her own use a copy of the original " Faust." This copy

as a suggestion for Goethe's drama. From being little
more than a tale of magical wonders, it became, in passing
through the alembic of his imagination, a conception
pregnant with thought and passion—a conception in
which were embodied all the most vital elements of the
intellectual life of his century. Faust, as Goethe presents him, is a man of magnificent intellect, endowed
originally with the purest and loftiest aspirations of
humanity. When the drama opens, he has devoted many
a year to study ; but, sitting alone in his Gothic chamber
at midnight, he feels sadly and bitterly that his labour
has been in vain. Dry, abstract knowledge he has in
abundance, but it does not satisfy him ; it seems to him
but a mockery of the knowledge for which he has always
yearned. He pants for something infinitely grander than
his books can tell him of. A Titan of the spirit, he would
mount the very heavens, and snatch from the universe
its inmost secrets. And so, despairing of finding truth
by ordinary means, he has recourse to supernatural
methods. Opening his book of magic, he sees the symbol
of the Macrocosmos ; and at once the scales fall from his
eyes ; he is confronted directly by the secret forces of
nature working together in glorious harmony. At last,
for a moment, joy wells up in his heart ; he asks himself
whether he has not become a god. But suddenly it
flashes upon him that he is but a spectator, and he longs

was recovered in 1887, and is printed in the edition of Goethe's
works now being published by order of the Grand Duchess Sophia
of Saxony. It has also been printed separately—" Goethes Faust,
in ursprünglicher Gestalt, nach der Göchhausenschen Abschrift,
herausgegeben von Erich Schmidt (Weimar : Hermann Bohlau,
1887)."

for so much more than can come to him by mere vision !
To drink at the infinite sources of existence, to feel his
soul quickened by contact with the very essence of life—
nothing short of this can give him a rapture corresponding to his needs. Looking again into his book, he finds
the symbol of the earth-spirit ; and through all his being
thrills a consciousness of energy and courage. There is
no achievement of which he does not feel himself capable;
he has an impulse to go out into the world, to experience
all its delights and woes, and even in the crash of shipwreck to exult in his strength and freedom. The earth-
spirit itself he must see, and it responds to his summons.
But it scoffs at his claim of equality, and, as it disappears,
leaves him once more in despair.

Baffled in his ideal aspirations, Faust gives himself up
to the enjoyment of such pleasures as may be accessible
through the senses. After the first monologue, and
before the introduction of Gretchen, we find in the
original "Faust" only Faust's first dialogue with Wagner ;
the scene, afterwards considerably modified, in which
Mephistopheles mystifies the ingenuous student ; a draft,
chiefly in prose, of the scene in Auerbach's cellar ; and a
few lines, ultimately struck out, indicating the perplexity
of Mephistopheles as he passes a cross by the wayside.
Goethe was apparently in haste to reach the tale of love
and sorrow, in which the destiny of Faust was to be
interwoven with that of Gretchen, and the full meaning
of his repudiation of the law of his spiritual being was
to be disclosed in its tragic consequences.

After the accidental meeting of Faust and Gretchen in
the street—when, struck by her beauty, he offers her his

arm, and she escapes from him—there are wanting "Wald und Höhle" and "Walpurgisnacht;" the part to be played by Gretchen's brother, Valentin, is only indicated; immediately before "Trüber Tag" there is a dialogue between Faust and Mephistopheles which was afterwards omitted; and the last scene of all, the scene in the prison, is in prose. In other respects this part of the drama received at Frankfort what was essentially its final form. When the work was to be published, some lines and expressions were altered; but these changes did not vitally affect the conception as it had originally taken shape in Goethe's mind.

Of all the products of Goethe's genius, his presentation of the story of Gretchen is the finest; and, if we exclude Shakespeare, it would be hard to find anywhere in modern dramatic literature an equally noble achievement. The original of Gretchen, as a fresh, simple, happy maiden, with a heart overflowing with love and confidence, was Frederika Brion; and it may be that in depicting the early scenes in which she talks with Faust Goethe was recalling what had actually happened at Sesenheim. Frederika, for instance, must often have been astonished and rather dismayed by strange opinions expressed by her lover, and it is likely enough that she questioned him about religion, and that his answer was in spirit akin to the matchless lines in which Faust makes confession of his faith. But Goethe never seeks in his poetry simply to reproduce his personal experience. He transports us into an ideal world in which all that he has to show us stands out clearly, stripped of the accidental qualities which in actual life so often obscure our vision and disturb our judgment. Gretchen is not merely Frederika; she is the living representative of an enduring type of character and feeling.

Unlike Frederika, Gretchen is tempted to stain the purity of her spirit, and is brought within the sweep of forces that work her destruction; but she is never allowed to pass beyond the range of our sympathies, and in the end we are made to feel that in a deeper sense than that of theological dogmas she is "saved." The last scene, as afterwards rendered in verse, has a more ideal character than it possesses in the original prose, yet in the process of transformation it lost some elements of tragic depth and force. In this great scene Goethe concentrates, with absolute truth to nature, all that is saddest and most terrible in human destiny.

Faust, as Goethe conceives the character, retains our interest through all the phases of his development; for we are often reminded that his was originally a noble nature, and that at the bottom of his heart there are still many survivals of humane and generous impulse. He is never a merely vulgar sensualist; he is an idealist who, having demanded of the universe more than it is capable of yielding, has given way to a mood of bitter and reckless spiritual despair. Mephistopheles is a creation not less remarkable in his own way than Faust, and upon the stage he is by far the more effective of the two, the outlines of his character being more distinct than those of his restless, wavering, unhappy comrade. In the Second Part, written long afterwards, his name is little more than a symbol for an abstract principle; but in the First Part, and especially in the scenes conceived at Frankfort,

Mephistopheles has all the freshness and vigour of thorough individuality. It would be impossible to imagine a more striking contrast to the struggle incessantly going on in Faust's mind than the settled purpose, the frank cynicism, and the grim humour of Mephistopheles. The character was suggested to Goethe by some qualities of his friend Merck. Merck, although honourable and good, had moods in which he took anything but an amiable or cheerful view of life; and his scoffs and sneers (as we may see from the description of him in "Dichtung und Wahrheit") produced a more lasting impression on Goethe than his better characteristics. Although suggested by Merck's cynical outbursts, Mephistopheles is not the less, of course, to be regarded as in the main a free creation of the imagination.

In "Faust" Goethe's art reached the highest level it was capable of attaining during the early part of his career; and from a biographical point of view it is even more deeply interesting than "Goetz von Berlichingen" and "Die Leiden des jungen Werthers." Goetz and Werther each represented a particular phase of his character in the course of its development. Faust represented his character as a whole just as it was about to enter upon a new stage of its growth. Goethe had not, indeed, allowed his will to be subdued by passion; but he had all the vehement cravings, all the restless aspirations, the disappointment of which is the secret cause of Faust's gnawing misery. Goethe at this time enjoyed many a hearty laugh with his friends, and wrote many a bright and genial letter; but beneath the surface he suffered from a profound agitation of spirit, often longing for he knew not what, and feeling that there was no anodyne for the pain of a yearning that the world, as he conceived it, could not still. In this respect also Goethe may be taken as a representative of his period. For the men of the "Sturm und Drang" nothing in the actual universe seemed to be good enough. Not institutions, not social conventions only, but the very conditions of life itself appeared to them to be unjust and injurious limitations of free individuality ; and with all their might they kicked against the pricks, and cried out angrily against the tyrannous order that would not bend or break at their bidding. It was inevitable that Goethe should feel the full power of the dominant influences of his epoch, and to the fact that he felt it, was due, in the springtime of his life, the splendid efflorescence of his genius.

It so happened that at the time when Goethe was striving to relieve his overburdened spirit in "Werther" and "Faust," the "Ethics" of Spinoza came into his hands. This was an event of great importance in his life, for Spinoza introduced him to a higher order of thought than he had yet known. He never accepted Spinoza's system of doctrine as a whole, yet the "Ethics" exercised a powerful influence over him, and for many years he returned to it again and again, always finding in it something that came home to him, and that he could make his own. Indeed, Spinoza was the only purely philosophical writer by whose teaching he ever largely and permanently benefited.

Apart altogether from the particular truths he learned from Spinoza, it was almost inevitable that in his restless and unhappy mood the "Ethics" should have for him a strong fascination. He, whose poetic temperament led him always to think with feeling and through the imagination, could not but be impressed by the calm and stately progress of an argument presented in passionless, abstract terms, and by means of an unswerving logical method. Again, it consoled Goethe to find that the philosopher who, of all others, had most completely stripped his mind of prejudice, could look at life steadily, and yet think of it, not in a spirit of resignation merely, but with hope, cheerfulness, and courage. Most earnestly, too, did he respond to the idea that while the ultimate powers of the universe reveal themselves in a vast and inexorable order, the individual mind can bring itself into harmony with that order only by remaining for ever true to the laws of its own being. The noble generosity of Spinoza's temper also, as Goethe himself explains, was one of the sources of his charm. "Whoso rightly loves God must not ask that God shall love him in return." That was a saying after Goethe's own heart. Did not he himself afterwards write, "If I love you, how does that concern you?"

During his residence at Frankfort Goethe did not attain, or nearly attain, to a position at which he could say that he was reconciled to himself and to the world. But Spinoza's teaching was to him like cool water to parched lips. Communion with this serene and lofty spirit put him on the track that was to lead to inward self-control and to the harmonious devolopment of his powers.

While Goethe was working with inexhaustible energy, he did not neglect his friends, and he had many oppor-

tunities of adding to their number. Lavater, who was
making active preparations for his much-talked-of book
on Physiognomy, wrote to Goethe from Zürich, and in
1774 spent a week as a guest in his father's house. Years
afterwards, Lavater, although always one of the most
popular clergymen of his time, repelled many of those
who had known him intimately by mingled fanaticism
and vanity; but now Goethe was strongly attracted by
his enthusiasm, and took an extraordinary interest
in his notions as to the possibility of understanding
the mind through its expression in the body, and
especially in the face. With Lavater's friend Basedow,
the ardent upholder of Rousseau's ideas on education,
Goethe was also on friendly terms. He was often,
however, irritated by Basedow's boorish talk; for,
notwithstanding his zeal for "nature" in social intercourse, Goethe detested rude and arrogant assumption.
He himself was the brightest and pleasantest of companions, with a manner made all the more attractive
by a touch of lively Bohemianism. It may be worth
noting that there was no trace of Bohemianism in his
appearance. He dressed well—so well, indeed, that it
was often hard for him (his father being by no means
generous) to pay his tailor's bills.

Another of his intimate friends was Johanna Fahlmer,
the aunt of the brothers Jacobi, both of whom were beginning to make a mark in literature. She settled at Frankfort with her mother in 1772, and Goethe, who made her
acquaintance soon after his return from Wetzlar, valued
few of his friends so highly as the young, genial, and clever
"Aunt Fahlmer." She was anxious that he should

enter into close relations with her nephews, but their
writings did not quite please him, and for a long time he
made no attempt to approach them.   In 1774, however,
he felt that it might be pleasant for him to know them,
and in the summer, having spent some weeks with Lavater and Basedow at Ems, he made his way with these
friends up the Rhine to Cologne—"a prophet to the
right, a prophet to the left, the child of the world in the
midst," as he wrote in a humorous little poem describing
their dinner at Coblenz.   At Cologne the party broke
up, and Goethe went on to Düsseldorf, where the Jacobis
lived.   As it happened, they were at Elberfeld, and thither
Goethe followed them.   The younger of the two brothers,
Frederick Jacobi, who was Goethe's senior by about six
years, made a most agreeable impression on him, and at
Pempelfort, Jacobi's country house near Düsseldorf, they
became fast friends.   They visited Cologne together, and
had so happy a day there that at night, when each had
retired to his room in the inn, Goethe could not resist
the impulse to renew their talk.   So he went to Jacobi's
room, and sitting at the open window, looking out on the
moonlit Rhine, they enjoyed an hour of unalloyed happiness in the free communion of mind with mind and heart
with heart.   Goethe had never before given to a friend
so deep a love, and the attraction was mutual. ·Jacobi,
who was a man of high intellectual power and fine character, knew well the real nature of the treasure he had
won in winning Goethe's friendship.   One of the most
absorbing subjects of discussion between them was the
philosophy of Spinoza, with which Jacobi also had been
making himself familiar.   Their opinions on the subject

did not agree, but that in no way lessened the cordiality or the pleasure of their intercourse.

In 1775 Goethe had pleasant intercourse with the Counts Stolberg, who afterwards achieved distinction. in literature.   They were about his own age.   During their stay at Frankfort they often dined with Goethe, whom they intensely admired ; and one day, when the wine had circulated, there was much poetic talk about an unquenchable thirst for tyrants' blood.   Goethe's father shook his head and smiled, but Frau'Aja, as they called his mother, knew nothing of tyrants, and was dismayed by the ferocious outcries of the young poets.   Going to her wine-cellar, she brought up a bottle of her oldest and best wine.   "There !" she said, " that is the true tyrants' blood.   Delight yourselves with that, and let there be an end of murderous thoughts."

In the history of Goethe's last year at Frankfort, 1775, the central name is that of Lili Schönemann.   Lili (Anna Elizabeth) and her two brothers lived with their mother, the widow of a wealthy banker.   They belonged to what was considered the highest rank of Frankfort society, and every evening kept open house for their friends.   Early in the year, probably in the evening of New Year's Day, Goethe was present at one of their parties, and saw Lili for the first time.   She was then in her seventeenth year, a beautiful fair-haired girl with blue eyes, graceful in all her movements, and with the ease and self-possession that came of constant association with people of her own class.   She was as different as possible from Frederika Brion and Charlotte Buff, but Goethe was fascinated by her beauty, and she in her turn could not resist the handsome young poet, whose work had made his name familiar to all educated Germans. After some misunder-standings they became engaged, and Lili gave Goethe a little golden heart which was fastened round his neck with a ribbon.

Notwithstanding his love for Lili, the engagement brought with it no happiness to Goethe. Her relatives, whom he disliked, thought he was not socially her equal, and he, to whom free expression was so essential, could not bear the restraints imposed upon him at Frau Schöne-mann's fashionable parties. It embittered him, too, to see the readiness with which Lili responded to the cour-tesies of men who would gladly have supplanted him. He had a suspicion that she could never belong to him absolutely, and that if they became husband and wife her ideas would go on diverging more and more widely from his own.

Torn by conflicting motives, Goethe felt at last that he must shake himself free for a while from the circumstances that caused him so much perplexity; and in the middle of May he started with the Counts Stolberg for Strasburg —all three, by the way, dressed in Werther's style. From Strasburg he visited his sister at Emmendingen, who urged him to break off an engagement that seemed to her wholly unsuitable. He then travelled to Zürich, where he was cordially welcomed by Lavater ; and after-wards he went southwards, thinking that he might per-haps go on to Italy. But, now that he was far away from Lili, she became dearer to him than ever. On her seven-teenth birthday he was at the Pass of St. Gotthard, and, as he kissed the golden heart she had given him, he was seized by so ardent a longing to be with her again that he immediately turned back and began his homeward journey.

On his return all the old difficulties presented themselves, and in the end, to the relief of Lili's mother and Goethe's parents, and not much apparently to the regret of the lovers themselves, the engagement was allowed to lapse. His relation to Lili had not moved him as he had been moved by his relation to Frederika and Lotte; nor did it become a source of inspiration in his later work. But to his love for her we owe two exquisite lyrics, " Neue Liebe, Neues Leben " (" New Love, New Life "), and " An Belinden " (" To Belinda "), and the finely humorous poem, " Lili's Park."

The time had now almost come when Frankfort, on which Goethe had shed so much lustre, was to lose him, and he was to surround himself with an entirely new set of conditions. Towards the end of 1774 he was presented at Frankfort to the Hereditary Prince of Weimar, who was then seventeen years of age, and to his younger brother, Prince Constantine. The meeting gave the Hereditary Prince so much pleasure that Goethe had to visit him at Mainz—a visit made memorable by the fact that during Goethe's absence from Frankfort, Fräulein von Klettenberg, for whom he had all his old affection and reverence, died. In the autumn of 1775 the Hereditary Prince became Duke of Weimar; and shortly afterwards, on his way to Stuttgart, where he was to be married, he begged that when he returned with his bride Goethe would visit them at Weimar. Goethe gladly accepted the invitation, and in October, when the young Duke and

Duchess came to Frankfort, it was arranged that within a few days he should follow them.

Geheimerath Kalb, the official with whom he was to travel, had been left behind at Stuttgart, and his coming was so long delayed that Goethe finally became impatient, gave up the idea of visiting Weimar, and set off for Italy. At Heidelberg he was aroused during the night by a messenger, who arrived with a letter announcing that Kalb was awaiting him at Frankfort. He hurried back, and on November 7, 1775, entered Weimar. He thought he was merely about to pay a short visit to a friendly prince; in reality he had come to a new home, and had formed relations which were to alter the whole complexion of his life.

CHAPTER V.

WEIMAR, pleasantly situated in the valley of the Ilm, is now known by name to all the world, thanks mainly to Goethe's association with it. At the time when he arrived there, it was an obscure little place, about which most people even in Germany had only the vaguest information. It was still a walled town, but had few picturesque or otherwise interesting buildings. The old Schloss had been burned down in 1774, and the Court was established in a temporary residence which was not well adapted for the purpose.

Goethe was received with enthusiasm by the young Duke, and all sorts of entertainments were got up for his benefit. These entertainments gave rise to much gossip, and soon it was whispered in many places in Germany that Goethe was leading a shamefully dissolute life at Weimar, and exercising on the Duke a most deplorable influence. By and by Klopstock, hearing a rumour of what was supposed to be going on, took it upon himself to write to his fellow poet a letter of reproof and expostulation. Goethe had the highest respect for Klopstock, and, when he had passed through Frankfort, had taken occasion to show him due honour. But now it was necessary to prove that there were limits beyond which even the author of " The Messiah," in his intercourse with younger men, had no right to pass. Accordingly Klopstock received a cool little letter in which it was indirectly and delicately intimated that he had interfered in matters which did not concern him, and about which he was inadequately instructed.

The worst that could be said about the lively proceedings that went on at Weimar after Goethe's arrival was that they took up a great deal of time, and wasted much good energy. As for the notion that the Duke was in any way misled by Goethe, nothing could be further from the truth. The Duke had in his blood the fiery impulses of many a wild ancestor, and even now it was Goethe's aim to restrain rather than to stimulate his passion for pleasure and excitement. Goethe knew him too well to think of troubling him with formal advice, but none the less he sought to suggest to the young prince that as a ruler he had obligations which honour required him to take seriously. Afterwards Goethe kept this object steadily before himself, and the result was that, notwithstanding occasional outbreaks of irregular passion, the Duke became one of the best of the minor German sovereigns, for, of all men, Goethe had the strongest hold over his imagination and feelings.

At first Goethe found some difficulty in arriving at a satisfactory relation with the young Duchess. For a time she also was disposed to think that he led her husband astray. She was, however, too frank and sincere not to see things in the end as they really were. She became

Goethe's true friend ; and he often had opportunities of showing how worthy he was of her confidence by acting as a mediator for the removal of domestic misunderstandings. With the Duchess Dowager Amalia he never had the slightest trouble. Although the mother of a reigning prince, she was only thirty-six years of age at the time of Goethe's arrival in Weimar. She was a woman of masculine intelligence, and during her son's minority had discharged firmly and discreetly her duties as regent. Handsome, amiable, endowed with delicate tact, and taking a sincere interest in art and literature, she could not but attract Goethe ; and he in his turn at once gained her good opinion. She saw clearly how wisely he was likely to guide the Duke, and was most eager that he should, if possible, be persuaded to settle in Weimar.

Among the residents of the little capital a high place was by universal consent conceded to Wieland, who had accepted, in 1772, an invitation sent to him by the Duchess Amalia, to come to Weimar as the tutor of her sons. Wieland was now forty-two years of age, and one of the most prominent writers in Germany. He had been grievously offended by the " Farce " written at his expense, but Goethe had by letter made some amends for the injury done to him, which, after all, was not very serious ; and Wieland had magnanimously let the matter slip from his mind. Now, when he met Goethe, he thought he had never seen any one who was more to his liking. He wrote to a friend that he was "as full of Goethe as a dewdrop of the morning sun." And the two poets continued to be on

pleasant terms with one another. When Wieland wrote
"Oberon," incomparably the finest of his poems, he was
enchanted by Goethe's warm appreciation of its merits.
It was natural for Goethe to praise lavishly anything that
pleased him. There was no room in his generous spirit
for even a touch of petty jealousy.

While living at Frankfort, he had for some time
had much reason to complain of the conduct of Herder,
who for no good cause had conceived a violent prejudice
against him. Happily, this had been dispelled; and at
Weimar Goethe was able to be of splendid service to his
friend. The office of Court preacher and general super-
intendent of matters ecclesiastical was vacant, and the
Duke asked Goethe whether he knew of any one to
whom it might be offered. He at once suggested
Herder, who was thoroughly tired of his position at
Bückeburg, and thinking of accepting a professorship
at Göttingen. The majority of the clergy of the duchy
were by no means delighted with the proposal, for
Herder had the reputation of being a heretic; but
Goethe never grudged labour undertaken for a friend,
and worked so hard, and with so much tact, in Herder's
interest, that all difficulties were overcome. Herder
came to Weimar in 1776, and soon made a great mark,
not only as a preacher, but as an earnest promoter of
every scheme for the public welfare. At Weimar he
wrote his "Ideen zur Philosophie der Geschichte der
Menschheit" ("Ideas towards the Philosophy of the History of Humanity"), which, although only a fragment,
displays so wide a knowledge, so firm a grasp of great
principles, and so deep an appreciation of all that makes

for the highest ideals, that it can never lose its place as one of the treasures of German literature. For many years Goethe and Herder had much pleasant intercourse in Weimar, and encouraged each other in work by mutual sympathy.

The Duke became so attached to Goethe that he was resolved they should never part, and accordingly he expressed to the high officials of his Government his wish that his friend should be admitted into the public service. The proposal met with vehement opposition, for grave old councillors found it impossible to believe that a poet could be capable of attending to business. The Duke, however, warmly supported by his mother, insisted on having his own way.

The elder Goethe strongly disliked the idea of his son entering the service of a prince. Brought up in a free imperial city, he had a decidedly Republican feeling, subject, of course, to loyalty to the Emperor, which was rather a nominal that a real obligation. Moreover, he had always hoped that his son would become an eminent Frankfort lawyer, and that he himself and his wife would have the pleasure of welcoming to their home a daughter-in-law whom they could love. Goethe, however, felt that it would be impossible for him to go back to Frank-fort. He had not been happy there; he still disliked the work of an advocate; he longed to be independent; and he knew that he would receive every consideration from the Duke, the Duchess, and the Duchess Dowager, for all of whom he had a sincere regard. On the other hand, he did not wish to bind himself absolutely to re-main in Weimar. It was necessary that he should be at liberty to leave it at any time when he might desire to go. This he stated to the Duke, and so the matter was arranged.

In the spring of 1776, Goethe was formally appointed a member of the Privy Council, with the title of "Geheimer Legationsrath," Privy Councillor of Legation. His salary, which was gradually increased, was at first 1,200 thalers (£180). The Duke, as a special mark of favour, provided for him a house overlooking the Ilm, and surrounded by a pleasant garden. It was in the Park beyond the town, so that Goethe was able to have perfect quiet, and to enjoy to his heart's content solitary strolls along the banks of the stream flowing past his dwelling. Here he lived for some years, his household consisting of his valet Seidel, whom he had brought with him from Frankfort; a man servant; and an elderly woman who acted as cook. Afterwards he took a house in Weimar, and spent only the summer months in his garden-house.

By the time he definitely took up his abode in Weimar, he had formed a relation which was to exercise a powerful influence over him during the following ten years— his relation to Charlotte von Stein. In Frankfort he had seen her silhouette, which was to appear in Lavater's book on Physiognomy. Under it he wrote, "It would be splendid to see how the world reflects itself in this soul. She sees the world as it is, yet through the medium of love. Mildness is, therefore, the general impression." So vividly did the face appear before him that it kept him awake during three successive nights. On the other hand, Frau von Stein was familiar with, and strongly admired, Goethe's writings. They were thus prepared to think well of one another.

When Goethe arrived in Weimar, she was at her estate, Kochberg; but she soon returned, and he was introduced to her at court by the Duke. She was six years older than Goethe, had been married eleven years, and was the mother of seven children; and she had no very remarkable intellectual gifts. She had, however, delicate grace and beauty, fine tact, and warm sympathy with all that seemed to her best and greatest in life and literature; and these qualities drew Goethe towards her with an irresistible attraction. At first his expressions of regard and admiration—after the fashion of the time—were so ardent that she was rather alarmed, and took care that he should not see her too often; but by and by he showed the most tender respect for her wishes, and so there grew up between them a true, pure, and noble friendship. There were few days when they did not meet. When either was from home, he sent her long letters telling her everything that happened; and even when both were in Weimar, little notes containing kindly greetings constantly passed between them. Goethe confided to her all his cares and anxieties, and she never failed to strengthen him, and give him fresh courage, by her sympathy. His thoughts, studies, and plans of work he also spoke of, and she sought not only to understand them and to share the pleasure they gave him, but to encourage him in all his high undertakings. If sometimes there were misunderstandings, they soon vanished, and Goethe could write to her that the torment due to such experiences was "the sunlit rain (Sonnen-Regen) of love."

With Frau von Stein's husband, who held the office

of master of the horse, Goethe was on the best of terms. He was a sensible, practical person, who did not interfere with his wife's friendships; and the idea that there was any reason why he should be jealous of Goethe seems never to have entered his mind. Goethe's letters to her were often enclosed in letters to her husband. Her children always welcomed Goethe with cries of delight. In this respect they were not different from other children; it was one of his characteristics that young people invariably felt, by a kind of instinct, that he was their friend.

While attending the University of Leipsic, he had been much impressed by the singing of a young public singer called Corona Schröter, and during a short visit to Leipsic in 1776, all his old enthusiasm for her was revived. The result was that she was asked to come to Weimar as a singer in the chamber concerts of the Duchess Dowager. She accepted the invitation, and spent at Weimar the greater part of the rest of her life. She was very handsome, and not only a good singer, but an admirable actress. Goethe was thrown much into her society, and liked her so well that she necessarily has a place in his biography. She was not, however, one of the women who left their mark deeply on his inward life and on his poetry.

A profound change passed over Goethe's character during the early years of his residence at Weimar. This change was partly a natural evolution, partly the result of deliberate and long-continued effort. He became painfully conscious of the fact that in the past he had allowed himself to be swayed too much by momentary impulses, that he had cherished wild desires which had no real relation to the facts of existence, that his happiness had been at the mercy of passing moods, some of the darkest of which had sprung from too intense a concentration of thought on his own feelings. It became his fixed purpose that all this should come to an end, that he should acquire firm control over himself, and that his powers should be disciplined to work steadily for lofty but clearly-defined and attainable ends. " A calm glance back on my past life," he wrote in his diary on the 7th of August, 1779, "on the confusion, restlessness, lust after knowledge, of youth, how it roams about everywhere to find something satisfying. How, especially, I found delight in mysteries—in dark, imaginary relations. How, when occupied with anything scientific, I only half attacked it, and soon let it pass ; how a sort of humble self-complacency goes through all I then wrote. With how little insight I moved round and round in human and divine things. How there was as little of action as of thought and poetry directed to an aim ; how many days were wasted in time-destroying sentiment and shadow-passions ; how little good came to me therefrom ; and how, now that the half of life is past, there is no way back, but I simply stand here as one who has saved himself from the water, and whom the sun begins beneficently to dry. The time I have spent in the rush of the world, since October, '75, I do not yet trust myself to review. God help further and give lights, so that we may not stand so much in our own way; cause us to do from morning to night what is fitting ; and give us clear ideas of the consequences of things, so that one may not be like men who complain all day of headache and dose themselves for headache, and every evening take too much wine ! May the idea of purity, extending itself even to the morsel I take into my mouth, become ever more luminous in me !" On the 13th of May, 1780, he wrote : "In my present surroundings, I have little, hardly any, hindrance outside of myself. In myself there is still much. Human frailties are thorough tapeworms; one tears away a piece, but the stock remains where it was. I will yet, however, be master. No one save he who wholly renounces self is worthy to rule, or can rule."

How sternly he disciplined himself, and with what magnificent success, we may see from the manner in which he discharged his duties at Weimar. It must have been hard for a poet of quick sensibilities to grapple with the difficulties of business, yet he shrank from no obligation, however severe the demands it might make on his temper and patience. The sittings of the Privy Council he attended with strict regularity, and he made a point of mastering every important document submitted to it, so that his judgment might be of real service to the State. He devoted especial attention to questions connected with finance, and so wisely did he deal with them, seeking to secure at once economy and efficiency, that he excited the astonishment and admiration of those who had doubted the fitness of a poet for the practical work of life.

It was not only in the Council that Goethe had to do difficult service. He was intrusted by the Duke with many special duties, all of which he fulfilled with scrupulous care. He had frequently, for instance, to carry on negotiations with the Estates of the two duchies, Weimar and Eisenach, both of which were subject to the Duke ; and in the exercise of this delicate function he displayed unfailing firmness and tact. It was the Duke's desire that the disused mines of Ilmenau should be reopened, and in connection with this scheme Goethe worked earnestly, studying the principles of mining, consulting with men who had a right to an opinion on the subject, and finally seeing that the undertaking was organized in accordance with the most advanced methods. He was made responsible for public works, and in this position had much to say as to the plans for the new Schloss and for the laying out of the Park in which his garden-house was situated. The University of Jena, which was the common property of the Saxon Duchies, he missed no opportunity of benefiting ; and he did what he could for popular education in Weimar. The small military force of the duchy, consisting of six hundred men, was put under his care, so far as administration was concerned ; and he not only brought it to a high state of efficiency, but made it less burdensome to the people by reforming the system according to which the troops were levied. He insisted that the soldiers should be treated by their officers with more consideration than was in those days thought to be safe or proper, and for soldiers' daughters he estab- lished a school of spinning and embroidery, which he placed under the charge of Seidel, whom he knew he could trust. As he had to ride about a great deal in attending to military matters, it was considered that no one could so well manage everything connected with public highways ;

and this duty also he readily undertook. It became his business, too, to look after the demesne lands, and here one is glad to think he had the aid of a thoroughly competent Englishman, George Batty, for whose energy, skill, and good sense Goethe had profound respect. This part of his work was congenial to his tastes, but we find him on one occasion complaining bitterly that those in high places consumed in a day more than could be produced in the same time by the labours of all the toilers on the estates under his charge.

In discharging the various duties imposed upon him, Goethe became the soul of the entire administrative system, and diffused through all its branches much of his own vigour and thoroughness. As he did his own work honestly, he would take no dishonest work from others ; and this came to be well understood by every one who had to carry out his orders. For a long time he was not unhappy in his labours. "The pressure of affairs," he wrote in 1779, "is very good for the mind; when it has disburdened itself, it plays more freely and enjoys life. There is nothing more miserable than a comfortable man without work." Again: "Many a time I feel as if I ought, like Polycrates, to throw my most precious jewel into the water. In everything I undertake I have luck."

During these years Goethe disciplined the body not less strictly than the mind. He slept on a straw mattrass, and drank only half the quantity of wine to which he had formerly accustomed himself. Riding, walking, fencing, and other forms of physical exercise he delighted in ; and—what must then have been thought an extraordinary eccentricity—he took cold baths regularly in winter as well as in summer. The result of all this was that he enjoyed better health than at any previous period of his life.

His manner necessarily changed to some extent in accordance with the change in his character. He was still occasionally capable of the frank and genial out-bursts of feeling that had so often delighted his com-rades in the days of "Sturm und Drang," but, upon the whole, he became more calm, sedate, and reserved. This did not mean that there was any diminution of the kindly impulses of his character. Every one who knew him well was aware that the fine spirit of humanity that had welled up so freely in his nature in the early part of his life never, as years went on, lost its original depth and freshness. In the winter of 1777 he went to the Harz mountains, and one of his objects in undertaking the journey was to see whether he could not help a young man who, although a perfect stranger to him, had ven-tured to tell him, by letter, of troubles that made life intolerable. An unfortunate man who, although also a stranger, appealed to Goethe, received an appointment at Ilmenau, where Goethe not only gave him material aid, but with constant kindness and sympathy encouraged him to maintain his own self-respect by doing valuable work. "Goethe," wrote Merck, while visiting his old friend, " directs everything, and every one is pleased with him, for he serves many and hurts none. Who can resist the unselfishness of the man?"

In 1778 Goethe spent some days with the Duke in Berlin, and in the autumn of the following year they went together to Switzerland. On the way to Switzerland

Goethe rode out from Strasburg to Sesenheim, and
spent a night in the parsonage. He was touched
by the frank and kindly way in which Frederika Brion
received him, and, as he said good-bye, felt with relief
that in future he might think of her with an easier mind.
In Strasburg he visited Frau von Türckheim, who was
no other than Lili, now the wife of a rich banker, and
a mother. At Emmendingen he stood by the grave
of his sister, who, to his great sorrow, had died in 1777.
"Aunt Fahlmer" had become Schlosser's wife, and it
made a strange impression on Goethe to see her in his
sister's place. At Frankfort the party were hospitably
received by his mother. His father, now an old
man, was less genial, for he had never quite recovered
from the disappointment caused by Goethe's choice of a
career at Weimar. Goethe did not again see his father,
who died in 1782.

A few days before he started for Switzerland Goethe
had been made a "Geheimerath," and in 1782 he
became President of the Chamber of Finance. In the
same year he received a patent of nobility, so that
he was from this time Johann Wolfgang von Goethe.
Any pleasure he may have derived from this honour
was due to the fact that it did away with some incon-
veniences arising from the etiquette of the petty German
Courts.

In 1783, being jaded by overwork, he restored himself
to fresh vigour by a second visit to the Harz mountains. This tour was made doubly pleasant by the fact
that he had with him Frau von Stein's son Fritz, a clever
boy for whom he had a warm affection. With Frau von

Stein's sanction, Goethe had taken Fritz to live with him, and it was a constant delight to him to have the boy's companionship, to direct his education, and to watch the gradual unfolding of his mind and character.

During this period Goethe entered upon the scientific investigations which were to occupy many of the best hours of his life. Almost from boyhood he had had a strong inclination for the study of science. At Leipsic he attended lectures on physics and medicine, and at Strasburg, as we have seen, he gave some attention to various branches of biology. Now he devoted himself to science with an enthusiasm not less fervent than that with which he had devoted himself to literature. He began with mineralogy, to which he was led by his labours in connection with the Ilmenau mines, and mineralogy soon made it necessary for him to turn his thoughts to geology. Afterwards he occupied himself chiefly with osteology and botany. For his investigations in all these subjects he had considerable advantages. The collections at the University of Jena were of course at his disposal, and the scientific professors were only too glad to have a chance of giving him what aid they could. In botany he was able to carry on long series of researches in his garden, and in the forests of the duchy, which he had frequently to visit as an administrator. He took up the study of science in a serious spirit, and, as the results proved, he had a high capacity for it. He was a careful and most exact observer, and his imagination, so far from standing in his way, was the power to which he owed the greatest and most fertile of his ideas.

It was in osteology that he made his first important

discovery. In the study of this branch of anatomy he was interested mainly in the points of comparison between the human skeleton and the skeletons of other vertebrates. It was generally held that the intermaxillary bone, which is found in the upper jaw of some animals, is wanting in man, and this was regarded as a proof of the doctrine that the physical nature of man is vitally distinguished from that of other living creatures. On March 27, 1784, while examining various bones with his friend Professor Loder, of the University of Jena, Goethe was greatly surprised to discover what he believed to be the intermaxillary bone in a human jaw. He lost no time in comparing it with the various forms assumed by the bone in different species of animals, and the more widely the comparison was extended the more sure he became that he was right. The results of his researches he set forth in an essay, illustrated by drawings. This essay, which is a model of lucid statement, was translated into Latin, and submitted to several men of science. It was not, however, published until about thirty years afterwards.

Goethe's discovery of the intermaxillary bone in a human jaw finally disposed of the notion that it is possible to draw a sharp line of distinction between the physical nature of man and that of other vertebrates. And it led Goethe to the theory that all organic beings of the same class are formed in accordance with ideal types or patterns, which Nature modifies indefinitely to suit varying conditions. This conception marked an epoch in the history of scientific thought, for by fastening attention on the fact that organic beings of the same class, however widely their organs may seem to differ from one another, have a fundamental agreement in structure, it directly prepared the way for the discovery of the law of evolution, in which this fact is taken up and explained.

It was impossible for Goethe, while occupied so much with science and public affairs, to devote his best energies to imaginative creation. He did not, however, wholly neglect literature. In 1776 he planned a great prose drama, "Iphigenie," and in 1779 it was written to his dictation. The play was represented with brilliant success at the Weimar Court, Corona Schröter taking the part of the heroine, and Goethe himself that of Orestes. It is wholly different, both in conception and execution, from his earlier dramas. It contains no violent outbursts of passionate feeling; the diction is measured and dignified; and the utmost pains are taken to secure that the various parts shall each have the place that properly belongs to them in the general scheme. It has often been said that the change in Goethe's method, from the frank, glowing style of the works by which he established his fame, to the consciously artistic style of his mature writings, was wholly due to the impressions derived during his visit to Italy. In reality, as the prose "Iphigenie" shows, it began long before he went to Italy; and no doubt we must to some extent associate it with the change which passed over his character as a whole. Goethe's aim was, above all things, to master himself, to have every element of his nature under control; and it was inevitable that the strenuous efforts he made to attain this object should leave their mark on his art as well as on his practical life.

In 1777 Goethe began "Wilhelm Meister;" and, stimulated by Frau von Stein, whom the work greatly interested, he returned to it again and again during the following eight years. He also wrote a part of a prose play, "Torquato Tasso," and various minor prose dramatic pieces, intended for the amusement of the Court, before which they were represented. To this period, too, belong various powerful poems, one of the most remarkable of which is the "Harzreise im Winter" ("The Harz Journey in Winter"), presenting his thoughts and feelings on the day when he climbed to the top of the Brocken in the winter of 1777. In another poem of this time, "Ilmenau," written in 1783 as a birthday-gift for the Duke, Goethe showed how high and sacred, as he conceived them, were the duties owed by a ruler to his subjects. A third poem, "Die Geheimnisse" ("The Secrets"), begun in 1784, is unfortunately only a splendid fragment. If completed, it would have given form to all that Goethe had thought about the relations of the great religious movements of the world to man's deepest spiritual needs.

While he was slowly working out a new ideal, both in his character and in his art, the intellectual movement in Germany, of which he had been considered the chief representative, retained all its original characteristics. In 1781 Schiller began his career with his wild play, "The Robbers;" and other young writers, with little of his power, found it easy to imitate his extravagance. To Goethe the prevailing tone of the literature of the time— although he himself was in some degree responsible for it —became deeply repugnant, and he turned from it with

more and more dislike, finding refuge in the calmer realms
of philosophy and science.   Even his friend Jacobi
contrived to displease him.   Jacobi's " Woldemar '
appeared in 1779, and its sentimentalism—reproducing
the sentimentalism of " Werther "—seemed to Goethe so
ridiculous that one day, in the Park at the Duchess Dowager's residence at Ettersburg, he climbed a tree and nailed
the book to a branch as a warning to literary evil-doers.
Unfortunately Jacobi heard of this mad prank, and took
serious offence.   After some time, however, Goethe
wrote to him in a tone of such sincere, although indirect,
apology that Jacobi understood at once that less had
been intended than he had thought.   In 1784 he came
to see Goethe at Weimar, and their friendship was never
again interrupted.

When Goethe had been about ten years at Weimar,
he began to feel that some change of life was absolutely
essential.   He had worked hard, steadily, and loyally in
the fulfilment of difficult duties, and longed for a time
of relief, during which his mind might expand freely and
be enriched by fresh impressions.   From early boyhood
he had often wished to visit Italy, and this yearning was
now revived with almost painful intensity.   At last he
decided that, at whatever cost, his desire should be
gratified.   Late in July, 1786, he went, as he had
repeatedly gone in previous summers, to Carlsbad, where
he met Frau von Stein, Herder and his wife, and the
Duke ; and a little more than a month afterwards he
started on his travels.   He had accompanied Frau von
Stein a part of the way back to Weimar, but even to
her he had said nothing about his approaching journey.

Nor, in writing to the Duke for leave of absence, did he speak of his destination. He had a kind of superstitious feeling that if the secret were let out his scheme might be thwarted.

Simultaneously with the return of his desire for Italy Goethe was conscious of a reawakening of his poetic genius. He began to think seriously of his unfinished plans, and to dream of new achievements. Finally he arranged with Göschen, a Leipsic bookseller (the grandfather of Mr. Goschen, the English statesmen), for the publication of a collected edition of his writings in eight volumes. The contents of four of these volumes he prepared for the press before quitting Carlsbad.

CHAPTER VI.

HARDLY had Goethe set foot on Italian ground when he began to feel something of the joy and elasticity of temper for which he had been longing. He was absolutely his own master again, and all around him was the sunny land which he greeted as, in some sense, the true home of his spirit. The people, too, with their natural grace and courtesy, delighted him, and their speech fell softly and pleasantly on his ears. He had never had keener pleasure than he felt in looking forward to the happy days and weeks that were before him.

During his visit to Italy he wrote a large number of letters, most of which were addressed to Frau von Stein. Long afterwards he issued some of them, carefully edited, as one of the supplements of his autobiography, giving them the general title, " Italienische Reise " ("Italian Journey "). These letters have all the freshness of immediate impressions, yet we find in them only so much detail as is necessary to give brightness and animation to his pictures of the central elements of interest that meet him on his way. In every letter we

feel the influence of a deep enthusiasm, but it is an
enthusiasm that never distorts his vision or injures the
noble simplicity and purity of his style.

He entered Italy from the Tyrol, and the first important town at which he stopped was Verona. From
Verona he went to Vicenza, and so, through Padua,
to Venice. At Venice he remained three weeks, allowing its splendours to impress themselves deeply on
his imagination. He then went to Bologna, which he
ever afterwards associated with the charm of Raphael's
St. Agatha. In his thoughts about Italy it had always
been Rome of which he had chiefly dreamed, and now
his longing to be there became so overwhelming that
he hurried over what remained of the journey, staying
only three hours at Florence. In view of the joy that
was to come he was scarcely conscious of the incon-
veniences of travel. "If I am dragged to Rome on
Ixion's wheel," he wrote, "I will not complain."

On October 29, 1786, he drove into Rome through
the Porta del Popolo. "Yes," he wrote a day or two
afterwards, "I have at last arrived at the capital of the
world! . . . All the dreams of my youth are now
realized. The first engravings I remember—my father
had hung the views of Rome in an entrance-hall—I
see now in reality, and all the things I have long known
from paintings and drawings, from copper-plates and
wood-cuts, from plaster casts and cork models, stand
together before me. Wherever I go, I find an acquaintance in a new world; it is all as I had conceived it,
and all new. The like I may say of my observations,
of my ideas. I have had no new thoughts, have found

nothing quite strange, but the old thoughts have been so defined, they have become so thoroughly alive, they have been brought into such harmonious relation to one another, that they may pass for new. When Pygmalion's Elise, whom he had formed absolutely in accordance with his wishes, and to whom he had given as much truth and reality as were within the scope of art, at last came to him, and said, 'It is I,' how different was the living woman from the sculptured stone!"

While at Rome, Goethe realized with new vividness all that the mighty city had been to the world in the remote ages when on her had been imposed the task of guiding it to higher destinies. And he worked hard to think himself back into the Rome of ancient times. This, he confesses in one of his letters, was no easy task. "It is a sour and sad undertaking," he writes, "to pick out the old Rome from the new. . . . One comes upon traces of a splendour and of a destruction, both of which go beyond our conceptions. What the barbarians allowed to stand, the architects of modern Rome have laid waste." Gradually, however, a living idea of the ancient city was formed in his mind. "Roman antiquities," he wrote about two months after his arrival, " begin to delight me. History, inscriptions, medals, of which I might otherwise have known nothing, all crowd in on me. As it happened to me in natural history, so it happens here; for in this place the entire history of the world centres, and I count as a second birthday, the day of a real new birth, that on which I entered Rome." With regard to the significance of the remains of ancient art in Rome, Winckelmann had introduced a wholly new order of ideas, and Goethe

owed much to him in the appreciation of the Apollo
Belvedere and all the other masterpieces of sculpture he
had now an opportunity of studying. He was astonished
to find how little he had learned from plaster casts. The
breath of life, it seemed to him, was to be felt only in the
original marble figures. The fascination exerted by
ancient statues led him to renew, but in a higher way,
the studies of the human body which he had formerly
carried on through anatomy. "In our medico-surgical
anatomy," he says, "all that is aimed at is a knowledge
of the part, and for this a wretched muscle is enough.
But in Rome the parts are worth nothing if they do not
at the same time present a noble, beautiful form."

The art of the Renascence, as represented in Rome,
stirred in Goethe an interest not less profound than that
awakened by ancient sculpture. Long before, when as a
young student he visited Dresden, the pictures which had
appealed to him most strongly were those of the Dutch
school. Now he felt the power of the ideal art of
Italy in her great period. He was fascinated by the
Loggie of Raphael, at the Vatican, but even they seemed
of slight importance in comparison with the masterpieces
of Michael Angelo in the Sixtine Chapel. " I could,"
he says, writing of these sublime conceptions, "only gaze
and stand amazed. The inward sureness and manliness
of the master, his greatness, go beyond all expression."

He did not fail, of course, to make pilgrimages to the
great churches, and in one of his letters he describes how,
after a visit to the Sixtine Chapel, he went with his friend
Tischbein to St. Peter's, "which received the most
beautiful light from the cheerful sky, and appeared in all

its parts bright and clear." " As men who had come to enjoy what we were to see, we delighted in its greatness and splendour, without allowing ourselves, this time, to be misled by a taste too fastidious and intelligent. We suppressed every unfavourable judgment, and delighted in what was delightful."

Anxious that nothing should stand in the way of his full enjoyment of "the capital of the world," Goethe avoided as far as possible all association with "the great." He had, however, several friends with whom he had pleasant intercourse. The most intimate of them was Tischbein, a good German artist, whom he had known for several years. Goethe occupied two rooms in Tischbein's house, and obtained from him much help in the study both of ancient and of modern art. Another of his friends at Rome was Meyer, a Swiss artist, who delighted him as much by the charm of his personal character as by his artistic skill and knowledge. Goethe was also greatly attracted by Moritz, a writer who had made some reputation as the author of a book of travels in England, and was now collecting materials for a like book on Italy. Angelica Kaufmann, who had settled in Rome after her departure from London, welcomed Goethe cordially to her home, and he soon held her in high esteem. With these and other friends he spent many happy hours, and his delight in the new world opened to him in Rome was, if possible, deepened and intensified by their sympathy.

From the time when Goethe had taken lessons in drawing from Oeser at Leipsic he had never lost the wish to become a skilful artist; and at Weimar he had displayed considerable aptitude for portraiture. Now, when he had so many opportunities of indulging his taste, he took great pains to improve himself in drawing, painting, and modelling. For some time he even debated with himself whether he ought not to become an artist by profession. He did not long, however, remain in doubt. Although, with Tischbein's help, he made good progress, he was obliged to admit that nature had denied to him the capacity of achieving, in art, work that in any way corresponded to his lofty ideal of what such work should be.

He had brought with him from Weimar many writings which he proposed either to complete or to re-cast for the new edition of his works. The first task undertaken was the transformation of "Iphigenie" from a prose to a poetical drama, and he had worked at it more or less steadily at all the places at which he had stopped before reaching Rome. It had also frequently occupied his thoughts while he travelled from one point of his journey to another. At Bologna, while he stood before Raphael's St Agatha, his conception of the character of Iphigenie assumed a new and higher form. " I remarked the figure well," he afterwards wrote ; " in mind I shall read my ' Iphigenie ' to her, and my heroine shall say nothing that the saint might not utter." In Rome the writing of "Iphigenie " formed from day to day, until the work was completed, the central interest around which all his other occupations grouped themselves. On the 12th of December the drama received its last touches, and it was soon afterwards read to a group of his friends. They had expected that the play would resemble "Goetz von

Berlichingen," and Goethe saw only too plainly that it disappointed them. Angelica Kaufmann alone had something like an adequate idea of its importance.

About this time Goethe received a friendly letter from the Duke of Weimar extending his leave of absence indefinitely. He resolved to profit to the utmost by the opportunity thus provided for him, and on the 22nd of February, 1787, he started with Tischbein for Naples. As they approached the city, he was powerfully impressed by the view of Vesuvius, from which great masses of smoke were issuing. The liveliness and good humour of the people of Naples enchanted him, and he found inexhaustible sources of delight in the beauty of the town itself, in the bright southern sky, and in all the splendours of nature that constantly presented themselves in new aspects both on land and sea. Twice he climbed Vesuvius, and on both occasions he described his experiences in letters that bring the scene before us almost with the vividness of reality. As in Rome, so in Naples he made himself familiar with every treasure of ancient and modern art that was accessible to him, and his conception of the old Roman world was at once enlarged and made more definite by visits to Pompeii, Herculaneum, and Pæstum. "I have seen much and thought still more," he wrote on the 17th of March ; "the world opens itself more and more ; even the things I have long known become now for the first time my own." In the same letter, however, he says : "Many a time I think of Rousseau and his hypochondriacal misery, and yet it becomes intelligible to me how so fine an organization might be thrown off its balance. Did I not take such

an interest in natural things, and did I not see that in the
apparent confusion a hundred observations are capable
of being compared and classified, as a land surveyor
corrects many single measurements by one line drawn
through them, I should often consider myself mad."

On the 29th of March, 1787, accompanied by Kniep,
a German artist settled at Naples, Goethe embarked for
Sicily. Sixteen days he remained at Palermo, where art
and nature combined to give him a happiness that seems
to have been absolutely unalloyed. He then made for
Alcamo and Segesta, visited Girgenti and Catania,
climbed a part of Mount Etna, and finally arrived at
Messina, whence he returned by sea to Naples. His
letters, written for Frau von Stein, in the form of a
diary, reproduce with astonishing power, yet with perfect
simplicity, the impressions produced upon him during
his visit to Sicily. He studied closely the remains of
Greek architecture, and at the same time carried on his
scientific investigations, which had occupied him at every
favourable opportunity from the day of his arrival in
Italy. These investigations had become more attractive
to him than ever, for he had now a clear conception
of the main outlines of his great discovery of the metamorphosis of plants.

On the 6th of June he was once more in Rome. It
was his intention to return to Weimar soon, but Rome
exercised so irresistible a power over him that nearly a
year passed before he could bring himself to leave it.
All that he had seen before his departure for Naples
he studied again and again, and almost daily he found
objects of interest that had been overlooked. During

this time his idea of Rome and of its greatest possessions became so full, accurate, and vivid that it was never in the faintest degree blurred by the events of his later life.

He looked forward with the deepest interest to the great ceremonies of the Roman Church during Passion Week, and they seem to have given him a wholly new conception of the service art may be made to render to religion. Writing of a Mass in the Sixtine Chapel, attended by the Pope and the Cardinals, he says he does not wonder that strangers are often unable to contain themselves in the presence of a spectacle at once so great and so simple. The ceremonies in the Sixtine Chapel on the morning of Easter Day filled him with admiration, and appeared to him a striking proof of the fact that at Rome the Church had penetrated deeply into the spirit of "the Christian traditions."

In his literary work his progress was less rapid than he had expected. He was able, however, to achieve some important results. Among his papers was an unfinished prose drama, "Egmont," which dated from about the time when he had written "Stella." He had often thought of completing it at Weimar, but had never accomplished his purpose. Now he gave the play its final form, partly re-casting it; but re-writing it, as originally planned, in prose. He also improved the less important works, "Erwin and Elmire" and "Claudine von Villa Bella."

Another of his papers, frayed at the edges and grey with age, was "Faust," in the form in which he had taken it from Frankfort to Weimar. It was hard for him, after so long an interval, to take up this work at the point at which he had left it. On the 1st of March, 1788, however, he wrote that he had "found the thread again," and that "the plan for 'Faust' was made." At Rome he wrote "Die Hexenküche" ("The Witches' Kitchen"), one of the most striking scenes in "Faust," a scene at which, no doubt, his imagination worked all the more freely from the strange contrast it presented to the actual world in the midst of which it was conceived. In this scene there is one slight indication of the difficulty he must have experienced in carrying on the work in the spirit in which it had been begun. Faust in the first monologue says he has had pupils for ten years. This means that he cannot be much more than thirty years old. In the "Hexenküche" he is presented as a man over fifty, for he speaks of the possibility of his youth being renewed by thirty years being struck out of his life. Goethe never detected this curious contradiction.

At last it became necessary for him to drag himself away from the city he now knew and loved so well. On the evening of the 21st of April, 1788, he strolled with some friends along the Corso in the moonlight, and visited for the last time the Capitol and the Colosseum. Next day he was travelling towards the North. On the way he spent some time at Florence and Milan, and on the 18th of June he re-entered Weimar.

CHAPTER VII.

GOETHE was in his thirty-ninth year when he returned to the little capital from which he was never again to be so long absent. His visit to Italy had done for him all, and more than all, he had hoped for. It had stilled a great longing; it had enriched his mental life by bringing him into contact with nature in some of her most alluring aspects and with many of the loftiest creations of human genius; it had renewed his consciousness of strength as a poet, and filled him with an ardent desire to exercise it in the achievement of higher results than any to which he had yet attained.

He knew well that if he allowed himself again to be absorbed by business he would necessarily be turned aside from his true destiny. This he had, in effect, communicated to the Duke in letters from Italy; and as the Duke not only had a sincere love for Goethe, but felt that he himself was now fitted to undertake, in reality as well as in name, the supreme control of affairs, he was willing to assent to any arrangement his friend might propose. It was therefore decided that Goethe should be relieved of most of the duties he had discharged before going to Italy. He retained, however, the position of a Minister of State, and continued for some years to take an active part in the direction of the Ilmenau mines, a work in which he was genuinely interested. To him was also intrusted the authority which belonged to the Duchy of Weimar in the government of the University of Jena.

Goethe had returned with the full intention of maintaining his friendship with Frau von Stein. It was, however, impossible that their old relations should be renewed. Her sympathy could not now be to him what it had been, for during nearly two years he had accustomed himself to live without the relief that had formerly come from confidential talk with her about his inmost thoughts and cares. Moreover, while he had come back with a world of new ideas in his mind, she had no interests with which he had not long been familiar ; and as she was now a delicate woman of forty-four, it was improbable that she would be accessible to fresh influences. With a woman's instinct, Frau von Stein at once detected the change in Goethe, of which he himself was only half conscious ; and she could not help showing that she resented it. He, on the other hand, was repelled by her coldness. Thus misunderstandings at once sprang up, and both knew that they could never be wholly removed.

A few weeks after his arrival at Weimar, Goethe was walking one day in the Park when he was approached by a girl of about twenty-three, of a humble position in life. Her name was Christiane Vulpius. She had brought with her a petition from her brother, who, after studying at Jena, had betaken himself to literature, and thought that Goethe might be willing to help him. Goethe read the paper, but was far more interested in the messenger than in the message. Christiane, although not tall, had a good figure and a fresh pretty face, with an honest, frank, lively expression in her fine blue eyes. Goethe was charmed with her, and the result was that she became his wife. At this stage their hands were not formally joined in a church, but from the beginning he never thought of their union as other than a true marriage. Much idle gossip has been printed to Christiane's disadvantage—for the most part an echo of the tittle-tattle of the Weimar Court, the ladies of which could not bear to think of Goethe as the husband of a woman who did not belong to their own class. In reality she was a good and most loyal wife, and retained to the last the warm love of her husband, who was never happier than in her presence. When he was from home he sent her long letters, all of which she kept as her most sacred possessions. He talked to her freely about his great botanical discovery, and did not find that the subject was beyond her intelligence; and when he intrusted her with important private business, she displayed, in attending to it, decision, good sense, and good feeling. She ruled his household, too, as he liked it to be ruled, firmly, yet with kindness and discretion. His mother received Christiane cordially as her "dear daughter."

For some time Goethe and Christiane lived in seclusion in his house in the Park, but their union could not long be kept secret. When it became known, Frau von

Stein was furious. She was about to visit the Rhenish
baths, and before starting she addressed to him a letter
so bitter in its tone that he could not answer it for some
weeks. For the time the break between them was complete. Afterwards they became good friends again, but
never, of course, on the old intimate terms. Frau von
Stein had the sympathy of all the Court ladies, with,
however, one notable exception, the Duchess, who
understood Goethe too well to speak of him harshly or
uncharitably.

No longer harassed by incessant business, and enjoying to the full his life with Christiane, Goethe had
resumed his literary work with enthusiasm. Its first-
fruits were his " Römische Elegien " (" Roman Elegies "),
in which he gave utterance to the delight he had experienced at Rome. Side by side with the poet stands a
beautiful girl, his love for whom is intimately connected
with all the other influences under which his heart expands
in the great city. In sketching this figure, Goethe was no
doubt thinking chiefly of Christiane, whom in imagination he transported to the land where life had seemed to
him so full of glory. In these poems there is an occasional warmth of expression that has sometimes given
offence, but, judged simply as works of art, they are as
near perfection as anything Goethe ever wrote. The
passion expressed in them is deep and ardent, yet the
forms and scenes with which it is associated stand out
as clearly as a landscape under the bright Italian sky.
The "Elegies" would have taken an enduring place in
literature if they had had nothing to commend them but
the splendour of their diction and melody.

While working at the " Elegies," Goethe strove to complete his drama, " Torquato Tasso," a part of which had been written long before in prose. In Italy he had hoped to be able, before returning to Weimar, to clothe the conception of this play in fitting verse. The task, however, was too hard to be accomplished quickly, and even at Weimar he did not bring it to an end until the summer of 1789. " Tasso " was the last of the series of plays either wholly or in part transformed in Italy.

We have seen that even before Goethe went to Italy his conception of the true aim and method of dramatic art had begun to undergo a profound change. In Italy this process of development was completed, partly by the influence of classical literature, but mainly by that of ancient sculpture. Here, following the track marked out by Winckelmann, he had found that the supreme aim of ancient artists was ideal beauty, and that they had sought to attain it by the harmonious combination of parts in a whole, so that the figures created by them should convey in action an impression of noble simplicity, dignity, and calm. This was the ideal he kept steadily before himself in most of the work begun or completed in Rome.

In " Egmont " this new conception could not find full expression, for the outlines of the scheme had been drawn at a time when Goethe worked under wholly different influences. Even in " Egmont," however, in the form in which he gave it to the world, his new method predominates. Goethe's Egmont, who differs in many particulars from the Egmont of history, is a man of most genial temper. He is sincerely devoted to the cause of freedom, and makes troops of friends by his frankness, his courage, his inexhaustible generosity. But he lacks the power to read the signs of hostile intention in others, and this defect, which necessarily springs from some of his best qualities, exposes him to deadly peril, and leads ultimately to his ruin. Interwoven with the history of his relations to the public movements of his age is the story of his love for Clärchen. Such a love at such a time would seem wholly unnatural if Egmont were a prudent statesman, conscious of the actual circumstances in which he and his country are placed ; but he has no doubt as to the triumph of his cause, for he trusts absolutely the King of Spain and his counsellors, believing their objects to be as honourable as his own. There is no incongruity, therefore, between Egmont's patriotism and his love, and in such a nature as his, were the conditions favourable, each feeling would purify and ennoble the other. Clärchen is in every respect worthy of him. She is one of the finest of the many fine feminine characters conceived by Goethe. She is capable of heroic action as well as of the tenderest love, and she obeys an irresistible impulse when, having heard of Egmont's imprisonment, she appeals with passionate fervour to the people for his deliverance. The concluding scene, in which Freedom in the form of Clärchen appears to Egmont in a dream as he lies in prison awaiting execution, produces exactly the impression that Goethe meant it to produce. It softens the effect of the tragic conflicts which have led to Clärchen's death, and are about to lead to her lover's, and we are reminded that there are in the world forces for good, the victory of which may be delayed, but cannot in the end be prevented, by individual defeat and sorrow.

Although less interesting than the two central figures, the other characters in this great drama are most vividly presented. William of Orange, the resolute patriot who never allows himself to be diverted from his path by mistaking appearance for reality, contrasts strongly with the heedless Egmont; and Alva, cold, cruel, and treacherous, is a fitting representative of a crushing and inhuman tyranny. The crowds which from time to time give voice to popular feeling play an essential part in the evolution of the tragedy, and are brought before us with extraordinary animation and truth to nature.

In composing the poetical drama, "Iphigenie," Goethe did not depart very widely from the substance of the original prose version. He gave to the entire conception, however, new dignity and beauty. The central interest attaches to the heroine, than whom there is not in all modern literature a nobler type of womanhood. Hers is a spirit of spotless purity, associated with a high serenity springing from the inward harmony of all the elements of her character. She has infinite tenderness and humanity, with an inflexible will, and a passion for truth and honour. Those who come into contact with her are overcome by a mingled feeling of love and reverence, and all that is best in their spiritual life is evoked by her presence. Iphigenie is only nominally a Greek priestess; in reality, she would have been impossible in a society in which women were supposed to be subordinate to men. In her aims, sympathies, aspirations, she is wholly modern, and it may be that some features of her character were reproduced from the character of Frau von Stein, as it revealed itself to Goethe in the happiest moments of their friendship. Orestes, Pylades, Thoas, are not less dominated by essentially modern motives. It is a striking proof of the power and subtlety of Goethe's art that there is no conflict between the modern substance and the antique form of this splendid drama. He rigidly excludes every thought and feeling that might conflict with his chosen method. There is no austerity of sentiment, but all is measured and stately, and capable, therefore, of being brought within the scope of a severely restricted scheme.

The development of the tale is not less admirable than the truth of the characters. As in the ancient statues which Goethe so warmly admired, each of the individual parts is in its proper place, and contributes what is demanded of it, and no more, to the idea as a whole. The diction and metre of the drama, always noble and harmonious, accord perfectly with its predominant spirit, and they may be said to have revealed for the first time the high capabilities of the German language as an instrument of dramatic expression. We cannot wonder that "Iphigenie" disappointed readers who expected to find in it volcanic explosions like those of his early writings. It belongs to a different period of Goethe's development, and must be estimated by altogether different standards.

Goethe found it hard to complete "Torquato Tasso," and the explanation probably is that the subject did not lend itself so readily as the subject of "Iphigenie" to classic treatment. Here he had to present a strange, abnormal type of character, with agitated feelings, the expression of which continually tended to press beyond the limits within which Goethe's scheme required him to retain it. Tasso, as Goethe presents the character, is a kind of Werther, of a highly excitable temperament, and morbidly sensitive to praise and blame. He reminds us, too, of Rousseau, and it is possible that in working out the conception Goethe may have taken some hints from Rousseau's "Confessions," for, as we have seen, he often thought, while in Italy, of "Rousseau and his hypochondriacal misery." When the play opens, Tasso is living as an honoured guest of the Duke of Ferrara, at the Castle of Belriguardo. He has just finished "La Gerusalemme Liberata," and in the garden of the castle presents the poem to the duke in the presence of the duke's sister, the Princess Leonore, and of her foster-sister, Leonore, the Countess of Scandiano. The gift is received with many expressions of delight, and, at a sign from the duke, the princess takes a wreath from a bust of Virgil and crowns the poet with it. He is enchanted, and cannot find words strong enough to utter his gratitude. The conversation is interrupted by the arrival of the duke's chief minister, Antonio, who has returned from an important mission. He is held in great respect, and is cordially received. After some talk about the work he has accomplished, reference is made to Tasso's wreath, and Antonio, who is not given to vehement applause, addresses Tasso rather coldly, but takes an opportunity of praising Ariosto. Something in Antonio's character jars on Tasso's feeling, and he is

bitterly jealous of the high place occupied by the wise
and successful statesman. In conversation with the
princess, for whom he cherishes a secret passion, he
pours forth his discontent. She strives to pacify him,
and her efforts are seconded by the duke and Leonore.
Tasso, trying to master himself, seeks out Antonio, and
offers to become his friend. The offer being received
in an ungenial spirit, Tasso feels insulted, speaks to
Antonio angrily, and finally draws his sword, demand-
ing that their quarrel shall at once be fought out. At
this point the duke comes ; and Tasso, who has exposed
himself to severe penalties, is ordered,' but not harshly,
to confine himself to his room. Antonio feels that he
has not acted with sufficient consideration, and is eager
to do what he can to make amends. The duke, too,
and the princess, and Leonore, are all most anxious that
Tasso shall be reconciled to Antonio and to himself.
Now, however, the young poet is violently excited; he
becomes bitterly suspicious, feels sure that he is surrounded by enemies, and that every one is plotting
against him. All that is done to restore him to good
humour he resents, attributing it to a wish to injure him.
In the princess alone he has confidence, and her he
shocks, when she is encouraging him to collect himself,
by suddenly throwing his arms around her and pressing
her to his breast. In the final scene, while the duke,
the princess, and Leonore drive away from the castle,
Antonio, who now fully realizes that the poet is a man
of morbid temper.who needs to be tenderly and patiently
dealt with, comes to him and addresses him kindly.
Tasso indulges in a furious outburst against all the world,

by which he is misunderstood, but at the last moment takes Antonio's hand, and clings to him as a shipwrecked sailor to a rock.

In none of Goethe's plays does he display finer or more penetrating observation of character. The Tasso of the drama is in some respects very unlike the real Tasso, but that does not prevent him from being a most striking representative of minds which, making self the centre of their thoughts, are thereby led to have a wholly distorted conception of life, and to poison what might be, and ought to be, perennial sources of happiness. The prince, the princess, Leonore, and Antonio resemble one another in being healthy natures, and in acting with an air of distinction; but otherwise each is marked off from the rest by special characteristics, indicated clearly, but with infinite delicacy. As usual in his plays, it is to the feminine characters that Goethe attributes the highest qualities. The princess is one of his greatest creations, combining, as she does, deep feeling with exquisite tact and a noble appreciation of the conditions of inward growth and peace.

The tale in itself is not one of absorbing interest, and the conclusion is hardly satisfactory, since no difficulty is really solved by it. But the scheme is developed with such perfect art that it exercises a strong fascination, which increases from scene to scene. The theme, even when Tasso becomes most vehement, is not once allowed to pass beyond control. With a light but sure touch Goethe moulds every part, securing that there shall not be even a minute detail without an organic relation to the whole. The scene of the action is not forced on our attention, but incidental allusions constantly remind us that all around the castle of Belriguardo are lovely sunny landscapes. The grace and purity of the style are unmatched in German dramatic literature, yet so easily do the lines flow into one another that we are almost tempted to think of them as utterances of nature herself; and in almost every scene there are individual lines or groups of lines concentrating the essence of Goethe's thought about life. In no other work by Goethe are there so many pregnant sayings fitted at once to guide and console those who are accessible to his influence.

The edition of his works in which these dramas were printed includes also "Faust: A Fragment." It appeared in the seventh volume, which was published in 1790. This "Fragment" did not contain all the scenes that Goethe had written at Frankfort; it concluded with the scene in the cathedral, where Gretchen is overcome with grief and remorse. On the other hand, it took in a part of Faust's second dialogue with Mephistopheles (beginning with the line, "Und was der ganzen Menschheit zugetheilt ist"), the short monologue in which Mephistopheles speaks of the inevitable ruin of a mind which despises reason and science, the "Hexenküche" (written in Rome), and "Wald und Höhle." The dialogue between Mephistopheles and the scholar was much altered, and the whole of the scene in Auerbach's cellar was presented in verse. The work, therefore, without being vitally changed, was considerably developed, and in the new passages as well as in those re-written there is ample evidence of the advance

Goethe had made in the mastery of poetic forms. Moreover, Faust's dialogue with Mephistopheles, and the monologue of Mephistopheles, show that Goethe had now a deeper appreciation of all that was involved in the conception of Faust turning from his high ideal aims to seek for satisfaction in the pleasures of the senses.

Another, and very different, work was published in this edition—"Die Metamorphose der Pflanzen" ("The Metamorphosis of Plants"). In this famous essay Goethe expounds the theory that the foliar organs of flowering plants are all to be regarded as various forms of the leaf. To this discovery he had been led by prolonged and delicate observation. The idea seems to have dawned upon him before he went to Italy, but it was in Italy, where he had many opportunities of studying plants he had not formerly known, that he became conscious of its full significance. The doctrine has long been accepted by botanists, and it acquired fresh importance when it came to be associated, as it is now associated, with the general law of evolution. Goethe delighted in the conception, not only for its own sake, but because it seemed to him a most striking illustration of the principle that in organic nature all things are created in accordance with enduring types. The doctrine of the metamorphosis of plants had been set forth, thirty years before Goethe's treatise was written, by K. F. Wolff. Goethe afterwards learned this, and was in no way disturbed by the fact that he had been anticipated. That the theory had suggested itself to two minds working independently gave him hearty pleasure as welcome evidence of its truth.

Early in 1790 Goethe was summoned to Venice to meet the Duchess Dowager, who, having travelled for some time in Italy, was now about to return to Weimar. Her coming was long delayed, and, being restless and impatient, he occupied himself in writing a series of rather bitter epigrams. After six weeks' absence he was delighted to find himself again in Weimar, for now his home was doubly dear to him, a son having been born on Christmas Day of the previous year. The child wa' baptized by Herder, and received the name Juliu: August Walther. Afterwards three children were born dead, and a fourth died in infancy. On each of these occasions Goethe suffered poignant grief, and wholly lost his self-control.

His second visit to Venice was made memorable by an important scientific discovery. He was standing with his valet Seidel in the Jews' cemetery, when Seidel lifted a piece of a sheep's skull, and handed it to Goethe, pretending that it was the skull of a Jew. As Goethe looked at it, it suddenly occurred to him that the bones of which the skull is composed are not essentially diffe- rent from vertebræ, but are, in fact, vertebræ transformed. The idea corresponds exactly with his conception of the foliar organs of flowering plants as transformed leaves. Goethe did not mean that in the course of long ages ver- tebræ had been developed into the bones of the skull, but simply that Nature, in creating these bones, modifies vertebræ to suit special needs. Like his earlier dis- coveries, however, this theory—which is only another application of his general doctrine of types—becomes thoroughly intelligible only when the facts to which it relates are explained by the law of evolution. It is the supreme merit of Goethe's contributions to biology that they all pointed in the direction of evolution, and were among the influences that made the recognition of it, sooner or later, inevitable.

About this time Goethe interested himself in the study of Newton's theory of colours, and, that he might under-stand it more fully, borrowed some prisms. When the owner asked that they should be returned, he thought he would like to try one of them again before sending them back. The result was that he began to suspect that Newton's doctrine was not true, and in this suspicion he was confirmed by further research. This subject had an extraordinary fascination for Goethe, and almost to the end of his life he worked at it at intervals, firmly con-vinced, not only that Newton was wrong, but that he himself had discovered the true scientific significance of colours ; and he attributed vast importance to his own doctrine. In old age he even told Eckermann one day that he did not at all pride himself on his poetry, but that his theory of colours did seem to him something to be proud of. Unfortunately, Goethe here dealt with problems for the solution of which he had not been ade-quately prepared. The subject appeared to him less complicated than it really is, and his conclusions have been unanimously rejected by men of science. His writings about it, however, have a certain interest, not merely because of their lucid style, but because he brings together much curious information relating to the history of opinion on the question, and also because it is hardly less instructive to understand the intellectual influences

by which a great man is misled than to understand those
by which he is guided to truth.

In 1791 the Duke established a Court Theatre in
Weimar, and asked Goethe to undertake the direction of
it. Goethe consented, and for many years this was one
of the duties to which he devoted most attention. His
aim was to provide representations that should appeal
to, and delight, a really cultivated taste, and he was
almost as anxious that the acting should be maintained
at a high level as that the dramas acted should be good.
He took immense pains to realize his ideal, and under
his control the Weimar Theatre ultimately became
famous. All over Germany it was recognized as the
theatre in which most was done for the development of a
great school of dramatic art.

The Duke, anxious to find some fitting way of expressing to Goethe his gratitude for the services he had
rendered, presented him, in 1792, with the house in
which he spent the rest of his life. Goethe changed it
to suit his own ideas, and made it the handsomest and
pleasantest private dwelling in Weimar. In altering it he
received much help from his friend Meyer, the Swiss
artist whose acquaintance he had made in Rome. Meyer
had come to Weimar at Goethe's urgent request, and
for several years lived as a guest in his house. He
painted for Goethe a portrait of Christiane with her
little boy in her arms in the position of the "Madonna
della sedia." This portrait was always kept under a cur-
tain, and Goethe counted it among the most precious of
his treasures.

We must think of Goethe at this time as often direct-

ing his attention gravely and anxiously to the progress of
events in France, where the movement of thought by
which he had been so profoundly influenced in youth had
at last led to its logical issues in action.   Some of the best
of Goethe's contemporaries in Germany hailed the French
Revolution as the beginning of a new and glorious era
for humanity. Their rejoicings were not shared by
Goethe. He knew well, indeed, the sufferings of the
oppressed population, not only of France, but of other
countries, his own included ; and he was eager that their
condition should be improved by just and wise government. But he found it impossible to believe that the end
could be attained by violence, and he had no doubt that
the tendency of the Revolution would be to check for
many a day every great and noble movement in art, literature, and science.   He fully recognized, however, that
the events he deplored were in the last resort due, not to
self-seeking agitators, but to the abuses of a thoroughly
corrupt society.   Long afterwards he said to Eckermann
that if he detested revolutionists, he detested not less
strongly the people who made revolutions inevitable ; and
that this was his feeling from the beginning is distinctly
indicated by several of his writings. "Gross-Cophta,"
a prose play written in 1791, deals with the story of the
diamond necklace, with which the impostor Cagliostro
was intimately connected. The play is not artistically
important, but it shows how dark a view Goethe took of
some elements of the social life of France in the period
immediately preceding the Revolution. In "Die Auf-
geregten," an unfinished prose play belonging to the
same time, he represents the peasantry of a French

estate as rising in revolt against the countess to wnom
they owe allegiance. The countess, being a woman of
enlightened opinions, does not dispute that they have
solid grievances, and readily meets them half way. The
moral evidently is that if the French nobles as a class
had possessed her elevation of character, the peril of
violent change might without difficulty have been averted.

In 1792 began the long series of revolutionary wars.
The Duke of Weimar served as a general in the Prussian
army, and at his request Goethe accompanied him during
the campaign in Champagne. Here Goethe realized
for the first time the terrible nature of the forces which
the Revolution had let loose on the world. During
the cannonade of Valmy, anxious to know what the
"cannon-fever" was really like, he rode to a spot exposed
to the enemy's fire. On the evening of this memorable
day, when the French gained their first success, Goethe
wrote in his tent: "From this place, and to-day, begins
a new epoch in the history of the world, and you may
say that you were there."

On his return, after an absence of four months, he
wrote in hexameters, as a satire on the political follies of
the day, his admirable version of the old Low Dutch tale,
"Reineke Fuchs." Next year, 1793, he was again with
the Duke, this time before Mainz, which the Prussians
were trying to recapture from the French. When the
town was given up, Goethe felt that he had had enough,
and more than enough, of war, and went back with relief
to his home and his studies at Weimar.

CHAPTER VIII.

DURING the next period of Goethe's life, extending from 1794 to 1805—that is, from his forty-fifth to his fifty-sixth year—the central facts are those relating to his friendship with Schiller.

Schiller, who was ten years younger than Goethe, came to Weimar from Dresden in 1787, when Goethe was in Italy. He was then twenty-eight years of age, and was known chiefly as the author of "The Robbers" and "Don Carlos." He had passed through many a harsh and stern experience, but retained in all their freshness the high, ideal impulses of his early youth. Of the many striking figures who arose in Germany during the second half of the eighteenth century, Schiller, not as a writer only but as a man, was one of the noblest. It was his destiny to have to endure much physical pain, but his sufferings were never allowed to embitter his spirit or to depress his courage. He marched steadily forward on his chosen path, keeping always before himself the loftiest aims, and kindling in other minds something of his own generous passion for truth, humanity, and freedom.

Dramatic work having been anything but profitable in a material sense, Schiller began, soon after his arrival at Weimar, to write his book on the revolt of the Netherlands, hoping that as an historian he might secure the independence that was necessary to enable him to do justice to his powers as a poet. He had the warmest admiration for Goethe's genius, and looked forward eagerly to his return.

The two poets met for the first time in the summer of 1788, at Rudolstadt, in the house of Frau von Lengefeld, whose daughter Charlotte afterwards became Schiller's wife. Goethe, who had no means of knowing that Schiller's ideas had been in some respects gradually approaching his own, thought of him simply as one of the vehement "Sturm und Drang" writers. On this occasion, therefore, their talk did not pass beyond the limits of ordinary politeness, and Schiller obtained the impression that they were so different from one another that friendship between them would be impossible. Nevertheless, he thought much about Goethe, and sometimes could not help rather enviously contrasting Goethe's prosperity with his own crushing difficulties.

In 1789 Schiller settled in Jena as a professor of history, having obtained this appointment through Goethe's influence. Early in the following year he married Charlotte von Lengefeld, his union with whom may have brought him repeatedly into contact with Goethe, who was an old friend of Charlotte's family. We know of one meeting between them in the autumn of 1790, when Goethe called at Schiller's house. They talked of the philosophy of Kant; and Schiller, in writing about the conversation to his friend Körner, spoke of Goethe as being, in his opinion, too much occupied with the laws of the outward world. He recognized, however, Goethe's great way of thinking, and his effort to detect the meaning of individual facts by combining them in a whole.

Broken in health, Schiller went with his wife, in 1793, to Würtemberg, in the hope that he might benefit by his native air. While staying at Stuttgart, he made arrangements with the publisher Cotta for the issue of a literary periodical, the *Horen* ("The Hours"); and after his return to Jena, in 1794, he wrote to Goethe, asking him to become a contributor. Goethe cordially undertook to give what help he could. Shortly afterwards they both happened to attend a meeting of a scientific society at Jena, and as they walked together towards Schiller's house they had an interesting discussion about the true method of science. In the course of this conversation Goethe was for the first time attracted by Schiller ; and he was drawn towards him still more strongly by a later talk, in which he found that they did not essentially differ from one another in their ideas about art.

In September of the same year Goethe invited Schiller to visit him, that they might come to an understanding about the nature of the work to be done for the *Horen*. Schiller gladly promised to spend a fortnight in Goethe's house, and it was during this visit that the deep and solid bases of their friendship were laid. Each gave his heart to the other without reserve, and to the end of Schiller's life nothing was permitted to stand in the way of their mutual love and confidence. Goethe often went to Jena, where he had rooms in the old Schloss, and Schiller was never happier than when he had an opportunity of spending some time at Weimar. On every occasion when they met, each seemed to find some new quality to intensify his admiration for the other's thought and character.

Goethe and Schiller took the purest delight in one another's achievements, and neither of them was ever tired of stimulating the other to bring forth the noblest fruits of his genius. The tendency of Schiller, who was hardly less a philosopher than a poet, was to give his ideas, even in poetry, an abstract expression. Through contact with Goethe he was led, almost unconsciously, to present his conceptions in more imaginative forms. His style became more direct, lucid, and animated, and deeper appreciation of the real world around him imparted fresh life and colour to his pictures of purely ideal realms. Goethe, whose genius was of an incomparably higher order, and responded to a wider range of influences, had nothing, so far as art was concerned, to learn from Schiller. Nevertheless, he owed to Schiller, as he himself was always eager to acknowledge, a deep debt of gratitude. From the time when he had finished "Tasso" and the "Roman Elegies," he had produced nothing that was worthy to rank with his best work. He had occupied himself chiefly with ministerial business and physical science, and seemed almost to have lost the impulse to visit the imaginative world in which he had for a while moved so freely and so happily. His power of poetic creation was, however, only slumbering; and by his intercourse with Schiller it was awakened to splendid activity.

Schiller's enthusiasm called forth in him what Goethe himself called "a second youth," "a new spring."

The *Horen*, which began to appear in 1795, excited much antagonism, and Schiller was excessively annoyed by the attacks directed against it. Goethe did not let himself be disturbed by hostile judgments, but towards the end of the year he proposed that they should amuse themselves by making their opponents the subjects of a series of epigrams, each epigram consisting of a distich. This suggestion delighted Schiller, and they lost no time in giving effect to it. The scheme widened as they went on, being made to include not only writers who had directly assailed them, but others whose methods and tendencies they disliked. They also seized the opportunity to do honour to various great writers, such as Lessing and Kant. A vast collection of epigrams soon accumulated, some by Goethe, some by Schiller, and some the work of both poets. They were called "Xenien" ("Xenia," hospitable gifts: a title borrowed from Martial), and published in the "Musenalmanach," a yearly volume of poems, edited by Schiller. These epigrams, many of which are bright and keen, fluttered the dovecots of criticism, and caused Goethe and Schiller, whose names were always henceforth closely associated, to be held in wholesome dread by pedants and literary impostors.

The first important work completed by Goethe after the beginning of his friendship with Schiller was "Wilhelm Meisters Lehrjahre" ("Wilhelm Meister's Apprenticeship"). In 1793 he had taken in hand the task of revising the part he had written before his sojourn in

Italy, but it is doubtful whether he would have gone on with it but for Schiller's influence. Schiller was intensely interested in the book, and often talked about it with Goethe, who sought his advice as to the best way of rounding it off. Encouraged by his friend's enthusiasm, Goethe carried on his labours steadily until it was finished in 1796.

In "Werther," Goethe's first romance, he deals only with one great crisis in the history of his hero. "Wilhelm Meister," on the contrary, is a picture of the entire course of a young man's life. Meister is the son of a merchant, and at the point where the tale begins he is associated with his father in business. He has a touch of poetry, and longs for a freer, more exciting, more interesting career, in which he may find scope for the development of his individuality. He is profoundly interested in the drama, and this feeling is deepened by his relation with Marianne, a beautiful actress whom he passionately loves. At last he decides to escape with Marianne from his commonplace surroundings, and to become an actor; and all his arrangements are made, when he is led, by some incidents which he misinterprets, to believe that the girl to whom he has been devoted is unfaithful to him. Shocked by this supposed discovery, he abandons her, and in a dejected mood continues to go through his ordinary duties. But by and by, when travelling to execute some business commissions, he meets several actors and actresses, and his old love for the stage is revived. A theatrical company is formed; the director receives from Meister enough money for the necessary expenses; and the players are invited by a count to give performances at his country house. Here Meister becomes acquainted with the works of Shakespeare, and his ideas about the drama are transformed. He is excited, too, by a romantic relation with the young and beautiful countess. When the players, after the fulfilment of their engagement, are leaving the castle, he is attacked by bandits, and, as he lies wounded and apparently dying, help is brought to him by "the Amazon," a woman who makes a deep impression upon him. She suddenly appears, and as suddenly disappears, and he hardly knows, when he thinks of her, whether she is real or only a figure in a dream.

He forms a connection with a regular theatre, and, when acting the part of Hamlet, is so startled by the Ghost (the mystery of whose appearance is explained in the course of the story) that he produces a powerful effect by the truth of his representation. He has not, however, the capacity of becoming a great player, the reason being—as one of the characters tells him—that, no matter what part he assumes, it is always his own personality that he represents. He does not possess the faculty of giving living form to the thoughts and feelings of a type of mind different from his own. One of the actresses of the company, Aurelia, excites his sympathy by her settled melancholy, which is due to the fact that she has been deserted by Lothario, a lover, of high station, whom she is unable to forget. Before her death she intrusts a letter to Meister, asking him to place it, when all is over, in Lothario's hands.

In fulfilment of this mission, Meister quits the stage; and by Lothario, who has many great qualities, he is

introduced to a circle widely different from anything he
has yet seen. He finds that there is a secret society by
which, unknown to himself, he has been closely watched
and in some measure guided. This society, of which
Lothario is one of the leading members, has been formed
for the cultivation of all that is highest and noblest in
humanity; and Meister, his "Lehrjahre" over, is admitted into it with much pomp and ceremony. He
learns the truth about his first love, Marianne, and at
the same time hears that she is dead. He then wins the
affections of a woman who appeals rather to his intellect
than to his feeling; but he is afterwards brought into
contact with "The Amazon," who had passed before him
so strangely and beneficently, and the tale ends with the
description of the somewhat complicated circumstances
which lead to their betrothal.

Meister does not convey the impression of having
profited very largely by his "Lehrjahre." About this,
Goethe appears to have given himself little trouble. His
object was to present a series of striking pictures of life,
and this purpose he accomplished with brilliant power.
The execution is, however, very unequal. The last part
lacks the life, vigour, and movement of the earlier
scenes, and all that relates to the secret society is
strained and unnatural. In this part Goethe appears to
have been misled by Schiller, who insisted that the
problems suggested in the course of the narrative should
be worked out and solved. The elements of the original
conception were not knit together closely enough for
this rigorous treatment.

In the books dealing with Meister's connection with

the drama Goethe displays to perfection his matchless power of giving charm, through sheer force of style, even to scenes and incidents that are not in themselves very impressive. The characters, too, have astonishing vitality. We are told little about them, and their motives are never elaborately analysed. They are simply made to act before us, and we thus learn to know them, each in his and her own clearly marked individuality, as if we had met them in real life. Meister himself, with his wavering impulses and vague strivings after an ideal existence, is revealed with absolute truth to nature, and, although he never wins (nor is intended to win) our full respect, we are compelled, almost in spite of ourselves, to follow him with interest from stage to stage of his career. The most important character, however, is not Meister, but Mignon, one of the strangest, most pathetic figures in the world's literature. Transported in childhood from "the land where the citrons blossom " to the cold North, she is never at home in the scenes in which we find her. Calm, gentle, self-possessed, she conceals a burning passion that in the end consumes her life ; yet she is of so ethereal a nature that she seems to glide through the world as one who in no way belongs to it. A more truly poetic conception never took form in a romance ; and Mignon alone, even if "Wilhelm Meister " had contained no other element of interest, would have sufficed to make the book immortal. In relation to her the hero is seen at his best, and it is she who gives the work such unity as it possesses—a unity of spirit rather than of form. The songs sung by Mignon and by the Harper (another highly poetic figure, marked out from the beginning, like Mignon, for a tragic doom) are among Goethe's lyrical masterpieces, remarkable equally for the depth of their meaning and the purity, sweetness, and grace of their expression. In almost startling contrast to Mignon is the gay, bright, coquettish Philline—the type of feminine Bohemianism; a character thoroughly self-consistent and full of bounding life until we hear about her in the unfortunate concluding scenes, when things are told of her that tend to make her utterly unintelligible.

In "Wilhelm Meister" Goethe gives us much dramatic criticism. It has, of course, no vital relation to the story, but it is penetrating and suggestive, and the famous criticism of "Hamlet" marked an era in the modern appreciation of Shakespeare's methods. "The Confessions of a Fair Soul," of which the sixth book consists, have no connection whatever with the romance except that Meister is described as reading them. Yet who would wish that this exquisite study had been excluded? The original of the "Schöne Seele" was Goethe's friend Fräulein von Klettenberg. In presenting the history of her inward life, he penetrates to the very depths of a spirit purified, calmed, and ennobled by mystic contemplation of the invisible world.

The next great work completed during this period was "Hermann und Dorothea," an idyllic poem in hexameters. The idea of using classic forms in the treatment of a domestic theme was suggested to Goethe by Voss's "Luise," an idyll in hexameters, which he had read again and again with warm interest. "Hermann und Dorothea" consists of nine cantos, each of which is headed with the name of one of the Muses. The first five cantos (originally four) were written in nine days in the autumn of 1796, when Goethe spent some weeks at Jena. The work was resumed from time to time, and finished in the following year.

Nothing could be simpler than the tale told in this poem. Hermann is the son of an innkeeper in a Rhenish town. A band of emigrants, driven from their homes by stress of war in the period of the French Revolution, happen to come to the neighbourhood in the course of their wanderings, and Hermann's good mother sends him to them with a supply of clothing and provisions. Among them he sees Dorothea, who at once wins his heart. On his return he finds his father and mother in conversation with the pastor and the druggist ; and the pastor, a man of insight, perceives at a glance, from Hermann's heightened colour and sparkling eyes, that something has happened to excite and gladden him. He relates what has happened, and his father suspects that he loves Dorothea. The old man has always wished that his son should marry a maiden of a prosperous family, and angrily declares that he will never receive as a daughter a common peasant girl. Hermann sorrowfully leaves the room, and is soon followed by his mother, who finds him seated in deep dejection under a pear-tree which, crowning vine-clad slopes behind the inn, serves as a landmark far over the country. He opens his heart to her, and she consoles him, and gives him hope that his father's resistance may be overcome. It is finally arranged that the pastor and the druggist shall go and see Dorothea, and form an opinion of her fitness

to be Hermann's wife, and that Hermann shall drive with
them to the place where the emigrants have for the time
taken up their abode.   The pastor and the druggist are
captivated by Dorothea, and return to the inn to communicate their impressions.   Hermann remains behind
to woo the maiden he loves.   He is, however, deterred
by seeing that she wears an engagement ring, and simply
asks whether she will come with him and help his mother
in her housewifely duties.   She supposes that he wishes
to engage her as a servant, and, on this understanding,
frankly accepts his offer.   Then they walk back together,
and by the time they reach the pear-tree the landscape is
lighted by the full moon, while heavy masses of clouds,
betokening the approach of a storm, gather over the sky.
They enter the house together, and after an animated
scene, during which Dorothea—while thunder is heard
to crash—tells her history, all is brought to a satisfactory
end by the happy union of the lovers.

The substance of this story is contained in an old
pamphlet describing the adventures of a group of Protes-
tant exiles who were expelled from the archbishopric of
Salzburg in 1731.   The tale, however, owes its charm,
not to the bare facts of which it consists, but to the life
breathed into them by Goethe's art.   In old age he said
that " Hermann und Dorothea " was the only one of his
greater poems which he could still read with pleasure,
and it is certainly as near perfection as any of his creations.   The central figure is Dorothea, and we readily
understand her sway over Hermann, for she combines
strength with tenderness, and acts nobly, not from a
sense of duty merely, but because she is impelled by the

instincts of a true and generous spirit. There is a striking fitness between her vigorous, handsome form and her
frank and wholesome character ; and we feel that of such
stuff the women are made who keep a nation's life sound
and pure. Hermann, who has not, like Dorothea, been
disciplined by hard experience, is less independent, but
he has qualities which, when he is fully matured, will
give his character the firmness of outline possessed by
that of the wife he has won. Already he has courage to
be true to his own choice, and he awakens our sympathy
by the depth and ardour of his love. His mother's
gentleness is finely contrasted with the rough, worldly,
but not essentially unkind disposition of his father ; and
the wise, good pastor, and the gossiping, self-important
druggist help to bring out one another's peculiarities
by the differences of their modes of thought and
feeling. Goethe never pauses to call our attention to
this or that element of the tale ; all is stir and movement,
and the imagination is excited to form for itself a series
of graphic pictures and to combine them into a living
whole. The story advances so simply and naturally that
it carries us on with growing interest to the end, and its
significance is deepened by the vast world-movement of
which we are continually reminded by the presence of
the emigrants. The antique form of the poem is in perfect keeping with the theme as Goethe conceives it. His
hexameters flow lightly and freely, and aid rather than
hamper the harmonious development of his ideas.

In 1796 Goethe wrote "Alexis und Dora," which
serves as a splendid pendant to the "Roman Elegies ;"
and in the summer of the following year, while he was

staying at Jena, he began, in friendly rivalry with Schiller, to compose a series of ballads. Goethe generously yielded the palm as a ballad-writer to Schiller ; and it is true that Schiller's ballads, which are among the finest of his works, have a dramatic force that makes them more akin than Goethe's to the old popular poems of this class. But such ballads as " Der Erlkönig" (" The King of the Erls or Elves "), " Die Braut von Corinth " (" The Bride of Corinth "), and " Der Gott und Die Bajadere " (" The God and the Bayadere ") have a subtle charm of expression that was far beyond Schiller's range.

Goethe's lyrical poems, too, many of which were written during this period, have a freshness and a lightness of touch which Schiller himself felt to be unapproachable. Whatever may be thought of Goethe as a dramatist or a writer of romance, there never has been, and never can be, any dispute as to his greatness as a lyrical poet. The secret of the unfading charm of his lyrics lies chiefly in their truth and spontaneity. Goethe never sought to express in writings of this kind what he himself did not feel ; but if a strong feeling took possession of his mind, he could not rest until it found lyrical utterance. And in passing into form in verse, his feeling lost all that was accidental or of merely passing interest ; its expression became the reflection, not of one man's experience only, but of the ever-recurring experience of humanity. There are few elements of the inward life that Goethe does not touch in his lyrics, and all that he approaches is within the scope of his art. The German language, often so harsh and obscure, has in these perfect products of his genius an exquisite softness, richness, and transparency.

Goethe, who knew well the difficulties it presented, found in it an organ equally fitted for the lightest play of fancy and the loftiest flights of the imagination.

In 1797 Goethe visited Switzerland for the third time, and enjoyed heartily a long holiday with his friend Meyer, who had been in Italy collecting materials for a work which they thought of writing in common. This work, in which they proposed to show the relation of Italian art to the physical features of the country and to its social and political development, was never begun ; but Goethe's studies for it gave a fresh impetus to his enthusiasm for art, and for years one of the objects he had most at heart was to communicate his enthusiasm to an ever-widening circle among the educated classes of Germany. In 1798 he started an art journal called " Die Propyläen" (the German form of τὰ προπύλαια, The Gateway) ; but the public had little interest in the questions with which it dealt, and after the appearance of four numbers the enterprise had to be abandoned. Another result of Goethe's labours in connection with art was his masterly book on " Winckelmann und sein Jahrhundert " ("Winckelmann and his Century "), published in 1805. In this work, to which contributions were made by Meyer and the great Homeric scholar Wolf, Goethe offered a magnificent tribute to the memory of the writer who, by his insight and learning, had opened the way to a true appreciation of the artistic achievements of the ancient world.

Among other prose writings of this period may be mentioned Goethe's translation of the autobiography of Benvenuto Cellini, a task undertaken for the *Horen ;*

and "Rameaus Neffe" ("Rameau's Nephew"), a translation of what is, on the whole, the most powerful of
Diderot's works. "Le Neveu de Rameau" had not
yet been printed, and Goethe's rendering was made from
a manuscript which had come into Schiller's hands. A
more searching study of the baser possibilities of human
nature has never, perhaps, been written, and Goethe
faithfully reproduced it with all its original force and
vividness.

Schiller occupied himself for several years, at intervals,
with his great drama "Wallenstein." The mass of
his materials made it hard for him to see his way to an
adequate treatment of the subject; but in 1798, having
discussed his scheme thoroughly with Goethe, he was able
to arrive at a final decision as to its form. The Prelude,
"Wallensteins Lager" ("Wallenstein's Camp"), in the
extraordinary vividness of which there are unmistakable
marks of Goethe's influence, was represented for the first
time at the Weimar Theatre in October, 1798. "The
Piccolomini" was given early in 1799; and soon afterwards the entire work, including "Wallenstein's Death,"
was performed, a night being devoted to each of its three
parts. Goethe, as the director of the theatre, worked
hard to secure that full justice should be done to his
friend's masterpiece, and his disinterested efforts were
crowned with what was then considered unparalleled
success.

The effect of this triumph was that Schiller resolved not
only to devote himself almost exclusively to dramatic
work, but to transfer his residence from Jena to Weimar,
where he would have the advantage of being near the

theatre, and possess unlimited opportunities of intercourse with Goethe. Before the end of 1799 this plan was carried out, and all the benefits Schiller hoped to derive from it were realized. Goethe and he became, if possible, more intimate friends than ever, and never tired in their efforts to make the Weimar Theatre a great centre for the creation of a truly national stage. They were virtually joint directors, but Goethe retained, of course, supreme control.

This was the most brilliant period in the history of Weimar, for it was now the home of four famous writers, Goethe, Schiller, Herder, and Wieland. Herder died in 1803, and during his last years he became bitter and morose, so that, to Goethe's intense regret, he brought to an end the relations which had formerly been a source of so much happiness to both. With Wieland, who survived Herder ten years, Goethe remained on friendly terms to the last.

The great philosophical movement of Germany was now in full progress. It began with the publication, in 1781, of Kant's "Critique of Pure Reason," and was continued in different directions, first by Fichte, then by Schelling, and afterwards by Hegel and Schopenhauer. Goethe was not so fascinated as Schiller by the suggestions which were being offered by so many fine minds for the solution of the highest problems ; but he was too keenly alive to every kind of intellectual influence to allow any deep current of contemporary thought to escape his notice. He read with profound interest the second of Kant's great works, " The Critique of Judgment," and thoroughly mastered Fichte's system of ideas as expounded in the "Wissenschaftslehre" ("Theory of Knowledge"). He was still more strongly attracted by Schelling, in whose philosophy he found much that accorded with his own conceptions of Nature. Fichte and Schelling were for several years professors at Jena, and Goethe, to whom they owed their appointments, had many opportunities of discussing with them the questions to the study of which they had devoted their lives.

Another important movement, closely connected with the philosophical ideas of Fichte and Schelling, began at this time to arrest attention. It was the movement which led to the formation of the Romantic School. The critical leaders of this school, August and Frederick Schlegel, were both for a while lecturers at the University of Jena, where they exercised a powerful influence through their literary journal, *The Athenæum.* With them, and with Tieck and Novalis, Goethe, always anxious to encourage young writers who seemed to give indications of genius, sought to maintain the most friendly relations. He even caused to be represented on the Weimar stage two rather crude plays, "Ion" and "Alarcos," the former by August Schlegel, the latter by Frederick Schlegel. The writers of the Romantic school ultimately diverged widely from Goethe's methods, but all that was really vital in their teaching had already been embodied in his works, and it was chiefly from him that they originally derived the best and most fruitful of their impulses.

In the winter of 1803–4 Madame de Staël paid her famous visit to Weimar. Goethe did not fail to do due honour to so distinguished a guest, but, like Schiller, he was soon fatigued by her restless curiosity and endless talk. He interested her the more deeply because she could not but see that the air of patronage with which she had been disposed to meet him was wholly out of place. For no other German writer did she conceive so strong a respect.

Meanwhile, Schiller, quickened by Goethe's unfailing sympathy, had been producing in rapid succession the great plays of his last years—"Mary Stuart," "The Maid of Orleans," "The Bride of Messina," and "William Tell." Goethe had at this period, so far as the drama was concerned, no corresponding period of activity. In 1800 and 1801 he produced only translations of Voltaire's "Mahomet" and "Tancred." He was working, however, at an important poetical drama, "Die Natürliche Tochter" ("The Natural Daughter"). This drama was intended to be the first member of a trilogy dealing with the ideas on which the French Revolution had been compelling all the world to reflect. The trilogy was to represent the overthrow and re-establishment of an ancient monarchy, its overthrow being due to corrupt government, its re-establishment to the frank recognition of popular rights. The only part of the scheme he succeeded in working out was "Die Natürliche Tochter," in which we are permitted to see some of the abuses that were to have led to revolution. The facts on which the idea of the play was based Goethe found in the "Mémoires historiques de Stéphanie Louise de Bourbon Conti," published at Paris in 1797. Eugenie, the heroine, is the natural daughter of a duke, the uncle of the king; and the question on which the interest depends is whether she shall allow herself to be publicly acknowledged as one in whose veins there is royal blood, or whether she shall remain, as she has been educated, in seclusion. Fascinated by the charm of a lofty social position, she decides to claim the rights which the king, at her father's intercession, is willing to confer upon her. Then she becomes a victim of treachery and violence. Of all Goethe's plays this is the one in which he allows the idea of necessity to exercise the most rigid control over the development of the action. The circumstances being such as are described, there is no way of escape from the consequences of Eugenie's decision; all is ordered in accordance with an inevitable law. The characters, therefore, have no very distinct individuality. They are so completely subordinated to the general scheme that only the heroine receives a special name. The other characters appear simply as the King, the Duke, the Secretary, and so forth. The play, if we estimate it from the point of view selected by Goethe, is one of great power; but had he devoted himself to works of this kind he could never have shown the true character of his genius. His strength lay in the development, not of plot, but of character.

From time to time Goethe worked at a scheme very different from "Die Natürliche Tochter." Schiller had been greatly impressed by the fragment of "Faust" published in 1790, and in season and out of season urged and entreated him to complete it. Goethe himself had a secret consciousness that this was to be the highest of his achievements, and took advantage of every favourable mood to return to it. He was in no hurry, however, to bring the work to an end. All the deepest elements of his life were being expressed in it, and he could afford to let the harvest ripen slowly.

Early in 1801 Goethe had a serious illness, and for a good many years afterwards he was liable to attacks of a painful malady. Schiller also suffered from bad health, and it was too certain that his life would not be greatly prolonged. The crisis came in the spring of 1805. Schiller and Goethe had both been ill, but on the 29th of April Goethe felt well enough to visit his friend. Schiller was about to go to the play, and Goethe would not hear of his changing his plan. So they parted, never to see one another again. While in his place in the theatre Schiller caught a severe chill, and on the 9th of May he died.

Goethe, who was confined to his room, suspected, when he heard of Schiller's condition, that the result would be fatal. " Destiny is inexorable," he said, sadly ; "man of little moment." When the tidings of death were brought to his house, Meyer, who was spending the evening with him, was called out of the room. He had not courage to give so dreadful a message, and went away without taking leave. Something in the manner of the members of his household made Goethe uneasy, but he would not put his doubts at rest by asking any direct question. " I observe," he said to Christiane, "that Schiller must be very ill." During the night he was heard to sob loudly. Next morning, again addressing Christiane, he said, " It is true, is it not, that Schiller was *very* ill yesterday ? " Christiane burst into tears. " He is dead ? " asked Goethe, in a firm voice. Christiane, still crying, at last told him the bitter truth. "He is dead!" Goethe repeated, and covered his eyes with his hand.   He had never lived through a sadder moment, and for several days no one dared to mention Schiller's name in his presence.

CHAPTER IX.

AT the time of Schiller's death, days of terrible public disaster were swiftly approaching. In the summer of 1806 the Confederation of the Rhine was formed, and the rickety Holy Roman Empire fell to pieces. Shortly afterwards came the war in which Prussia, as an independent kingdom, was all but annihilated. The decisive battle was fought near Jena on October 14, 1806, and in the morning, standing with his family in the garden behind his house, Goethe heard the distant boom of cannon. Later in the day a skirmish was fought near the garden between some French and Prussian troops. When all was over, the French broke into the town, and plundered the inhabitants to their hearts' content, for, as the Duke of Weimar was an ally of the King of Prussia, his capital was held by the victors to be fair game. Two wild French soldiers burst into Goethe's house, and his life would probably have been lost but for the presence of mind of Christiane, who was able to secure help in time to avert a calamity.

On the day after the battle Napoleon himself entered the town, and on the 16th he ordered that the harrying should be brought to an end. He would probably have deprived the Duke of his territory but for the influence of the Duchess, for whom the French Emperor had high respect. The Duke was allowed to retain sovereign power on condition that he should at once withdraw from the Prussian army. Soon afterwards he was compelled to join the Confederation of the Rhine, and he had also to pay a huge indemnity.

Much energy had to be expended before the desolation due to these fearful days could be made good. The people, however, set to work with a will, and in the well-tried Minister, Goethe, they found the guidance and support they needed. He was full of resource and courage, saw exactly what had to be done, and the means of doing it, and stimulated every one by the example of his own zeal and activity. At this great testing-time, when Goethe's character shone forth in all its radiance, the inhabitants of the Duchy would have been much astonished if they had heard what afterwards became the foolish parrot-cry about his being an "egoist," a "Pagan," a man indifferent to the welfare of his neighbours, and caring only for his own culture. They would have felt that, if the cry was true, Goethe's "egoism" had a strange resemblance to other people's unselfishness.

Meanwhile, a great event had happened in Goethe's life. Christiane had become his wife, not only in reality, but in name. Many a time he had felt bitterly that he had committed a terrible mistake in defying, in this matter, the ordinary customs of society. He had paid a heavy penalty for the assertion of his independence ; for the presence of Christiane in his house in a position which—although perfectly honourable, so far as his own feeling was concerned—was misunderstood by the rest of the world, had been an occasion of much wretchedness both to her and to him. Moreover, his ideas about the respect due from the individual to great social rules had undergone a complete change. He himself needed no ceremony to bind his conscience, but he felt, as he had not felt eighteen years earlier, that a ceremony might be essential in the interests of the community at large. So, anxious that in a time of public confusion her true position should be put beyond doubt, he wrote to the Court preacher of Weimar, saying that a purpose which had often been in his mind had come to maturity—and might the formal union be concluded on the following Sunday or earlier? On Sunday, October 19, 1806, Goethe and Christiane became, in the face of the world, what they had all along been in their own esteem, husband and wife. The only persons present were their son August and Goethe's secretary, Riemer.

August was now a youth of seventeen, and had already been legitimated. He was a handsome young fellow, with dark hair and dark eyes, and endowed with good abilities. He was idolized by his father, and no one could please Goethe better than by showing kindness to his boy. About two years after the marriage August went to Heidelberg to study law, and it was with a heavy heart that Goethe let him go.

About this time Weimar became the home of Johanna Schopenhauer, the novelist, the mother of one of the most illustrious philosophers of the modern world. She was very bright and clever, and had an intense admiration for Goethe. "He is," she wrote, "the most perfect being I know, even in appearance. A tall, fine figure, which holds itself erect, very carefully clad, always in black or quite dark blue, the hair tastefully dressed and powdered, as becomes his age, and a splendid face with two lustrous brown eyes, which are at once mild and penetrating." Goethe was grateful to Frau Schopenhauer for receiving his wife with the respect that was her due. Not every woman of her standing was equally considerate.

A few years after Goethe's death a strange book took the world by surprise—Bettina von Arnim's "Goethes Briefwechsel mit einem Kinde" ("Goethe's Correspondence with a Child"). Bettina was the daughter of Goethe's old friend Maximiliane Brentano. While still a very young girl she fancied that there was some resemblance between herself and Mignon; and, as Mignon loved Wilhelm Meister, so she loved Goethe. In 1807, when she was about twenty-two, she came to Weimar, and soon gave evidence of her remarkable passion, which was, of course, an affair rather of the fancy than of the heart. Goethe talked with her kindly, but took care that her enthusiasm should be kept within reasonable bounds. Some years afterwards (in 1811) Bettina married the poet Arnim. She had the bad taste to insult Christiane, who very properly responded by forbidding her to enter Goethe's house again. To Bettina's surprise, he energetically supported his wife's decision. There was nothing about which he was so sensitive as the treatment accorded to his wife, and Bettina had to reconcile herself to the discovery that in her relation to

Goethe she was, in comparison with the woman whom she had held in such low esteem, of very little importance. The letters published after his death, and attributed to him, are in reality as much Bettina's work as Goethe's.

In 1808 he had to pass through a sorrow which he felt most keenly. Ever since his father's death his mother had continued to live at Frankfort. She was a woman of a genial and expansive nature, with a deep vein of poetry ; and her real character was fully recognized only when she had to confront the world, alone. Every one loved her, and she was adored by young girls, whom she delighted to gather around her. To her great joy, Goethe repeatedly visited her, and she was also able to welcome to her home his wife and son. She was so generous that, after Schlosser's death, the trustees for his children by his first wife, Cornelia, Goethe's sister, wished to put some legal limit to her expenditure ; and Goethe was asked to sanction their proposal. Goethe, however, who had inherited much of his mother's disposition, replied that she had a right to spend her fortune as she pleased, and so the good Frau Rath went on living the life that best suited her kindly, happy temper. She corresponded regularly with Goethe, and it would be impossible to conceive a more beautiful relation than that which existed between mother and son. She died on September 13, 1808, at the age of seventy-seven, and Goethe mourned for her with a grief that cut deeply into his inward life.

He sent his wife to Frankfort to make the necessary arrangements with regard to the inheritance that was to be divided between him and his sister's children. Christiane showed on this occasion not only a thorough faculty for business, but a liberal spirit that won golden opinions from all whom the matter concerned.

In the autumn of 1808 took place the famous meeting of Napoleon and Czar Alexander at Erfurt. Napoleon had read a French translation of "Werther," and expressed a wish to see the author. Accordingly, on the morning of October 2nd, Goethe was presented. As the poet entered, the Emperor looked searchingly at him, and, turning round, exclaimed, "Voilà un homme!" Napoleon talked of "Werther," and had also much to say about the French drama, frequently stopping to ask, "Qu'en dit M. Göt?" A few days afterwards Napoleon and his "pitful of kings" were present at a representation of Voltaire's "La mort de César" at the Weimar Theatre. After the play there was a ball, in the course of which Napoleon repeatedly took occasion to converse with Goethe. He condemned Voltaire's drama, and suggested that Goethe should write a better one on the subject, showing how Cæsar, if he had been allowed to live, would have done great things for Rome. The Emperor formed so high an opinion of Goethe that he begged him to come to Paris, assuring him of a fitting welcome.

Goethe had arranged with Cotta, in 1805, for the publication of a new edition of his collected works. The appearance of this edition is memorable, because one of the volumes, issued in 1808, contained the First Part of "Faust," as we now possess it.

There is no sound reason for supposing that when

Goethe first thought of making the Faust legend the subject of a drama he conceived the work as a whole, including the Second Part.   On the contrary, there is ample evidence that the dominant idea of the Second Part was a later development.[1]   The Frankfort "Faust" contains not a line or a suggestion which indicates that he intended the work to end otherwise than as a tragedy.   The whole scheme of the drama implies that the conclusion is to be tragical.

Long before the First Part was completed, however, the conception had taken another form.   It was one of Goethe's vital characteristics that his mind often reverted, by an inward necessity, to the consideration of the vast problems with which, at the earliest dawn of independent thought, man finds himself confronted.   He was especially fascinated by the terrible problem of evil.   What is its real nature?   Is it an essential element of the universe, and will it therefore abide for ever?   Or is it an appearance merely, a negation, which the human spirit may by some means shake off, and so recover its true freedom?   Goethe wrestled with these questions long and earnestly,

---

[1] This question has given rise to much discussion among students of Goethe's writings.   Herman Grimm is one of those who emphatically maintain that the First and Second Parts were from the beginning in Goethe's mind.   See his "Goethe," Zweiter Band, 273.   A full and clear statement of the opposite view will be found in Karl Biedermann's "Deutschland im Achtzehnten Jahrhundert," Zweiter Band, 1034.   Herman Grimm and those who agree with him rely mainly upon some expressions used by Goethe a few days before his death, in a letter written to William von Humboldt (one of the dearest and most highly esteemed of his friends).   Biedermann, however, shows conclusively that this letter has been misunderstood.

and at last he felt himself able to answer them deci-
sively.

No one who knows anything of Goethe will suppose
that he was a thinker of a light, optimistic temper. He
realized as few can realize—for few have his capacity for
piercing intuition—how deep are the roots of evil in
man's nature, and how profound the sources of his
misery. It is worthy of note that there is not one of
Goethe's works in which he tries to present a flawless
male character. Schiller loved to roam in an imaginative
world where men have no impulses except such as are
high, pure, and heroic. Goethe, on the contrary, held
fast by reality. Both in his dramas and his romances
most of his leading male figures have some radical defect
that either leads, or might conceivably lead, to disaster.
Even in "Goetz," the hero of which, if not perfect, is
thoroughly sound and good, he gives us Weislingen,
whose weakness brings him to a tragic doom. Kindred
weaknesses appear in the heroes of "Werther," "Clavigo,"
"Stella," "Tasso," "Wilhelm Meister." This is not an
accident, it is an essential element of Goethe's art, and it
in part explains why his work is so much more potent
than Schiller's. For, after all, however pleasant it may
be to dream of characters who float in an ideal realm far
above us, it is by characters in whom we find ourselves
reflected that we are most closely touched and most
deeply moved. Some of Goethe's feminine characters
are conceived in a different spirit. We cannot imagine
his Iphigenie, for instance, diverging from the straight
path. But he also presented Adelheid; and Lotte and
Gretchen, warmly as he loved them, are not prevented

from making experience of evil—the former by hovering on its verge, the latter by plunging into the abyss.

Goethe, then, was under no illusions as to the darker aspects of the world. He knew and felt that an awful conflict goes on between two mighty powers, the one fair and beneficent, the other hideous and malign. But he convinced himself—or, perhaps, it would be truer to say, the conviction grew in his mind—that this struggle is not necessarily eternal ; that in spirits which, in spite of failure and suffering, have always an inward longing for light and freedom, the good power ultimately triumphs, and crushes evil for ever under its feet.

To have a great conviction was in Goethe's case to be conscious of an urgent demand for its expression. Some time or other, therefore (perhaps in 1788, when, at Rome, he wrote of "the plan" having been "made"), it must have occurred to him that "Faust" provided him with precisely such a medium of expression as he needed. Faust has turned from all the highest influences to which his spirit in its inmost depths responds. In a mood of despair he has abandoned his ideals, and is seeking through the world for some rapture that will satisfy his cravings. So far, he is a type of humanity in one aspect of its life. But— Goethe seems to have asked himself—why should not Faust be a type of humanity in a larger, greater sense? If it is the destiny of evil to be conquered and to pass away, might not Faust become the representative of this sublime world-process? In his deep, imaginative spirit might we not see the entire course of the struggle, from the moment when evil seems to attain supremacy until that in which it will have to give way to the ultimate and absolute sway of good?

Nothing short of this was Goethe's aim in his final conception of "Faust." The poem was to embody all that his thought and his experience of life had taught him as to the spiritual history and the spiritual destiny of man.

Hence, in the completed First Part, the work no longer begins, as it began in its earliest form, with Faust's monologue. The Prologue in Heaven introduces us to a scene in which it is symbolically brought home to us that Faust, whatever may be his errors or crimes, will not always remain under their power, but will in the end recognize his true nature, yield his will to its laws, and so attain to liberty and peace. And, in accordance with this symbolic assurance, Goethe, in the body of the poem, brings into clearer prominence those qualities of Faust's character which show that at heart he is a man capable of fine impulse and generous aspiration. Every one knows how, after the second monologue, when he is about to end his unhappiness by death, he is affected by the chorus of angels and women on the morning of Easter Day. We obtain the conviction that, however deeply a man who can be so touched may fall, he can never place himself beyond hope of recovery. This is suggested, too, by the form of his pact with Mephistopheles. He is to yield himself wholly to Mephistopheles only if a moment shall come when he will be disposed to say "Oh, stay! thou art so fair!" We know that to a man of Faust's nature no such moment can ever come through evil agency.

In other respects the poem is not vitally changed; it is merely extended and developed in the sense in which it was originally conceived. The working-out of the idea of Faust's deliverance Goethe reserved for the Second Part.

The "Fragment" published in 1790 had passed almost unnoticed. The completed First Part, on the contrary, was received with general astonishment and admiration. Most people had begun to think of Goethe as one who had practically closed his literary career. He was now on the border-land between middle life and old age, and it had been supposed that no further work of importance was to be expected from him. Yet here was a poem of a depth and range that surpassed anything he had yet produced. For the first time his countrymen began to realize the true extent of his power, and, during the rest of his life, all who were capable of sound critical judgment regarded him as incomparably the greatest figure in the literature of Germany.

Two years after the publication of " Faust " he issued the third of his prose romances, " Die Wahlverwandtschaften " (" Elective Affinities "). The idea of this book had been for a long time in his mind. He originally intended to make it the subject only of a short study, but he ultimately felt that its full significance could be brought out only in an elaborate tale. The work displays high imaginative energy, and must be classed among the finest of Goethe's prose writings. Its most striking characteristic is the power with which he convinces us that the relations he calls " elective affinities," although they lead in the story to no outward wrong-doing, must necessarily, in such circumstances as he presents, have a deeply tragic meaning.

Another work belonging chiefly to this period is " Aus Meinem Leben. Dichtung und Wahrheit " (" From My Life. Poetry and Truth "), the first two parts of which appeared in 1811, the third in 1814. The fourth he did not finish until 1831. The narrative brings the story of Goethe's life down to the time when he quitted Frankfort for Weimar. His object was to describe the influences under which his character both as a man and as a writer was formed. Hence the stress he lays on his relations to Gretchen, Annette, Frederika, and Lili. To have omitted these figures from his picture, or to have sketched them only slightly, would have been to convey a wholly wrong impression of the conditions under which his peculiar powers were developed. The style in which the story is told is light, pliant, and graceful, and it has an especially delicate charm in the passages relating to the maidens whom he has loved. Some details of the narrative are incorrect, but that his reminiscences are substantially accurate we know from the fact that they accord in the main with his early works and letters. Goethe's intellectual relations even in youth were so far-reaching that " Dichtung und Wahrheit " is much more than a record of his personal experience. It contains a full and most vivid account of all the great currents of thought and feeling in Germany during an important transitional period in the history of her literature.

During the time when he was writing his autobiography, Goethe studied with much interest Von Hammer's translation of the Persian poet Hafiz. This led to the pro-

duction of the "West-Oestlicher Divan" (West-Eastern
Divan"). The work was not published until 1819, but
the greater part of it was written in 1815. It consists of
several series of short poems, and is remarkable chiefly
for the deep practical wisdom of many of its verses, for
the variety and perfection of its metres, and for the splendour of its diction. The "West-Oestlicher Divan" became
a source of inspiration to several poets of the new generation—among others, to Rückert, Platen, and Bodenstedt.

Meanwhile, Germany had been passing through a great
and stirring period of her history, and Goethe, like other
people, had been anxiously watching the progress of
events. It cannot, however, be said that he was one of
those who in any way aided the national cause. This
was not due to lack of patriotism, for although he could
not share the hatred with which most of his countrymen
at this time regarded France, he realized fully of what
vital importance it was for Germany that French supremacy should be brought to an end. But it did not seem
to him, when the War of Liberation began, that the time
had come for a final struggle for national independence.
Napoleon, notwithstanding his disasters in Russia, still
had vast resources at his disposal, and Goethe was con-
vinced that his military genius made him all but invinci-
ble. On the other hand, the German sovereigns, as he
had known them, had generally been self-seeking and
untrustworthy, and it appeared incredible to Goethe
that they would be able to act harmoniously for a high
common object. Happily, his forebodings proved to be
without foundation, and he was heartily pleased when he
had to admit that he had been mistaken.

One small result of the great national uprising was that the Duke of Weimar became a Grand Duke and received an accession of territory. As he proposed to establish a constitutional system of government, it was necessary that the method of administration should be considerably modified ; and Goethe, who was not consulted about the measures which were about to be taken, supposed that there might be some change in his own position. The Grand Duke, however, knew too well what he owed to his old and loyal friend to do anything to his disadvantage. Early in the winter of 1815, Goethe was informed that he had been appointed the First Minister of State.

A few months afterwards, he had to mourn the loss of his wife. She died on the 6th of June, 1816. This was a bitter grief to Goethe, who had never loved her more warmly than during the last years of her life.

CHAPTER X.

AFTER his wife's death Goethe became anxious that
arrangements should be made for the marriage of
his son August, who had for some time had an official
appointment at Weimar. Goethe's choice fell upon Ottilie
von Pogwisch, a handsome, clever girl, the granddaughter
of a lady for whom he had much regard. August was of
opinion that a better wife could not have been selected
for him, and so they were married on the 17th of June,
1817. Goethe laughingly warned Ottilie that she was
never to contradict her husband, and that if she
ever wanted to have the rapture of a quarrel, she
must come and have it out with *him*. They occupied the
top floor of Goethe's house, the rooms of which had been
carefully prepared and furnished for them ; and by and
by they received as a permanent inmate of their home
Ottilie's sister Ulrica. Two children were born of the
marriage, and his grandsons were to Goethe an inexhaustible source of delight.

Much as Goethe had done for the Weimar Theatre, the
business connected with it had often been an occasion of
trouble and annoyance, due chiefly to the intrigues of the

actress Fräulein Jagemann, who had great influence over the Grand Duke. Early in 1817 it was decided, in opposition to Goethe's wishes, that the birthday of the Grand Duchess should be celebrated by the representation of one of Kotzebue's plays. The performance was a failure, and Goethe handed in his resignation of the directorship. He was persuaded to withdraw it, but later in the year, when, in deference to Fräulein Jagemann, the Grand Duke sanctioned the representation of a play in which a leading part was to be taken by a dressed-up poodle, Goethe felt that it was impossible for him to retain a position in which his authority was disregarded. From this time he confined himself exclusively, in his official duties, to the control of institutions for the promotion of science and art. He devoted attention especially to the University of Jena, the prosperity of which he had missed no opportunity of furthering ever since his settlement at Weimar.

Goethe, who seemed to have the secret of eternal youth, carried with him into middle life and old age much of the fresh vivacity of his early years. He was especially remarkable for his sensitiveness to feminine influence. While writing the "Wahlverwandtschaften" he had been strongly attracted by the beauty, thoughtfulness, and amiability of Wilhelmine Herzlieb, the foster-daughter of the wife of Herr Frommann, a bookseller at Jena, at whose house he was a frequent and welcome guest. Some of Wilhelmine's qualities were reproduced in Ottilie, the lovely and pathetic figure who is overtaken by so sad a fate in the "Wahlverwandtschaften." At the time when most of the poems in the "West-Oestlicher Divan" were written, he had a still more cordial relation with

Marianne, the fascinating wife of his friend Geheimerath von Willemer, of Frankfort.   In 1814 and 1815 he had much pleasant talk with Marianne in her home, and in 1815 she and her husband spent some happy days with him at Heidelberg.   Marianne was not only a handsome woman, of a sound and affectionate character, but had a touch of poetic genius.   She followed with warm interest and sympathy Goethe's progress in the composition of the poems of the " Divan." Some of them were addressed to her, and she responded with original verses, of which Goethe thought so highly that he interwove them with his own work.

Goethe's relations to Wilhelmine Herzlieb and Marianne Willemer were much the same as Dr. Johnson's relations to Frances Burney and Mrs. Thrale. Both women interested him, appealed to his imagination, and liked him as heartily as he liked them ; and, as a poet and a German, he could give warm expression to his regard for them without running the slightest risk of being misunderstood by either.   When he sent to Frau Willemer the exquisite little lyric, " Nicht Gelegenheit macht Diebe," and she, as Suleika, replied with the equally beautiful poem, " Hochbeglückt in deiner Liebe," they would have been astonished and dismayed had any one been stupid enough to suppose that, so far as their relations to one another were concerned, either set of verses represented more than a light and delicate play of fancy.

Afterwards, however, Goethe passed through a deeper experience.   This was his love for Ulrica von Levezow, whom he met with her mother, an old friend of his, at

Marienbad in 1822, when he was in his seventy-third year. Goethe was charmed by the beautiful maiden, and loved her as ardently as if he had been fifty years younger. In the following year he met her again with her mother at the same place, and the fascination she exerted over him was so obvious that gossips began to talk of an approaching betrothal. When Ulrica left Marienbad, Goethe felt sadly depressed. He found relief, however, while listening to the playing of the Polish pianist, Madame de Szymanowska, and then he was able to give in the fine poem " Aussöhnung " (" Reconciliation ") full expression to his sense of what seemed for the moment his recovered freedom. It cost Goethe a hard struggle to overcome this late-flowering passion. He was determined that it should be mastered, and in the end succeeded in suppressing it.

On the 3rd of September, 1825, the fiftieth anniversary of the Grand Duke's accession was celebrated. Goethe was deeply moved by the memories which crowded in upon him on this occasion. It was arranged that early in the morning a cantata should be sung in front of the Roman House, in the Park, where the Grand Duke was staying; and, while this was being done, Goethe entered, anxious to be the first to congratulate the sovereign he had served so well. The Grand Duke took Goethe's hands in his own, and said, " To the last breath together!" About two months afterwards the fiftieth anniversary of Goethe's arrival at Weimar was also celebrated. The Grand Duke presented him with a gold medal struck for the occasion, and expressed in a letter all that he felt about the magnificent services Goethe had for half a century rendered to himself and his people. By the Grand Duke's order, a copy of this letter was posted on a wall opposite Goethe's house. Seeing a crowd, Goethe sent a friend to find what was interesting them. " That is he ! " cried Goethe, when he learned what had been done. In the evening " Iphigenie " was represented, and the town was brilliantly illuminated.

Goethe was saddened, almost beyond the power of expression, by the death of the Grand Duke in 1828, and that of the Grand Duchess in 1830. He had been associated with them so long, and had loved them, and been loved by them, so truly, that their death, in the first moments of grief, seemed like the breaking-up of all that had made life valuable. Happily, he had every reason to be satisfied with his relations with the young Grand Duke and Grand Duchess. They looked up to him with reverence, and delighted to do him honour.

In his home Goethe had much wearing anxiety and distress. His son August, although endowed with many good qualities, was of a wayward and uncertain temper, and at last took to hard drinking. He loved his father deeply, but even Goethe's influence was not strong enough to deliver him from this hideous tyranny. In 1830 he went to Italy, and he died at Rome on the 27th of October. It was found that he had been suffering from malformation of the brain.

In 1821 a student at Göttingen, Johann Peter Eckermann, submitted a copy of his poems to Goethe, with a sketch of his life; and Goethe, as was his wont on such occasions, sent a friendly answer. Two years afterwards Eckermann, encouraged by this reply, despatched a manuscript to Goethe, begging that he would forward it to Cotta. On the 10th of June, 1823, an interview took place, and Eckermann made so good an impression that Goethe gave him some work to do, and ultimately made him his secretary. The result was that many years afterwards the world received Eckermann's "Conversations with Goethe." Eckermann was not, like Boswell, a great artist, and Goethe does not live in his book as Johnson lives in Boswell's. Nevertheless, these "Conversations" present a most striking picture of Goethe in old age, and it is impossible to read them without feeling that they bring us into contact with an intellect and character of superb quality. Almost every subject interests Goethe, as he is here revealed; and on all matters, from the humblest to the most lofty, about which he expresses an opinion, he has something to say that indicates a mind fresh, vigorous, and richly stored with the fruits of a life of thought, action, and study. Above all, the reader is impressed by the noble feeling of humanity that pervades his utterances. Goethe has seen as much of the world as it is given to men to see; yet in his judgments there is no trace of a bitter or querulous temper. He is mild, serene, and helpful.

Weimar had now become a place of pilgrimage for young poets, who looked to Goethe as the supreme master of their craft. Among those who came to him was the poet who was destined to take, after Goethe's death, the first place in the imaginative literature of Germany—Heinrich Heine. Heine visited Weimar when he was twenty-five years of age, and had already taken rank among the most powerful writers of his day. Long afterwards, in "Ueber Deutschland," he said that in talking with Goethe he involuntarily looked at his side for the eagle of Zeus. "I was nearly," he says, "addressing him in Greek." Many a time, when he had thought of visiting Goethe, he had reflected on all sorts of sublime things he would like to say. When he found himself actually in the great man's presence, he remarked that the plums by the wayside between Jena and Weimar were uncommonly good! So, at least, we are assured by Heine, whose reminiscences were seldom intended to be taken quite seriously. Goethe appreciated Heine's rare gifts, but said to Eckermann that with all his brilliance one thing was wanting to him—love. He predicted, however, that Heine would be greatly feared.

From abroad, as well as from all parts of Germany, testimonies of admiration were from time to time sent to Goethe. On his last birthday he received from fifteen (or perhaps nineteen) Englishmen, among whom were Sir Walter Scott, Wordsworth, Southey, and Carlyle, a seal bearing the motto from one of his poems, "Ohne Hast, aber ohne Rast" ("Without haste, but without rest"). The suggestion that this tribute of respect and gratitude should be offered to Goethe had been made by Carlyle, with whose translation of "Wilhelm Meister" he had been greatly delighted. Goethe, although he never saw Carlyle, recognized his genius, and foretold his future greatness.

During his last years Goethe took little interest in the public affairs of Europe. Least of all did he interest himself in the proceedings of Liberal politicians. On the day when the tidings of the French Revolution of

1830 reached Weimar, his friend Soret went to see him. When Soret entered his room Goethe was in a state of intense excitement, and began to talk of the mighty volcanic eruption at Paris. Soret replied that nothing else was to be expected from such a Ministry. Goethe looked at him in astonishment. What had the Ministry to do with the matter? He had not been speaking of "those people," but of the contest in the French Academy between Cuvier and Geoffroy St. Hilaire!— a contest in which St. Hilaire had supported Goethe's ideas as to the true way of conceiving organic Nature.

The essential aim of the Liberal party all over Europe in those days was to secure a political system in which the functions of the Government should be restricted within the narrowest possible limits. Every interest of life was to be submitted to the operation of the principle of free competition. Goethe could have no sympathy with a movement of which this was the ultimate object, for it was one of his deepest convictions that strong government is an enduring necessity of society, and that the path of free competition is a path that leads to ruin. And have events proved that in this opinion he was utterly mistaken? So far as industry and trade are concerned, the Western world has had ample experience of free competition, and can we take much pride in such of its results as are seen in the foul and pestilent dens in which, in every great city, multitudes of men, women, and children are compelled to lead degraded and unhappy lives? Goethe did not mean by strong government a system which should crush thought and true individuality. On the contrary, to him thought and true individuality

seemed the vital conditions of human progress.   But he
wished, too, that the weak should be protected against
the tyranny of the strong ; that the State should be the
supreme organ of practical reason for the establishment
and maintenance of wholesome relations between man
and man, and for the execution of measures designed to
promote the free development, not of this class or of
that only, but of the community as a whole.

Many Liberal politicians were never tired of talking of
Goethe as one who cared nothing for the practical
interests of the world.   They mistook indifference to
their party for indifference to humanity.   The truth
is, he was in one sense far ahead of those who
virulently assailed him as a reactionary.   As we know
from many passages in " Wilhelm Meisters Wanderjahre,"
he saw that the real problems of the future were not
merely political but social; that communities could never
hope to solve these problems by simply giving free scope
to the forces contending for mastery ; and that for the new
conditions of the world new forms of co-operative industrial organization would become inevitable.   He
devoted much earnest attention to the principles expounded during this period by St. Simon, and his ideas
about social progress have a close affinity to some of
those with which the English-speaking world has been
made familiar by the most illustrious of its modern
spiritual teachers, Carlyle and Ruskin.

Even in old age Goethe never paused in his labours
as a man of letters.   One of the works now issued by
him was " Wilhelm Meisters Wanderjahre " (" Wilhelm
Meister's Years of Travel ").   It was published in its

earliest form in 1821, but afterwards it was recast, the work as we now have it being finished in 1829. This book has little real connection with the " Lehrjahre," and ought not to be read as a complete work of art, for Goethe hardly even attempts to give unity to the various elements of which it is made up. Much of it is rather tiresome, but it also contains tales and passages as remarkable for nobility of style as for depth of thought. Especially valuable are those parts of the book in which he develops his mature convictions with regard to education, and the conditions of the high and enduring welfare of industrial societies. Here he anticipates much of what is most deeply characteristic of the thought of our own day.

In all directions Goethe continued to exercise his widely varied powers. He edited a periodical called for some time " Kunst und Alterthum in den Rhein und Maingegenden " (" Art and Antiquity in the districts of the Rhine and the Main "). Afterwards he called it simply " Kunst und Alterthum," and included in it, besides papers o n art and archæology, some of his poems and essays in literary criticism. He also published, between 1817 and 1824, a scientific periodical, in which he printed his treatise on the intermaxillary bone, and communicated his discovery as to the constitution of the bones of the skull. This discovery had in the interval been independently made by Oken, but to Goethe the question of priority appeared to be one of absolutely no importance.

During this time, too, he went on writing lyrical and other poems, as he had done during all the earlier periods of his career; and he devoted great attention to

the preparation of a complete edition of his works, the
first volume of which was published in 1827. He also
found time to write or dictate an extraordinary number of
letters. Goethe had always been a model correspondent,
and the various collections of his letters are of inestimable
value for the light they throw upon his character. He
himself issued, in 1828-29, his correspondence with
Schiller; and he prepared for publication his correspondence with Zelter, the genial and eccentric Berlin
musical composer, to whom he was warmly attached.
We now possess a vast series of Goethe's letters, some
dating from early youth, others written immediately before
his death. They reflect accurately many different moods,
corresponding to the different stages of his development ;
but in the letters of all the periods of his life the mind
which unconsciously discloses itself is one dominated by
a passion for truth, by a lofty sense of honour, and by
manly, humane, and generous impulses.

The most important work of his old age is the Second
Part of " Faust." Some portions of it had been written
even before the appearance of the First Part ; but the
work belongs in the main to his latest period. He
finished it before his last birthday, and told Eckermann
that, this task being done, he would regard the rest
of his life as "a pure gift."

"Faust," therefore, had accompanied him during the
entire course of his literary career. In it he had represented all the various phases of evolution through which
his thought and character had passed.

As a work of art, the Second Part is far inferior to the
First. It lacks the unity which is to some extent given

to the First Part by Faust's relation to Gretchen ; and it contains a multitude of symbolical ideas, the meaning of which it is hard to unravel. We miss, too, the fire and glow of the scenes conceived in Goethe's early days, when "Faust" served as the direct imaginative expression of his own tumultuous thoughts and longings. Nevertheless, there are individual passages, especially in the scenes relating to Helen of Troy, full of splendid power ; and the idea in which all is summed up is in every way worthy even of the grandest of the original elements of Goethe's scheme. Before dying, Faust feels that a moment might come to which, with all his heart, he could say, "Oh, stay! thou art so fair!" But it is a moment which Mephistopheles, the representative of the evil in his nature, could never have secured for him. It is a moment of pure delight springing from the contemplation of the results of disinterested labour in the service of humanity.

This was Goethe's last word to the world ; the expression of his deepest and most settled conviction. To make selfish joy, as Faust had done, the supreme object of existence—that way lie perpetual evil and misery ; to sacrifice self, to bring the will into harmony with ideal law, in all things to think and act in a spirit of love and brotherhood, as Faust, after fierce struggle, learns to do —in that, and in that alone, can man find a life truly fitted to his nature and capable of satisfying his deepest, inmost wants. The idea with which Goethe seeks to solve the problem of "Faust" is the old, yet ever new, doctrine—"He that loseth his life for my sake shall find it."

For many years Goethe enjoyed excellent health, and from day to day his work went on without serious interruption. The end—described simply and graphically in Düntzer's "Goethes Leben"—came somewhat suddenly, when he was in his eighty-third year. On Thursday, March 15, 1832, when the young Grand Duchess paid him her usual weekly visit, he had much to say about a drawing which a friend had sent him from Pompeii. It was a sketch of an ancient design in mosaics, representing a scene in the life of Alexander the Great. The Grand Duchess saw in her friend no sign of an approaching illness, nor was Goethe, when he retired to his room in the evening, conscious of any physical change. During the night, however, he could not sleep, and next morning it was obvious that he had lost much of his usual vigour. Between the 19th and the 20th of March, about midnight, he had severe pains in the chest and suffered from an attack of breathlessness. Even these symptoms did not alarm him, and on the 20th he had strength enough to sign an official paper securing that aid should be granted to a lady whose talents as an artist had excited his admiration. But life was gradually ebbing away. On the morning of the 22nd of March, he sat in his armchair, holding the hand of his daughter-in-law, Ottilie, in his own, and conversing with her brightly. As he talked, his words came with increasing difficulty, and at last he wholly lost the power of speech. He made signs in the air, and, when his arm dropped, moved his fingers as if writing on his knee. Shortly before midday, leaning back in a corner of his chair, he softly passed away.

If we look back upon the course of Goethe's long life, it is impossible not to be struck with admiration when we think of the extraordinary range of his activity. There are few departments of intellectual life into which he did not penetrate, and in everything which, as a thinker and writer, he undertook, he displayed the highest order of mental power. As a man of science, he ranks among the foremost investigators of his age. He had no sooner begun to reflect seriously on scientific problems than he placed himself in what proved to be the central current of modern thought. The supreme idea of the nineteenth century is the idea of evolution, and the position of those inquirers who immediately preceded Darwin is necessarily determined by the answer which must be given to the questions — Were they, in their observations and speculations, guided by aims which in the main accord with Darwin's principle? Were they among the forerunners who prepared the way for the doctrine in which all that was best and most vital in pre-Darwinian scientific thought is summed up? In regard to Goethe, these questions must be answered emphatically in the affirmative. His discoveries, resulting almost equally from the exercise of his perceptive and imaginative faculties, were on the lines which led directly to the theory of evolution. It is only, indeed, since the law of evolution was detected, that the world has recognized the full meaning and importance of his contributions to scientific progress.

As a writer on art, Goethe was less original than as a man of science. But here also he was on the track that has been followed by the greatest of his succes-

sors. Greek architecture and sculpture Winckelmann
had made in part intelligible ; and, having absorbed his
teaching, Goethe, as the result of his own observations
in Italy, had many a luminous suggestion to offer as to
masterpieces of ancient art, and as to the general
processes of development with which they were related.
In his study of modern art it was to the painters and
sculptors whose technical skill was used in the service of
high imaginative ideas that he instinctively turned ; and
no writer of his day sought more earnestly to show how
little can be achieved in art if it is divorced from serious
and noble thought. He felt, too, as only a few of the
world's intellectual guides have yet felt, how great is the
place which properly belongs to art as one of the influences capable of giving dignity and refinement both to
individual and to social life.

Great, however, as were Goethe's achievements in the
criticism of art and in science, they are of almost slight
importance in comparison with his work as an imaginative
writer. As a writer of romance, as a dramatist, as a
lyrical poet, he towers high above all other men of
letters whom Germany has produced. In the literature
of his country he takes the rank which in that of Greece
belongs to Homer, in that of Italy to Dante, in that of
England to Shakespeare. Almost every element of
human life is touched in his creations, yet he has told us
that his writings are to be regarded as parts of one great
"confession." However remote they may seem to be
from his own experience, they are directly or indirectly
rooted in the facts of his personal history. To this is
due one of the most distinctive qualities of his work

both in verse and in prose — the extraordinary vitality
of his ideas ; the vividness with which all that he depicts
is made to pass before us, as if it were a part of the
outward and visible world. He cannot, however, be
truly described as a realist, if by a realist is meant
one who seeks to do no more than represent exactly
what he himself has seen or felt. In taking reality as
the basis of ideal structures, Goethe severed from it
associations which were only of temporary or accidental
interest. He brought it into new relations, touched it
with the transforming power of the imagination, and gave
to individual facts universal significance. Hence the
greatest of his works are as fresh to-day as when he
wrote them ; and they could lose their living power
only if human nature itself were radically changed.

As a critic of literature, he had the sanity of judgment
and the intuitive insight which mark all poets of the
highest genius. He has never, perhaps, been surpassed
in his power of detecting the signs of a genuinely
creative capacity ; and this power, remarkable even in
his youth, did not desert him in old age. He was constantly on the outlook for new intellectual forces, and,
when they appeared, seldom failed to divine the direction
in which they were moving, and the nature of the results
they were likely to accomplish. Byron, Scott, Manzoni,
Victor Hugo, Carlyle—all were hailed by Goethe as, in
different ways, potent representatives of the later periods
of the era to which he himself belonged. It did not
occur to him to think of them as rivals. He thought
only of his good fortune in having lived to see them
carry on the movement of European literature.

When a writer achieves world-wide fame, we cannot resist the impulse to ask what he has to tell us as to the great, enduring spiritual problems of existence. We have seen how deeply Goethe, in youth, was influenced by Spinoza; and during the whole of his mature life his conception of the universe in some respects closely resembled that of the teacher whom he had so profoundly revered. Atheism was not only repugnant to his feeling, but seemed to him the last development of human folly. To him the world was but the manifestation of Divine energy; he thought of it as "the living garment of the Deity." So far, his idea of the ultimate nature of things was simply Spinoza's idea; but, when he had fought his way to an independent conviction, he differed widely from Spinoza in his mode of conceiving the Reality which reveals itself in the phenomenal order. The God in whom Goethe believed was not simply "Substance." The enduring types or patterns to which, in his interpretation of Nature, he attributed such vast importance, imply the existence of something more and deeper than abstract force. They are Divine ideas, and would be unintelligible apart from Mind or Reason. That the word Reason, when applied to the creative energy of the universe, expresses absolute truth, Goethe nowhere says; but he held that man cannot but form for himself some representation of the Unknowable Power, and that to represent it as Reason is the least inadequate way in which we can catch some glimpse of its unutterable splendour.

The notion that the world was formed for man seemed to Goethe the offspring of extravagant self-conceit. Yet he had no mean estimate of the greatness of the human spirit. He recognized in it powers capable of indefinite growth and expansion, and did not doubt that there is an invisible realm in which, after it has fulfilled its mission in the present world, it passes to new and higher destinies. It appeared to him, however, strange and most unreasonable that men should miss what is great and worthy in this life by dreaming vaguely about a life to come. He conceived that the truest preparation for whatever may be in store for us in other states of existence must be the wise cultivation of the faculties with which we are endowed ; and among these faculties he gave the highest place to the impulses which bring men into intimate and helpful association with their fellows.

The conduct of life he made a subject of profound reflection, and no modern writer illuminates it with a light at once so clear and so steady. It is for this reason that a quite peculiar relation springs up between Goethe and those who feel the power and the charm of his genius. They go back again and again to his works, his letters, his " Conversations," and never fail to find in them some fruitful word that brings with it fresh hope and courage. His wise and noble sayings are the more inspiring because they almost invariably suggest deeper meanings than they directly utter. The mind, in appropriating them, is placed in contact, not with abstract dogmas, but with life itself, and is stimulated to the free exercise of its own energies.

Goethe had an almost unequalled opportunity of developing his powers, and apprehended vividly the full extent of the obligation it imposed. His life, therefore, has the note of greatness which distinguishes his writ ings.   It was a life of lofty aim and strenuous endeavour, and left a mark, wide, deep, and abiding, on the thought and aspiration of mankind.

THE END.

INDEX.

———•♦•———

BIBLIOGRAPHY.

BY

JOHN P. ANDERSON

(British Museum).

[The Compiler has found it impracticable to give more than the first edition of the separate works in the original. All the English translations known to him have, however, been included.]

I. WORKS.

D. Goethens Schriften. Mit Kupfern. 4 Th. Berlin, 1775-79, 8vo.

J. W. Göthens Schriften. 4 Bd. Carlsruhe, 1778-80, 8vo.

Goethe's Schriften. [With engravings.] 8 Bd. Leipzig, 1787-90, 8vo.

Goethe's Schriften. 4 Bd. Leipzig, 1787-91, 8vo.

Goethe's Schriften. 8 Bd. Wien und Leipzig, 1790, 8vo.

Göthe's Neue Schriften. 7 Bd. Berlin, 1792-1800, 8vo.

Goethes Werke. 13 Bd. Tübingen, 1806-10, 8vo.

Goethe's Werke. 20 Bd. Stuttgart und Tübingen, 1815-19, 8vo.

Original-Ausgabe. 26 Bd. Wien
und Stuttgart, 1816-1821,
12mo.
Vollständige Ausgabe letzter
Hand. (Goethe's nachgelass-
ene Werke. Inhalts-und-
Namen - Verzeichnisse über
sämmtliche Goethe'sche Werke,
Ausgabe 1827-1834, Verfertigt
von C. T. Musculus unter
Mitwirkung des Hofraths Dr.
Riemer.) 61 Bd. Stuttgart
und Tübingen, 1827-42, 8vo.
Göthe's sämmtliche Werke. Mit
Bildnisse und Facsimile. 5 Bd.
Paris, 1836, 8vo.
Goethe's poetische und prosaische
Werke. 3 Bd. Stuttgart und
Tübingen, 1836-47, 4to.
Vollständige, neugeordnete Aus-
gabe. 40 Bd. Stuttgart, 1840,
16mo.
Goethe's poetische und prosaische
Werke. Mit Stahlstichen.
Zweite Auflage. [Edited by F.
W. Riemer and J. P. Ecker-
mann.] 2 Bd. Stuttgart und
Tübingen, 1845-46, 8vo.
Goethe's sämmtliche Werke, etc.
30 Bd. Stuttgart, 1850-51,
8vo.
Goethe's sämmtliche Werke.
Vollständige, neugeordnete
Ausgabe. 30 Bd. Stuttgart,
1857-58, 8vo.
Vollständige Ausgabe. 6 Bd.
Stuttgart, 1860, 8vo.
Vollständige neu durchgesehene
Ausgabe. 3 Bd. Stuttgart,
1869, 8vo.
Goethe's sämmtliche Werke. Mit
Einleitungen von K. Goedeke.
15 Bd. Stuttgart, 1872-75,
8vo.
Der Junge Göthe. Seine Briefe
und Dichtungen von 1764-1776.
Mit einer Einleitung von M.

Bernays. 3 Bd. Leipzig, 1875,
8vo.
Goethe's Werke, Revidirte Ausgabe. (Thl. 1-3, 5-10, 11 ;.
Abtheil 2, 14-16, 25, 26, 28, 30·
32; herausgegeben mit Anmerkungen von F. Strehlke. Nebst
der Biographie des Dichters
[Thl. 1.] von F. Förster, Thl. 4,
11, Abtheil 1, 12, 13, 19-23
herausgegeben von G. von
Loeper. Thl. 17, 18, 24 heraus-
gegeben von W. Frh. v. Bieder-
mann. Thl. 33-36 herausgegeben
von S. Kalischer.) 36 Thl.
Berlin, Leipzig [printed, 1868-
79], 8vo.
Goethe's Werke. Erste illustrirte
Ausgabe, mit erläuternden
Einleitungen [by Wendt and
others]. Neunte verbesserte
Auflage. 20 Bd. Berlin,
Leipzig [printed] 1880, 8vo.
Goethe's sämmtliche Werke.
Vollständige Ausgabe. Mit
Einleitungen von K. Goedeke,.
15 Bd. Stuttgart, 1881, 8vo.
Goethe's Werke. [Edited by K.
G.—i.e., K. Goedeke.] 36 Bd.
Stuttgart, 1882-67-81, 8vo.
Goethe's Werke. Herausgegeben
von H. Düntzer. Berlin,
Leipzig [printed, 1882, etc.],.
8vo.
  Forming part of the "Deutsche
National Litteratur, herausgegeben
von J. Kürschner.
Goethes Werke, illustrirt von den
ersten deutschen Künstlern.
(Eine ausgewählte Sammlung.)
Herausgeber H. Düntzer. 5
Bd. Stuttgart [printed] und
Leipzig, [1883-85,] 8vo.
Goethe's Werke. Herausgegeben
im Auftrage der Grossherzogin
Sophie von Sachsen. Weimar,.
1887, etc., 8vo.

This edition, now being issued, is divided into four parts :—I. Abtheilung : Goethe's Werke, 50 Bände ; II. Abtheilung : Goethe's Naturwissenschaftliche Schriften, about 10 Bände ; III. Abtheilung : Goethe's Tagebücher ; IV. Abtheilung : Goethe's Briefe.

II. TWO OR MORE WORKS.

Nachträge zu Goethe's sämmtliche Werken. Gesammelt und herausgegeben von E. Boas. 3 Thl. Leipzig, 1841, 16mo.

Neue Ausgabe, etc. 3 Thl. Leipzig, 1846, 8vo.

Göthe's Singspiele Claudine v. Villa Bella und Erwin und Elmire. In ihren ursprünglichen Gestalt herausgegeben von Dr. H. Döring. Arnstadt, 1843, 8vo.

Clavigo. Ein Trauerspiel in fünf Akten. Die Geschwister. Schauspiel in einem Akt. 2 pts. Stuttgart, 1868, 8vo.
Forming No. 28 of a series entitled, "Classische Theater-Bibliothek aller Nationen."

Goethe's Italiänische Reise ; Aufsätze und Aussprüche über bildende Kunst. Mit Einleitung und Bericht über dessen Kunststudien und Kunstübungen. Herausgegeben von C. Schuchardt. 2 Bd. Stuttgart, 1862-63, 8vo.

The Autobiography of Goethe. Truth and Poetry : From my own Life. Translated from the German, by J. Oxenford. Thirteen books. — Vol. 2. The Autobiography, etc. The concluding books [14-20]. Also letters from Switzerland and Travels in Italy. Translated by A. J. W. Morrison. (*Bohn's Standard Library*). 2 vols. London, 1848-9, 8vo.

Dramatic Works of Goethe : comprising Faust, Iphigenie in Tauris, Torquato Tasso, Egmont, translated by Anna Swanwick, and Goetz von Berlichingen, translated by Sir Walter Scott. (*Bohn's Standard Library*). London, 1850, 8vo.

The Dramatic Works of J. W. Goethe. Translated from the German by Sir W. Scott, E. A. Bowring, A. Swanwick, and others. (*Bohn's Standard Library*.) London, 1879, 8vo.

Essays on Art. Translated by S. G. Ward. Boston [Mass.], 1845, 16mo.

Miscellaneous Travels of J. W. Goethe ; comprising Letters from Switzerland (translated by A. J. W. Morrison) ; the Campaign in France, 1792 (translated by R. Farie) ; the Siege of Mainz ; and a Tour on the Rhine, Maine, and Neckar, 1814-1815. Edited by L. Dora Schmitz. (*Bohn's Standard Library*.) London, 1882, 8vo.

Novels and Tales by Goethe. Elective Affinities ; The Sorrows of Werther ; German Emigrants ; The Good Women ; and a Nouvelette, translated chiefly by R. D. Boylan. (*Bohn's Standard Library*.) London, 1854, 8vo.

III. SINGLE WORKS.

Aus meinem Leben, Dichtung und Wahrheit. Abth. 1 ; and Th. 1-2 of Abth. 2. [6 Th.] Tübingen und Stuttgart, 1811-22, 8vo.

——Memoirs of Goethe : written by himself. (Biographical notices [by the translator] of the principal persons mentioned in these memoirs.) 2 vols. London, 1824, 8vo.

——Goethe's Boyhood, 1749-1764. Being the first five books forming part 1 of Goethe's Autobiography. Translated by J. Oxenford. (*Bohn's Shilling Library*.) London, 1888, 8vo.

—— ——Die Idylle von Sesenheim. Aus Göthe's "Dichtung und Wahrheit," etc. Berlin, Leipzig [printed], 1872, 32mo.

—— ——The New Paris. A child's tale. [An extract from "Aus meinem Leben."] (*Tales from the German, by John Oxenford and C. A. Feiling*.) London, 1844, 8vo.

Beiträge zur Optik. 2 Stücke. Weimar, 1791-2, 8vo.

Der Bürgergeneral. Ein Lustspiel in einem Aufzuge [and in prose]. Berlin, 1793, 8vo.

Campaign in France, in the year 1792. Translated by R. Farie. London, 1849, 12mo.

Claudine von Villa Bella. Ein Schauspiel [in prose] mit Gesang. Berlin, 1776, 12mo.

—— ——Arien und Gesänge des Singspiels Claudine von Villa Bella, etc. Berlin, 1818, 8vo.

Clavigo. Ein Trauerspiel [in five acts and in prose]. Leipzig, 1774, 8vo.

Egmont. Ein Trauerspiel in fünf Aufzügen. Ächte Ausgabe. Leipzig, 1788, 8vo.

——Another edition, with English notes, etc. London, 1864, 8vo. Forming part of "Thimm's Classical German Drama."

——Another edition. Annotated by E. A. Oppen. (*German Classics*, etc.) London, 1868, 12mo.

——Another edition. With explanatory notes and vocabulary by H. Apel. London, 1868, 8vo.

——Another edition. German Classics. Edited, with English notes, by C. A. Buchheim. Vol. i. Egmont, a tragedy by Goethe. (*Clarendon Press Series*.) Oxford, 1869, 8vo.

——Egmont. Translated from the German. Boston [Mass.], 1841, 12mo.

——Egmont. Translated from the German. London, 1848, 16mo.

——Egmont. Translated (with entr'actes and songs by Beethoven, newly arranged from the full score, and Schubert's song "Freudvoll und Leidvoll") by A. D. Coleridge. With an illustration by J. E. Millais. London, 1868, 8vo.

Des Epimenides Erwachen. Ein Festspiel [in one act and in verse. With a preface signed K. L.] Berlin, 1815, 8vo.

Erwin und Elmire : ein Schauspiel mit Gesang. Frankfurt, 1775, 8vo.

Faust. Ein Fragment. Ächte Ausgabe. Leipzig, 1790, 8vo.

Faust. Eine Tragödie. Tübingen, 1808, 8vo.

Faust. Eine Tragödie. Zweyter Theil in fünf Acten. Stuttgart und Tübingen, 1833, 8vo.

Faust in ursprünglicher Gestalt nach der Göchhausenschen Abschrift herausgegeben von E. Schmidt. Weimar, 1887, 8vo.

——Retsch's Series of twenty-six outlines, illustrative of Goethe's tragedy of Faust, engraved from the originals by Henry Moses. London, 1820, 4to.

——Faustus: from the German of Goethe. [The greater part of Thl. 1., translated in verse, and connected by a prose narrative. With 27 illustrations in outline by Moritz Retzsch]. London, 1821, 4to.

——Metrical version of the Walpurgisnacht, entitled, "May-Day Night," by Percy Bysshe Shelley. (*The Liberal. Verse and prose from the South*, vol. i, pp. 121-137). London, 1822, 8vo.
Re-published in Shelley's "Posthumous Poems," 1824.

——Faust [Part the First]: a drama by Goethe; and Schiller's Song of the Bell. Translated by Lord F. L. Gower. London, 1823, 8vo.

——Faustus, from the German of Goethe, with Retzsch's illustrations, re-engraved by H. Moses. London, 1824, 4to.

——Faust, a Drama by Goethe, and Schiller's Partition of the Earth, and Song of the Bell, translated by Lord Francis Leveson Gower. New edition. 2 vols. London, 1825, 8vo.

——Faust. By Goethe. From the German. By John Anster. London, 1828, 8vo.

——Faust, a dramatic poem, translated into English prose, with remarks on former translations, and notes, by the translator of Savigny's "Of the vocation of our age for legislation and jurisprudence. [A. Hayward]. London, 1833, 8vo.

——Faust; a dramatic poem translated into English prose, with remarks on former translations, notes [and an appendix], by A. Hayward. Second edition. London, 1834, 8vo.

——Faust [Part 1], a tragedy. Translated into English verse, with notes and preliminary remarks, by J. S. Blackie. Edinburgh, 1834, 8vo.

——Faust [Part 1]; a tragedy; translated from the German by D. Syme. Edinburgh, 1834, 12mo.

——Faustus [Part 1]; a tragedy. Translated from the German of Goethe. London, 1834, 12mo.

——Goethe's Faust [Part 1], illustrated with outlines by M. Retzsch, engraved by H. Moses. London, 1834, obl. 4to.

——Faustus [Part 1]; The Bride of Corinth; The First Walpurgis Night. Translated from the German by J. Anster. London, 1835, 8vo.

——The Faust [Part 1] of Goethe attempted in English rhyme, by R. Talbot. London, 1835, 8vo.

——Original Poems. Translations of Demetrius and three Scenes from Faust. By C. Hodges. Munich, 1836, 12mo.

——Goethe's Faust [Part II], illustrated with fourteen outline illustrations, by Moritz Retzsch. London, 1836, obl. 4to.

——Faust: a Tragedy, by Goethe; German text with English notes. London, 1836, 12mo.

——Faust, a tragedy in two parts, rendered into English verse. 2 vols. London, 1838, 12mo.
Only 50 copies printed.

——Faust: a Tragedy. Part II, as completed in 1831, translated into English verse (by John Macdonald Bell). Dumfries, 1838, 8vo.

——Faust: a Tragedy; translated into English verse by J. Birch;

embellished with engravings on steel (by J. Brain) after Moritz Retzsch. 2 pts. London, 1839-43, 8vo.

——Goethe's Faust. Mit gegenüberstehenden englischer Uebersetzung und erklärenden Noten versehen vom Honorable Robert Talbot. Erster Theil. The Faust of Goethe. Part 1. Translated into English rhyme, by the Hon. Robert Talbot. Second edition, revised and much corrected, with the German text on alternate pages and additional notes. London, 1839, 8vo.

——Goethe's Faust. Parts I and II. translated into English from the German, partly in the metres of the original, and partly in prose. By Leopold J. Bernays. London, 1839, 8vo.

——Faust; Part 11, translated from the German, partly in the metres of the original, and partly in prose; with other poems, original and translated, by Leopold J. Bernays. London, 1839, 8vo.

——Ceracchi, a drama, and other poems. (Passages translated from the Faust of Goethe.) By Samuel Naylor. Maidenhead [1839], 8vo.
Privately printed.

——Faust, by Goethe. Translated into English prose, with remarks on former translations, and notes, by A. Hayward. Third edition. London, 1840, 8vo.

——Faust; a tragedy, translated into English verse by J. Hills. London, 1840, 16mo.

——Faust. Parts I and II. With other poems, original and translated, by J. L. Bernays. Carlsruhe, 1840, 8vo.

——Faustus: a Dramatic Mystery; The Bride of Corinth; The First Walpurgis Night. Translated from the German of Goethe by John Anster. Frankfort a. M., 1841, 16mo.

——Faust [Part 1.], a Tragedy by Goethe. Translated by L. Filmore. London, 1841, 8vo.
Forming part of the collection entitled, "Smith's Standard Library."

——Faust [Part 1], translated into English verse by Sir George Lefevre. London [1841], 12mo.

——Faust, a Tragedy. Part II. Rendered from the German by Archer Gurney. London, 1842, 8vo.

——Faust: a Dramatic Poem. Translated into English prose by A. Hayward. Reprinted from the third English edition, corrected and revised. Erfurt and Leipzig, 1842, 16mo.

——Faust, a tragedy. Part II, as completed in 1831. Translated into English verse [by John Macdonald Bell]. Second edition. London, 1842, 8vo.

——Goethe's Faust [Part 1], translated into English verse. By Sir G. Lefevre. Second edition. Frankfort a. M[ain], 1843, 16mo.

——Retzsch's Twenty-six Outlines to Goethe's Tragedy of Faust. Engraved from the originals by Henry Moses, with an illustrative analysis of the Tragedy. London, 1843, 4to.

——Goethe's Faust, complete. The forty outlines by M.

Retzsch, engraved on steel for J. Birch's translation of Faust, by J. Brain. London [1843], obl. 4to.

——Goethe's Faust (being the "preface" or opening to that poem, and the "Prologue in Heaven." The literal translation by G. F. Duckett, etc.). [London ? 1845 ?], 4to.

——Faust, a tragedy by Goethe. Translated into English verse by Lewis Filmore. New edition. London, 1847, 12mo.

——Faust, a dramatic poem, by Goethe. Translated into English prose, with notes, by A. Hayward. Fourth edition. London, 1847, 8vo.

——Faust, a tragedy. Translated by Captain Knox. London, 1847, 8vo.

——Faust, a tragedy by Goethe; and Selections from Schiller, translated by Anna Swanwick. London, 1849, 8vo.

——Dramatic Works of Goethe: comprising:—Faust, Iphigenia in Tauris, etc. Translated by Anna Swanwick. (*Bohn's Standard Library*, Goethe's Works, vol. iii.) London, 1850, 8vo.

——Faust, a drama, with glossary and notes. By Dr. Tiarks. London, 1850, 12mo.

——Faust, by Goethe. Translated into English prose, with notes, by A. Hayward. Fifth edition. London, 1851, 12mo.

——Faust [Part 1]: a Tragedy. With copious notes, grammatical, philological and exegetical, by Falck Lebahn. *Germ.* London, 1853, 8vo.

——Faust, translated by L. Filmore. (*Universal Library*, *Poetry*, vol. i.) London, 1853, 8vo.

——Faust, by Goethe. Translated into English prose, with notes, by A. Hayward. Boston [Mass.], 1854, 16mo.

——Goethe's Faust: the First Part, with an analytical translation, and etymological and grammatical notes. By L. E. Peithmann. *Germ.* London [1854], 16mo.

——Faust: a dramatic poem. Translated into English prose, with notes. By A. Hayward. Sixth edition. London, 1855, 8vo.

——Goethe's Faust: the first part, with an analytical translation [or rather vocabulary] and etymological and grammatical notes. By L. E. Peithmann. Second edition, etc. *Germ.* London, 1856, 12mo.

——Faust, a tragedy. Translated into English prose from the German of Goethe, with notes, by Charles T. Brooks. Boston [Mass.], 1856, 8vo.

——Faust, a tragedy, translated, with notes, by C. T. Brooks. Second edition. Boston [Mass.], 1857, 8vo.

——Goethe's Faust [Part 1], with critical and explanatory notes by G. G. Zerffi. *Germ.* London, 1859, 8vo.

——Faust: a tragedy. Translated into English verse from the German of Goethe. By J. Galvan. Dublin, 1860, 12mo.

——Faust, by Goethe. Translated into English prose, with notes, by A. Hayward. Seventh edition. London, 1860, 8vo.

——Faust, by Goethe. Translated into English verse by

Lewis Filmore. New edition. London, 1861, 8vo.

——Faust, translated from the German by v. Beresford. Cassel, 1862, 8vo.

——Goethe's Faust. Translated into English verse, by J. Cartwright. London, 1862, 12mo.

——Faust. Part 1. With critical and explanatory notes, by G. G. Zerffi. Second edition. London, 1862, 8vo.

——Poems; original and translated. [From Goethe's Faust, etc.] By Theodore Martin. London, 1863, 8vo.
Printed for private circulation.

——Faustus. Part 1. From the German of Goethe. By John Anster. New edition. London, 1864, 8vo.

——Faustus: the Second Part. From the German of Goethe. By John Anster. London, 1864, 8vo.

——Faust. Translated by A. Hayward. Eighth edition. London, 1864, 8vo.

——Translation of Goethe's Faust. By W. B. Clarke. Freiburg, 1865, 8vo.
First and Second Parts.

——Faust [Part 1]: a dramatic poem. Translated into English verse by Theodore Martin. Edinburgh, 1865, 8vo.

——Faust [Part 1], translated by L. Filmore. (*Masterpieces of Foreign Literature.*) London, 1866, 8vo.

——Faust [Part 1]: a dramatic poem. Translated into English verse by Theodore Martin. Second edition. Edinburgh, 1866, 8vo.

——Faust, von Goethe. Der Tragödie, erster Thiel. With English notes. New York, 1866, 12mo.

——Faust. From the German, by J. Anster. (*Tauchnitz Collection of German Authors,* vol. v.) Leipzig, 1867, 12mo.

——Faust, a dramatic poem, translated by J. W. Grant. London, 1867, 8vo.

——Historical Pictures [in verse] from the Campagna of Rome. With lyrics from "Faust." By J. W. Grant. London, 1867, 8vo.

——Faust, a dramatic poem. Translated into English verse by Theodore Martin. Third edition. Edinburgh [printed] and London, 1870, 8vo.

——Faust: a tragedy. Translated in the original metres by Bayard Taylor. 2 vols. London, 1871, 8vo.

——Faust. The first part. Translated, in the original metres, by Bayard Taylor. Boston [Mass.], 1871, 8vo.

——Faust, a tragedy. Part 1. Translated in the original metres by Bayard Taylor. Leipzig, 1872, 8vo.

——Faust. Translated, in the original metres, by Bayard Taylor. Boston [Mass.], 1873, 8vo.

——Goethe's Faust. With copious notes, grammatical, philological, and exegetical. By Falck Lebahn. New edition. *Germ.* London, 1872, 8vo.

——Faust, a tragedy. Translated in rime by C. K. Paul. London, 1873, 8vo.

——Faust. Translated into English prose, by A. Hayward. Ninth edition. London 1874. 12mo.

——Outlines to Goethe's Faust. Twenty-six etchings by Moritz Retzsch. [With illustrative text in English.] London, 1875, obl. 4to.

——Faust, a tragedy. Part II. Translated in the original metres by Bayard Taylor. Leipzig, 1876, 8vo.

——Faust, by Goethe. Translated by Bayard Taylor. Illustrated by E. Seibertz, A. Liezen-Mayer, and L. Hofmann. New York, 1876, fol.

——Faust von Goethe. Der Tragödie, erster Theil. With English notes. New edition. New York, 1876, 12mo.

——Faust, a tragedy. The first part. Translated, in the original metres, by T. J. Arnold. With 50 illustrations after original designs by A. L. Mayer, and with vignettes, ornamental borderings, etc., by R. Seitz. Munich, London [1877], fol.

——Faust ; a tragedy. Translated by T. Martin. Illustrated by A. von Kreling. London, 1877, fol.

——Faust. [Part 1.] Translated into English verse by C. K. Bowen. London, 1878, 8vo.

——The Faust of Goethe. In English verse. By W. H. Colquhoun. Part 1. London, 1878, etc., 8vo.
No more published.

——Faust. A tragedy. Translated into English verse by W. D. Scoones. London, 1879, 16mo.

——Goethe's Faust. In two parts. Translated by Anna Swanwick. (*Bohn's Standard Library.*) London, 1879, 8vo.

——Goethe's Faust. [Part 1.]

Translated by A. Swanwick. With illustrations after the designs of M. Retzsch. London, 1879 [1878], 8vo.

——Faust [Part 1.], a tragedy, by Goethe. Translated in the original metres by Bayard Taylor. New edition. Boston, 1879, 12mo.

——Faust [Part 1.], a tragedy. Translated, chiefly in blank verse, with introduction and notes, by J. A. Birds. London, 1880, 8vo.

——Faust : a tragedy. [Part the First.] Translated into English verse, with notes and remarks, by J. S. Blackie. Second edition, largely rewritten. London, 1880, 8vo.

——Goethe's Faust, Part 1. The German Text, with English notes, and introductory remarks, by A. M. Selss. London, 1880, 8vo.

——Goethe's Faust : a Tragedy. Translated by Theodore Martin. Illustrated by A. v. Kreling. London, 1880, fol.

——Faust [the First Part], from the German of Goethe, by T. E. Webb. (*Dublin University Press Series.*) Dublin, 1880, 8vo.

——Faust, a tragedy. Part 1. Translated in the original metres by Bayard Taylor. Second edition. Leipzig, 1881, 8vo.

——Faust : a tragedy. Part 1., edited and annotated by F. H. Hedge, metrical versions by Miss Swanwick. Part II., translated by Miss Swanwick. New York, 1882, 8vo.

——Goethe's Faust. [Part 1. The text, with English notes

and verse translations, by E. J. Turner and E. D. A. Morshead. *Germ.* London, 1882, 8vo.

——Marlowe's Faustus. Goethe's Faust from the German, by John Anster. With an introduction by Henry Morley. London, 1883, 8vo.

——Goethe's Faust, translated by Anna Swanwick. New York, 1883, 16mo.

——Faust: a tragedy. Translated by Bayard Taylor. With explanatory notes. (*Chandos Classics.*) London [1886], 8vo.

——Goethe's Faust. Translated from the German by J. Anster. (*Routledge's World Library.*) London, 1886, 12mo.

——Faust, a dramatic poem by Goethe. Translated into English verse by Sir Theodore Martin. Part 1. Eighth edition. Edinburgh, 1886, 12mo.

——Faust, a dramatic poem by Goethe. Translated by Sir Theodore Martin. Edinburgh, 1886, 12mo.

——The Tragedy of Faust, translated into English verse by F. Claudy. Washington, 1886, 8vo.

——Faust. [Part I.] A Tragedy. Translated in the original metres by Bayard Taylor. London [1886], 8vo.
   Ward, Lock, & Co.'s "Popular Library of Literary Treasures."

——Faust, with an introduction and notes by Jane Lee. Part 1 followed by an appendix on part II. (*Macmillan's Series of Foreign School Classics.*) London, 1886, 8vo.

——1. Marlowe's Faustus. 2. Goethe's Faust, the first and second parts complete, from the German by J. Anster. With an introduction by H. Morley. London, 1887 [1886], 8vo.
   One of the "Excelsior Series."

——Faust. Translated in the original metres, by Bayard Taylor. Authorised edition. London [1887], 8vo.
   Part of "The People's Standard Library."

Der Feier des fünfzigsten Dienstjahrs Herrn C. G. von Voigt gewidmet von den Grossherzoglichen Bibliotheken zu Weimar und Jena. [Verses by Goethe.] Weimar, 1816, 4to.

Zur Feier des zweyten Februars. [Verses by Goethe.] Weimar, 1823, 4to.

Die Fischerinn, ein Singspiel. [Weimar], 1782, 8vo.

Bei Allerhöchster Anwesenheit Ihro Majestät Maria Feodorowna in Weimar. Als Festspiel Charade, etc. [In verse.] [Weimar?], 1818, 4to.

Bei Anwesenheit Ihro Majestät Maria Feodorowna in Weimar. Als Festspiel Gemälde. Darstellung in zwei Abtheilungen [and in verse.] [Weimar?], 1818, 4to.

Die Geschwister. Ein Schauspiel [in one act and in prose]. Ächte Ausgabe. Leipzig, 1787, 8vo.

——The Sister, a drama, etc. (*Dramatic Pieces from the German, etc.*) Edinburgh, 1792, 8vo.

Götter, Helden, und Wieland. Eine Farce. Leipzig, 1774, 8vo.

Götz von Berlichingen mit der eisernen Hand. Ein Schauspiel [in five acts, and in prose.

First edition]. Frankfurt-on-the-Main], 1773, 8vo.

——Another edition. [Hamburg], 1773, 8vo.

The Museum copy contains a MS. Note by L. Tieck.

——Goethe's Götz von Berlichingen. Edited by H. A. Bull. (*Macmillan's Series of Foreign School Classics.*) London, 1883, 8vo.

——Goetz of Berlichingen with the Iron Hand : a Tragedy translated from the German of Goethe by Walter Scott. London, 1799, 8vo.

——Gortz of Berlingen [Goetz von Berlichingen] with the iron hand. An historical drama of the fifteenth century [in five acts and in prose]. Translated from the German of Goethe [by Rose Lawrence, with a preface by J. Currie]. Liverpool [1799], 8vo.

Der Gross-Cophta. Ein Lustspiel in fünf Aufzügen. Berlin, 1792, 8vo.

Hermann und Dorothea. Berlin, 1798, 8vo.

——Zweite verbesserte Auflage. [With illustrations.] Brunswick, 1799, 8vo.

——Goethe's Hermann und Dorothea. With corresponding English Hexameters on opposite pages, by F. B. Watkins. *Germ. and Eng.* London, 1875 [1874], 8vo.

——Herman and Dorothea. A poem, from the German by T. Holcroft. [With illustrations.] London, 1801, 8vo.

——Herman and Dorothea, translated from the Hexameters of Goethe [by W. Whewell]. [London ? 1840 ?], 8vo.

—— Herman and Dorothea. Translated into English hexameters, from the German hexameters of Goethe. With an introductory essay. [By Charles Tomlinson.] London, 1849, 8vo.

——A new edition, revised. London, 1887, 8vo.

——A translation of the Hermann and Dorothea of Goethe in the old English measure of Chapman's Homer. By M. Winter. With notes. Dublin, 1850, 12mo.

——Herman and Dorothea. From the German of Goethe, by J. Cochrane. Oxford [1853], 8vo.

——Hermann and Dorothea. Translated by T. C. Porter. New York, 1854, 8vo.

——Goethe's Hermann and Dorothea. Translated by H. Dale. Dresden, 1859, 8vo.

——Goethe's Hermann and Dorothea : translated into English verse [by J. Cartwright]. London, 1862, 8vo.

——Goethe's Hermann and Dorothea. Translated [in verse] by E. Frothingham. With illustrations. Boston [Mass.], 1870, 8vo.

——Goethe's Hermann and Dorothea. Translated by H. Dale. With illustrations by W. Kaulbach and L. Hofmann. Munich [1874], 4to.

——Goethe's Hermann and Dorothea, translated into English hexameter verse by M. J. Teesdale. London, 1874, 8vo.

——Second edition. London, 1875, 8vo.

Jery und Bätely. Ein Singspiel. Achte Ausgabe. Leipzig, 1790, 8vo.

Erste Nachricht von dem Fort-
gang des neuen Bergbaues zu
Ilmenau, etc. (Signed J. W.
Goethe and C. G. Voigt.)
Weimar, 1785, 8vo.

Iphigenie auf Tauris. Ein
Schauspiel [in five acts, and in
verse]. Ächte Ausgabe. Leipzig, 1787, 8vo.

—— Goethe's Iphigenie auf
Tauris. With notes, vocabulary, and interlinear translation of the first scenes. By M.
Behr. London, 1850, 12mo.

——Iphigenie auf Tauris. Annotated by E. A. Oppen. (*German
Classics.*) London, 1868, 8vo.

——Iphigenia in Tauris. Edited
with notes in English by Henry
Attwell. *Germ.* London,
1885, 8vo.

——Iphigenia in Tauris : a
tragedy. [Translated by
William Taylor.] London,
1793, 8vo.

——Iphigenia in Tauris. From
the German by G. L. Hartwig.
Berlin, 1841, 8vo.

——Iphigenia in Tauris, a drama
in five acts. Translated from
the German by G. J. Adler.
New York, 1850, 12mo.

——Iphigenia in Tauris, from the
German of Goethe. With
(translations from the Italian
and) original poems. Liverpool,
1851, 12mo.
    Privately printed.

——Iphigenia in Tauris. Trans-
lated from the German into
English blank verse by P. M.
E. [*i.e.*, Phillis Marion Ellis].
London, 1883, 8vo.
    Only 50 copies ; privately printed.

Die Leiden des jungen Werther's.
2 Thle. Leipzig, 1774, 8vo.

——The Sorrows of Werter ; a
German story. 2 vols. London, 1779, 12mo.

——Second edition. 2 vols. London, 1780, 8vo.

——Third edition. 2 vols. London, 1782, 16mo.

——A new edition. London,
1785, 16mo.

——The Sorrows of Werter ; a
German story. Translated
from the French edition of M.
Aubry [or rather of Count F.
W. K. Schmettau ?] by J.
Gifford. 2 vols. London,
1789, 8vo.

——The Sorrows of Werter ;
translated from the German of
Goethe, by W. Render. (Appendix containing an account
of a conversation which the
translator had with Werter, a
few days preceding his death).
London, 1801, 12mo.

——The Sorrows of Werter ;
translated by F. Gotzberg.
London, 1802, 8vo.

——The Sorrows of Werter.
Translated from the German.
By Dr. Pratt. The second
edition. London [1813], 8vo.

——The Sorrows of Werter. London [1815 ?], 12mo.

——The Sorrows of Werter.
[Translated by S. J. Pratt.]
Chiswick, 1823, 16mo.

——The Sorrows of Werter. A
new edition. Belfast, 1844,
12mo.

——The Sorrows of Werter.
(*Illustrated Literature of all
Nations,* No. 14.) London
[1852], 4to.

——Classic Tales : comprising
the most esteemed Works of
Imagination. Rasselas, Vicar of
Wakefield . . . Sorrows of

Werter, etc. London, 1852, 8vo.

——The Sorrows of Werther, from the German of Goethe [translated by F. Gotzberg]. (*Cassell's National Library*, vol. xxxvi.) London, 1886, 8vo.

——Essay on Novels, a poetical epistle. With six sonnets from Werter. By Alexander Thomson. Edinburgh, 1793, 4to.

Bey Allerhöchster Anwesenheit Ihro Majestät der Kaiserin Mutter Maria Feodorowna in Weimar. Maskenzug. Stuttgard, 1819, 8vo.

Maskenzug zum 30sten Januar 1809. [In verse.]—[1809], 8vo.

J. W. von Goethe. . . . Versuch die Metamorphose der Pflanzen zu erklären. Gotha, 1790, 8vo.

Die Mitschuldigen. Ein Lustspiel [in three acts and in verse]. Achte Ausgabe. Leipzig, 1787, 8vo.

Nachricht von dem ilmenauischen Bergwesen. (*Goethe und die lustige Zeit in Weimar, von A. Diezmann.*) Leipzig, 1857, 8vo.

Die Natürliche Tochter. Trauerspiel [in five acts and in verse]. Tübingen, 1804, 16mo.

Neueröffnetes moralisch - politisches Puppenspiel. Leipzig und Frankfurt, 1774, 8vo.

Goethe's Novel. Translated from the German. London, 1837, 12mo.

Paläophron und Neoterpe. Ein Festspiel zur Feier 24 Octobers 1800. An die Herzogin Amalia. Nach einer kleinen theatralischen Vorstellung gesprochen. (*Kleine Schriften*, Bdch. 1.) Weimar, 1801, 12mo.

——Paläophron and Neoterpe ; a Masque. From the German of Goethe, by the translator of Herman and Dorothea, etc. [J. C. Mellish ?]. Weimar, 1801, 4to.

Pandora. Ein Taschenbuch für das Jahr 1810. Wien und Triest [1810], 16mo.

Pflanzen und Gebirgsarten von Marienbad gesammelt und beschrieben von seiner königlichen Hoheit, dem Prinzen Friedrich, und von J. W. von Goethe, etc. Prag, 1837, 8vo.

Philipp Hackert. Biographische Skizze, meist nach dessen eigenen Aufsätzen entworfen von Goethe. Tübingen, 1811, 8vo.

Göthe's Reinecke Fuchs. Ein Gedicht in zwölf Gesängen. Berlin [1794], 8vo.

——Reynard the Fox ; after the German version of Goethe. By T. J. Arnold. With illustrations from the designs of W. v. Kaulbach. London, 1860 [1859], 4to.

——Reynard the Fox, after the German version of Goethe, with illustrations by J. Wolf. London, 1853[-55], 8vo.

——Reynard the Fox. After the German version of Goethe, by A. D. Ainslie. London, 1886, 8vo.

——Reynard the Fox after the version of Goethe, by T. J. Arnold. With sixty illustrations from the designs of W. von Kaulbach, and twelve engravings by J. Wolf. London, 1887 [1886], 8vo.

Goethe's Roman Elegies, translated into English verse, in the

original metre. By L. Noa.
Boston [1876], 8vo.

Sammlung zur Kenntniss der
Gebirge von und um Karlsbad
Angezeigt und erläutert von
Goethe. Karlsbad, 1807, 8vo.

Scherz, List und Rache. Ein
Singspiel. Ächte Ausgabe.
Leipzig, 1790, 8vo.

Stella. Ein Schauspiel für
Liebende in fünf Akten. Berlin,
1776, 8vo.

——Stella, translated from the
German [by Benjamin Thomp-
son]. London, 1798, 8vo.

The Tale. Translated by T.
Carlyle. [With preface signed
O. Y. — *i.e.,* Oliver York.]
Boston, 1877, 16mo.

Torquato Tasso. Ein Schauspiel
[in five acts and in verse].
Leipzig, 1790, 8vo.

——Torquato Tasso ; a dramatic
poem, from the German of
Goethe, with other German
poetry. Translated by C. Des
Voeux. London, 1827, 8vo.

——Second edition. Weimar,
1833, 8vo.

——Torquato Tasso, from the
German of Goethe and other
poems, translated and original.
By M. A. H. London, 1856,
8vo.

——Goethe's Torquato Tasso.
Translated into English verse
[by C.—*i.e.,* J. Cartwright].
London, 1861, 8vo.

Der Triumph der Empfindsam-
keit. Eine dramatische Grille
[in six acts and in prose].
Leipzig, 1787, 8vo.

Ueber Kunst und Alterthum.
6 Bde. Stuttgart, 1816-32, 8vo.
Each Bd. is in 3 pts. separately
paged, excepting Bd. 6, which has a
continuons pagination throughout.

Die Wahlverwandtschaften. Ein
Roman. 2 Thle. Tübingen,
1809, 8vo.

Was wir bringen. Vorspiel bey
Eröffnung des neuen Schauspiel-
hauses zu Lauchstädt. Tübingen, 1802, 8vo.

West-oestlicher Divan. Stuttgard,
1819, 8vo.

——Goethe's West - Easterly
Divan. Translated, with intro-
duction and notes, by J. Weiss.
Boston, 1877, 16mo.

Wilhelm Meisters Lehrjahre. Ein
Roman. 4 Bde. Berlin,
1795-96, 16mo.

——Wilhelm Meister's Ap-
prenticeship. A novel. From
the German of Goethe. [Trans-
lated by Thomas Carlyle.] 3
vols. Edinburgh, 1824, 8vo.

——Wilhelm Meister's Ap-
prenticeship and Travels.
[Translated by Thomas Carlyle.]
A new edition, revised. London, 1842, 12mo.

——Wilhelm Meister's Ap-
prenticeship. A novel from the
German of Goethe translated by
R. D. Boylan. (*Bohn's Standard
Library.*) London, 1855, 8vo.

——Wilhelm Meister's Ap-
prenticeship. From the German
by Eleanor Grove. (*Tauchnitz
Collection of British Authors,*
vols. xxv., xxvi.) 2 vols. Leipzig, 1873, 12mo.

Wilhelm Meisters Wanderjahre
oder die Entsagenden. Ein
Roman. Th. 1. Stuttgard
und Tübingen, 1821, 8vo.
This novel was finished in 1829, and
appeared in 3 vols. in the "Werke,"
1830, Bde. 21-23.

——Wilhelm Meister's Travels.
(*German Romance,* vol iv.)
Edinburgh, 1827, 8vo.

——Wilhelm Meister's Travels. Translated [by A. H. Gunlogson] from the enlarged edition of the German, and edited by E. Bell. (*Bohn's Standard Library.*) London, 1882, 8vo.

Winkelmann und sein Jahrhundert. In Briefen und Aufsätzen herausgegeben von Goethe. Tübingen, 1805, 8vo.

Aus Goethe's Knabenzeit, 1757-59. Mittheilungen aus einem Original-Manuscript der Frankfurter Stadt-bibliothek. Erläutert und herausgegeben von H. Weismann. Frankfurt a. M., 1846, 16mo.

Zur Farbenlehre. Nebst einem Hefte mit sechzehn Kupfertafeln. 2 Bd. Tübingen, 1810, 8vo.

——Theory of Colours; translated from the German, with notes, by C. L. Eastlake. London, 1840, 8vo.

Zur Naturwissenschaft überhaupt, besonders zur Morphologie. 2 Bde. Stuttgard und Tübingen, 1817-1823, 8vo.

IV. POEMS.

Göthe's neueste Gedichte. Mit Kupfern. Berlin, 1800, 8vo.

Goethe's Gedichte. Tübingen, 1812, 8vo.

Goethe's Gedichte. 2 Thl. Stuttgart und Tübingen, 1815, 12mo.

Goethe's Gedichte. Neue Auflage. 2 Thl. Stuttgart und Tübingen, 1821, 8vo.

Goethe's Gedichte. 2 Thl. Stuttgart, 1829, 8vo.

Goethe's ältestes Liederbuch. Herausgegeben von L. Tieck. Berlin, 1844, 8vo.

Goethe's Gedichte, erläutert und auf ihre Veranlassungen, Quellen und Vorbilder zurückgeführt, nebst Variantensammlung und Nachlese, von H. Viehoff. 3 Thl. Düsseldorf und Utrecht, 1846-53, 16mo.

Goethe's sämmtliche Gedichte. Kritische Textrevision von H. Kurz. 2 Bd. Hildburghausen, 1869, 8vo.

Goethe's Gedichte, erläutert von H. Viehoff. Zweite Auflage. 2 Bd. Stuttgart, 1869-70, 16mo.

Goethe's Gedichte. Mit einem bisher noch nicht gedruckten Sonett und Epigramme. Für deutsche Frauen ausgewählte von A. Lutze. Coethen, 1870, fol.

Goethe's Gedichte. Diamant-Ausgabe mit Illustrationen. Zweite Auflage. Berlin, 1870, 16mo.

Gedichte. Mit Zeichnungen von L. Pietsch, F. Piloty, etc. Berlin, 1871, 8vo.

Goethe's Minor Poems. Selected, annotated, and rearranged by A. M. Selse. *Germ.* London, 1875, 8vo.

Select Poems of Goethe, edited by E. A. Sonnenschein and A. Pogatscher. *Germ.* (*Annotated German Classics.*) London, 1883, 8vo.

Specimens of the German Lyric Poets; consisting of translations in verse from the works of Bürger, Goethe, etc. Second edition. London, 1823, 8vo.

Employment. [Poems translated from the German of Schiller and Goethe.] Bath, 1828, 8vo.

The Song of the Bell, and other poems from the German of Goethe, Schiller, Bürger, etc.

Translated by J. J. Campbell. Edinburgh, 1836, 8vo.

Select Minor Poems, from the German of Goethe and Schiller. (*Specimens of Foreign Standard Literature, ed. by George Ripley,* vol. iii.) Boston, 1839, 12mo.

The Drama of a Life. [In 10 scenes. In verse. Followed by poems, and translations from Goethe.] By John Edmund Reade. [Bath], 1840, 8vo.

Designs and Border Illustrations to Poems of Göthe, Schiller, Uhland, etc. With translations. London, 1841, fol.

German Ballads, Songs, etc. Comprising translations from Schiller, Uhland, Bürger, Goethe, etc. London [1845], 12mo.

English Hexameter Translations from Schiller, Göthe, Homer, etc. London, 1847, 8vo.

Metrical translations from the German of Goethe, Schiller, Uhland, Heine, and others, by a German lady. Hamburg, 1852, 8vo.

The Poems of Goethe translated in the original metres, with a sketch of Goethe's life. By E. A. Bowring. London, 1853, 8vo.

The Minor Poetry of Goethe. A selection from his songs, ballads, and other lesser poems. Translated by W. G. Thomas. Philadelphia, 1859, 4to.

Poems and Ballads. Translated by W. E. Aytoun and Theodore Martin. Edinburgh, 1859, 8vo.
——Second edition. Edinburgh, 1860, 8vo.

Goethe's Minor Poems. Translated by E. Chawner, etc. London [1866], 8vo.

The Poems of Goethe : translated in the original metres, by E. A. Bowring. Second edition, etc. (*Bohn's Standard Library.*) London, 1874, 8vo.

Favourite Poems. Translated by W. E. Aytoun and Theodore Martin. Illustrated. Boston 1877, 16mo.

Goethe's Poems translated in the original metres by P. Dyrsen. New York, 1878, 8vo.

The Poems of Goethe, consisting of his ballads and songs, and miscellaneous selections, done into English verse, by W. Gibson. London, 1883, 8vo.

V. TRANSLATIONS.

Benvenuto Cellini. Eine Geschichte des xvi Jahrhunderts. (Nach dem Italien'schen. Von J. W. von Göthe.) 3 Bde. Braunschweig, 1798, 8vo.

——Another edition. Leben des Benvenuto Cellini, etc. 2 Thl. Tübingen, 1803, 8vo.

Mahomet. Trauerspiel in fünf Aufzügen, nach Voltaire. Tübingen, 1802, 8vo.

Rameau's Neffe. Ein Dialog von Diderot. Übersetzt von Goethe. Leipzig, 1805, 8vo.

Tancred. Trauerspiel in fünf Aufzügen, nach Voltaire, von Goethe. Tübingen, 1802, 8vo.

Thomas Carlyle Leben Schillers. Aus dem Englischen. Eingleitet durch Goethe. Frankfurt am Main, 1830, 8vo.

Die Vögel. Nach dem Aristophanes. Ächte Ausgabe. Leipzig, 1787, 8vo.

VI. MISCELLANEOUS.

Als Nicolai die Freuden des junger Werthers geschrieben hatte. [Satirical Verses on C. F. Nicolai.] Berlin, 1837, s. sh., 12mo.

Herr Nicolai auf Werther's Grabe. [A satire against C. F. Nicolai as the author of a parody of "Die Leiden des jungen Werthers." Signed by J. W. G. [*i.e.* Goethe.] [Berlin, 1837], s. sh. fol.

Apotheose des Hochverdienstes am 27 September 1816, von dem Secretariat bei Grossherzoglicher Kammer. [Verses on the anniversary of the 50th year of service of C. G. von Voigt, by J. W. von Goethe.] Weimar, 1816, 4to.

Der deutsche Gilblas, eingeführt von Goethe. Stuttgart und Tübingen, 1822, 8vo.

Von deutscher Baukunst. [In *Von deutscher Art und Kunst.*] Hamburg, 1773, 8vo.

Der junge Feldjäger in französischen und englischen Diensten während des Spanisch-Portugiesischen Kriegs von 1806-1816, (Des jungen Feldjägers Kriegskamerad, etc. Des jungen Feldjägers Landsmann, etc. Des jungen Feldjägers Zeitgenosse, etc. Eingeführt durch J. W. von Göthe. 6 Bdchen. Leipzig, 1826-31, 12mo.

——The Young Rifleman's Comrade: a narrative, etc. [Translated from the German of "Des jungen Feldjägers Kriegskamerad," etc.] London, 1826, 12mo.

Observations on Leonardo Da Vinci, a picture of the Last Supper. Translated from the German, with an introduction and notes by G. H. Noehden, J. Booth, etc. London, 1821, 4to.

Positiones juris quas . . . publice defendet J. W. Goethe. Argentorati, 1771, 4to.

Prolog von Goethe, gesprochen im Königl. Schauspielhause vor Darstellung des dramatischen Gedichts Hans Sachs, von Deinhardstein. Berlin, 1828, 8vo.

Rede bey Eröffnung des neuen Bergbaues zu Ilmenau. [Weimar? 1784], 4to.

Das Römische Denkmal in Igel und seine Bildwerke. . . . mit einem Vorworte von Goethe. Weimar, 1829, 4to.

Das Tagebuch, 1810. Wien, 1879, 8vo. The authorship of this work is doubtful.

Taschenbuch auf das Jahr 1804. Herausgegeben von Wieland und Goethe. Tübingen [1804], 8vo.

A tribute to the memory of Ulrich of Hutten. Translated from the German of Goethe, by A. Aufrere, illustrated with remarks by the translator, etc. London, 1789, 8vo.

Wieland's Andenken in der Loge Amalia zu Weimar gefeyert den 18 Februar 1813. [Weimar, 1813], 4to.

Wilkommen! [Poems, edited by J. W. von Goethe.] Weimar, 1814, 8vo.

VII. LETTERS.

Goethe's Briefe in den Jahren 1768 bis 1832. Herausgegeben von Dr. H. Döring. Ein

Supplementband zu des Dichters sämmtlichen Werken. Leipzig, 1837, 8vo.

Göthe's Briefe, worunter viele bisher ungedruckte. Mit geschichtlichen Einleitungen und Erläuterungen. Berlin, 1856, 16mo.

Briefwechsel zwischen Schiller und Goethe in den Jahren 1794 bis 1805. 6 Thle. Stuttgart, 1828-9, 8vo.

Kurzer Briefwechsel zwischen Klopstock und Goethe im Jahre, 1776. Leipzig, 1833, 12mo.

Briefe von Goethe an Lavater. Aus dem Jahren 1774-1783. Herausgegeben von H. Hirzel. Nebst einem Anhange (einer Briefe an den Buchändler Reich) und zwei Facsimile. Leipzig, 1833, 8vo.

Briefwechsel zwischen Goethe und Zelter in den Jahren 1796 bis 1832. Herausgegeben von Dr. F. W. Riemer. 6 Th. Berlin, 1833-34, 8vo.

Eine Correspondenz Goethe's mit Madame Karschin. (*Schriften in bunter Reihe, etc., Herausgegeben von T. Mundt.*) Berlin, 1834, 8vo.

Schauspiele von Franz v. Elsholtz. Zweite Vermehrte und mit Goethe's Briefen über "Die Hofdame" versehene Ausgabe. 3 Thle. Leipzig, 1835, 8vo.

Goethe's Briefwechsel mit einem Kinde [*i.e.*, Elisabeth Brentano, afterwards Frau Von Arnim]. Seinem Denkmal. 3 Thle. Berlin, 1835, 8vo.

——Goethe's Correspondence with a Child. 3 vols. London ; Berlin [printed], 1837-39, 8vo.

Theater-Briefe von Goethe und freundschaftliche Briefe von

Jean Paul. Nebst einer Schilderung Weimar's in seiner Blüthezeit. Berlin, 1835, 8vo.

Briefwechsel zwischen Goethe und Schultz. Bonn, 1836, 8vo.

Goethe's Briefe an die Gräfin Auguste zu Stolberg. [Edited by A. von Binzer.] Leipzig, 1839, 8vo.

Ungedruckte Briefe von Schiller, Goethe und Wieland. Breslau, 1845, 8vo.

Briefe Schillers und Goethes an A. W. Schlegel, aus den Jahren 1795 bis 1801 und 1797 bis 1824, nebst einem Briefe Schlegels an Schiller. Leipzig, 1846, 8vo.

Briefe und Aufsätze von Göthe aus den Jahren 1766 bis 1786. Zum erstenmal herausgegeben durch A. Schöll. Weimar, 1846, 8vo.

Briefe von und an Göthe. Desgleichen Aphorismen und Brocardica. Herausgegeben von F. W. Riemer. Leipzig, 1846, 8vo.

Briefe von Goethe und dessen Mutter an Friedrich Freiherrn von Stein. Nebst einigen Beilagen. Herausgegeben von J. J. H. Ebers und A. Kahlert. Leipzig, 1846, 12mo.

Briefwechsel zwischen Göthe und F. H. Jacob herausgegeben von M. Jacob. Leipzig, 1846, 12mo.

Briefe aus dem Freundeskreise von Goethe, Herder, Höpfner und Merck. Eine selbständige Folge der beiden in den Jahren 1835 und 1838 erschienenen Merckischen Briefsammlungen. Aus den Handschriften herausgegeben von Dr. K. Wagner. Leipzig, 1847, 8vo.

Goethe's Briefe an Frau von

Stein aus den Jahren 1776 bis 1826. Zum erstenmal herausgegeben durch A. Schöll. [With a biographical sketch of Frau von Stein.] 3 Bd. Weimar, 1848-51, 8vo.

Goethe's Briefe an Leipziger Freunde. Herausgegeben von Otto Jahn. Leipzig, 1849, 12mo.

Briefwechsel zwischen Goethe und Reinhard in den Jahren 1807 bis 1832 [with a preface by C. von Reinhard]. Stuttgart, 1850, 8vo.

Briefwechsel zwischen Goethe und Knebel (1774-1832). [Edited by G. E. Guhrauer.] 2 Thle. Leipzig, 1851, 8vo.

Briefwechsel und mündlicher Verkehr zwischen Göthe und dem Rathe Grüner. Leipzig, 1853, 8vo.

Briefwechsel zwischen Goethe und Staatsrath Schultz. Herausgegeben und eingeleitet von H. Düntzer. Leipzig, 1853, 8vo.

Der Aktuar Salzmann, Goethe's Freund. . . . Ein Lebens-Skizze, nebst Briefen von Goethe, Lenz, L. Wagner, etc. Herausgegeben von A. Stöber. Mülhausen, 1855, 8vo.

Aus Weimars Glanzzeit. Ungedruckte Briefe von und über Goethe und Schiller, nebst einer Auswahl ungedruckter vertraulicher Schreiben von Goethe's Collegen, Geh. Rath von Voigt. Zum funfzigsten Jahrestage des Todes Schillers herausgegeben von A. Diezmann. Leipzig, 1855, 8vo.

Goethe und Werther. Briefe Goethes, meistens aus seiner Jugendzeit, mit erläuternden Documenten. Herausgegeben von A. Kestner. Zweite Auflage. Stuttgart, 1855, 8vo.

Briefe an Herder. (*Aus Herders Nachlass*, Bd. i.) Frankfurt a. Main, 1856, 8vo.

Briefe des Grossherzogs Carl August und Göthes an Döbereiner. Herausgegeben von O. Schade. Weimar, 1856, 8vo.

Freundschaftliche Briefe von Goethe und seiner Frau an N. Meyer. Aus den Jahren, 1800 bis 1831. Leipzig, 1856, 8vo.

Vier Briefe von Goethe an die Marquise Branconi. Herausgegeben von A. Cohn. [Berlin], 1860, 8vo.

Briefwechsel des Grossherzogs Carl August von Sachsen-Weimar-Eisenbach mit Goethe in den Jahren von 1775 bis 1828. 2 Bde. Weimar, 1863, 8vo.

Briefwechsel zwischen Goethe und Kaspar Graf von Sternberg (1820-1832). Herausgegeben von F. T. Bratranek. Wien, 1866, 8vo.

Goethe's Verkehr mit Gliedern des Hauses der Freiherrn und Grafen von Fritsch [containing several letters from Goethe]. Von W. Freiherr v. Biedermann. Leipzig, 1868, 8vo.

Goethe's Briefe an C. G. von Voigt. Herausgegeben von O. Jahn. Leipzig, 1868, 8vo.

Goethe's Briefe an F. A. Wolf. Herausgegeben von M. Bernays. Berlin, 1868, 8vo.

Goethe's Briefe an Eichstädt. Mit Erläuterungen herausgegeben von W. Freiherrn von Biedermann. Berlin, 1872, 8vo.

Neue Mittheilungen aus J. W. von Goethe's handschriftlichen

Nachlasse. 3 Thl. Leipzig, 1874-76, 8vo.

Thl. 1 and 2 contain "Naturwissenschaftliche Correspondenz;" Thl. 3, "Briefwechsel mit den Gebrüdern von Humboldt."

Briefe von Goethe, Schiller, etc., an Karl Morgenstern, herausgegeben von F. Sintenis. Dorpat, 1875, 8vo.

Briefe von Goethe an Johanna Fahlmer. Herausgegeben von L. Urlichs. Leipzig, 1875, 8vo.

Briefwechsel zwischen Goethe und Mariannevon Willemer (Suleika). Herausgegeben mit Lebensnachrichten und Erläuterungen von T. Creizenach. Stuttgart, 1877, 8vo.

Goethe Briefe aus F. Schlosser's Nachlass. Herausgegeben von J. Frese, etc. Stuttgart, 1877, 8vo.

Goethe's Briefe an Soret. Herausgegeben von H. Uhde. Stuttgart, 1877, 8vo.

Ungedrucktes. Zum Druck befördert von A. Cohn. [A collection of the letters of Schiller, Goethe, etc.] Berlin, 1878, 8vo.

Goethe und der Komponist P. C. Kayser. Von C. A. H. Burkhardt. [Contains 24 letters from Goethe to Kayser.] Leipzig, 1879, 8vo.

Briefe Goethe's an Sophie von La Roche und Bettina Brentano, nebst dichterischen Beilagen herausgegeben von G. von Loeper. Berlin, 1879, 8vo.

Briefwechsel zwischen Goethe und K. Göttling in den Jahren 1824-1831. Herausgegeben und mit einem Vorwort begleitet von K. Fischer. München, 1880, 8vo.

Jugendbriefe Goethes. Ausgewählt und erläutert von Dr. W. Fielitz. Berlin, 1880, 8vo.

Goethe und Gräfin O'Donell. Ungedruckte Briefe nebst dichterischen Beilagen herausgegeben von Dr. R. M. Werner. Berlin, 1884, 8vo.

Goethes Liebesbriefe an Frau von Stein, 1776 bis 1789. Herausgegeben mit Uebersichten und Anmerkungen von H. Duentzer. Leipzig, 1886, 8vo.

Correspondence between Schiller and Goethe, from 1794 to 1805, translated by G. H. Calvert. Vol. 1. New York, 1845, 12mo.

Correspondence between Schiller and Goethe, from 1794 to 1805. Translated from the third edition of the German, with notes. By L. D. Schmitz. (*Bohn's Standard Library.*) 2 vols. London, 1877-9, 8vo.

Goethe's Letters to Leipzig Friends. Edited by O. Jahn. Translated by R. Slater, Jun. London, 1866, 8vo.

Goethe's Mother. Correspondence of C. E. Goethe with Goethe, etc. Translated from the German by Alfred S. Gibbs. New York [1880], 8vo.

Early and Miscellaneous Letters of J. W. Goethe, including Letters to his Mother. With notes and a short biography by Edward Bell. (*Bohn's Standard Library.*) London, 1884, 8vo.

Correspondence between Goethe and Carlyle. Edited by C. E. Norton. London, 1887, 8vo.

Goethe's Letters to Zelter, with extracts from those of Zelter to Goethe, selected, translated, and annotated by A. D.

Coleridge. (*Bohn's Standard Library*.) London, 1887, 8vo.

VIII. SELECTIONS.

Gedankenharmonie aus Goethe und Schiller. Lebens - und Weisheitssprüche aus Goethe's und Schiller's Werken. Gesammelt und herausgegeben von R. Gottschall. Hamburg, 1862, 16mo.

Geistesworte aus Goethe's Briefen und Gesprächen. Fortsetzung der Geistesworte aus Goethe's Werken. Herausgegeben von L. von Lancizolle. Berlin, 1853, 16mo.

Goethe-Buch. Goethe'sche Lebens- und Weisheitssprüche zur Einführung in des Dichters Denk-und Sinnesweise nach den Tagen des Jahres zusammengestellt und mit Commentar, etc. Leipzig, 1881, 8vo.

Goethe's Erzählungen Gewachsnen Mädchen zu eigen gemacht von F. Siegfried, etc. Leipzig, 1874, 8vo.

Goethe Gedenk-Buch. [Quotations for every day in the year.] Achern, [1880], 8vo.

Göthe's Genius. [Selections in prose and verse.] (*Miniatur-Bibliothek der Deutschen Classiker*, vol. iv.) 3 Bdchen. Hildburghausen, 1829, 16mo.

Goethe in Briefen und Gesprächen. Sammlung der brieflichen und mündlichen, Bemerkungen und Betrachtungen Goethe's über Welt und Menschen, Wissenschaft, Literatur und Kunst, etc. Berlin, 1852, 8vo.

Goethe's Opinions on the World, Mankind, Literature, Science, and Art. Translated by O. Wenckstern. London, 1853, 8vo.

Goethe's Philosophie. Eine vollständige, systematisch geordnete Zusammen-stellung seiner Ideen über Leben, Liebe, Ehe, Kunst und Natur aus seinen Werken. Herausgegeben von F. K. J. Schütz. 7 Bde. Hamburg, 1825, 26, 8vo.

Goethe's Prosa. Auswahl für Schule und Haus. Herausgegeben von Dr. J. W. Schaefer. 2 Bde. Stuttgart und Augsburg, 1859, 8vo.

Göthe über Art und Unart, Freud und Leid der Jugend und ihrer Erzieher [selections from his works], mit illustrationen von J. F. E. Meyer. Cutin, 1851, 8vo.

Göthe-und Schiller-Sprüche, etc. Breslau, 1843, 8vo.

Goethe's vaterländische Gedanken und politisches Glaubensbekenntniss. Frankfort a. M., 1853, 12mo.

Lieder und Worte von Goethe, etc. Altenburg, 1870, 8vo.

Law's New German Series. Buchheim's Deutsche Prosa. Goethe's Prosa, consisting of selections from G.'s Prose Works, etc. By C. A. Buchheim. London, 1876, 8vo.

Many colored threads from the writings of Goethe. Selected by C. A. Cooke. With an introduction by A. McKenzie. Boston [Mass., 1885], 8vo.

The Roman Martyr : a youthful essay in dramatic verse by Nominis Umbra. With translations (from Goethe) by the editor. London, 1859, 8vo.

Selections from the dramas of Goethe and Schiller, translated, with introductory remarks, by A. Swanwick. London, 1843, 8vo.

Sprachbilder, aus Goethe's Werken gesammelt, etc. Wien [1886], 8vo.

Vom Morgen zum Abend ; Worte von Goethe, Rückert, Uhland und Andern, etc. Berlin [1865], 4to.

The Wisdom of Goethe. By J. S. Blackie. [Translated from the German.] Edinburgh, 1883, 8vo.

Worte der Liebe. Aus unseren Dichtern Schiller, Goethe gesammelt, etc. Von E. von Beckendorff und E. Leistner. Leipzig [1874], 16mo.

IX. APPENDIX.

BIOGRAPHY, CRITICISM, ETC.

[*The Foreign Literature upon Goethe and his Works being very extensive, it has been only possible to include English works in the following list.*]

Arnold, Matthew.—Mixed Essays. London, 1879, 8vo.
    A French Critic on Goethe, pp. 274-314.

Bancroft, G.—Literary and Historical Miscellanies. New York, 1855, 8vo.
    The Age of Schiller and Goethe, p. 167, etc.

Bell, James. — Letters from Wetzlar, written in 1817, developing the authentic particulars on which the Sorrows of Werter are founded, etc. London, 1821, 8vo.

Blackie, John Stuart.—The Wisdom of Goethe. [With an estimate of the character of Goethe, by J. S. B.] Edinburgh, 1883, 8vo.

Boyesen, Hjalmar H. — Goethe and Schiller : their lives and works ; including a commentary on Goethe's Faust. New York, 1879, 8vo.

Buchanan, Robert—A Look Round Literature. London, 1887, 8vo.
    The Character of Goethe, pp. 54-95

Calvert, George H.—First Years in Europe. Boston, 1866, 8vo.
    Weimar, pp. 165-198.
——Goethe. His Life and Works. An Essay. Boston, 1872, 8vo.
——Brief Essays and Brevities. Boston, 1874, 8vo.
    Goethe's Faust, pp. 123-128.
——Coleridge, Shelley, Goethe. Biographic Aesthetic Studies. Boston [1880], 8vo.

Carlyle, Thomas.—The Life of Friedrich Schiller, etc. London, 1825, 8vo.
    References to Goethe.
——Goethe. Boston, 1877, 12mo.
    Reprinted from the "Critical and Miscellaneous Essays."
——Essays on Goethe. New York [1881], 4to.
    Reprinted from the "Critical and Miscellaneous Essays."

Dawson, George. — Shakespeare and other lectures. London, 1888, 8vo.
    Faustus, Faust, and Festus, pp. 342-392.

De Quincey, Thomas.—Works. Edinburgh, 1863, 8vo.
    Goethe's Wilhelm Meister, vol. xii., pp. 191-229; Goethe, vol. xv., pp. 143-179.

Düntzer, Heinrich. — Goethe's Leben. Mit authentischen Illustrationen. Leipzig, 1880, 8vo.

Düntzer, Heinrich.—Life of Goethe. Translated by T. W. Lyster. With authentic illustrations and facsimiles. 2 vols. London, 1883, 8vo.

Eckermann, Johann P.—Gespräche mit Goethe in den letzten Jahren seines Lebens, 1823-1832. 2 Thle. Leipzig, 1836-48, 8vo.

——Conversations with Goethe from the German of Eckermann (*Specimens of Foreign Standard Literature, ed. by George Ripley,* vol. iv). Boston, 1839, 12mo.

——Conversations with Goethe and Soret. Translated from the German by John Oxenford. 2 vols. London, 1850, 8vo.

——Conversations of Goethe with Eckermann and Soret. Translated from the German by J. Oxenford. (*Bohn's Standard Library.*) London, 1874, 8vo.

Eliot, George.—Essays and Leaves from a Note-Book. Edinburgh, 1884, 8vo.
Three Months in Weimar, pp. 290-321.

Emerson, Ralph Waldo.—The Works of R. W. Emerson. London, 1883, 8vo.
Goethe; or, The Writer, vol. iv., pp. 453-476. Appeared originally in Emerson's "Representative Men," 1850.

Encyclopædia Britannica. Encyclopædia Britannica. Ninth edition. Edinburgh, 1879, 4to.
Goethe, by Oscar Browning, vol. x.

Falk, Johannes D.—Goethe aus nähern persönlichen Umgange dargestellt. Leipzig, 1832, 8vo.

——Characteristics of Goethe. From the German of Falk, Von Müller, etc., by Sarah Austin. 3 vols. London, 1833, 8vo.

Fuller, Margaret.—Life without and life within; or, reviews, narratives, etc. Boston, 1874, 8vo.
Goethe, pp. 23-60.

Goethe, J. W.—Goethe-Jahrbuch. 7 Bde. Frankfort a. Main, 1880-6, 8vo.

——Schriften der Goethe-Gesellschaft. 2 Bde. Weimar, 1885-6, 8vo.

——Publications of the English Goethe Society. 2 pts. London, 1886, 8vo.

Godwin, Parke.—Out of the Past, etc. New York, 1870, 8vo.
Goethe, p. 341, etc.

Gostwick, Joseph. — German Culture and Christianity, etc. London, 1882, 8vo.
Goethe, pp. 267-317.

Gostwick, Joseph, and Harrison, Robert.—Outlines of German Literature. Second edition. London, 1883, 8vo.
Goethe, pp. 225, 226, 241, 242, 256-303, 439-443.

Grimm, Herman.—The Life and Times of Goethe. Translated by S. H. Adams. Boston, 1880, 8vo.

Griswold, Hattie Tyng.—Home Life of Great Authors. Chicago, 1887, 8vo.
Goethe, pp. 9-23.

Haeckel, E. H. P. A.—Natürliche Schöpfungsgeschichte. Gemeinverständliche wissenschaftliche Vorträge über die Entwickelungslehre im Allgemeinen und diejenige von Darwin, Goethe und Lamarck, etc. Berlin, 1868, 8vo.

——The History of Creation; or, the development of the earth and its inhabitants by the action of natural causes. The translation revised by E. R. Lan-

kester. 2 vols. London, 1876,
8vo.

Hayward, A.—Goethe, by A.
Hayward. (*Foreign Classics for
English Readers*, ed. *by Mrs.
Oliphant.*) Edinburgh,1878,8vo.

Hedge, Frederic H.—Prose Writers
of Germany. New edition. Philadelphia [1871], 8vo.
  Goethe, pp. 264-364.

Hedge, F. H.—Hours with German Classics. Boston,1886,8vo.
  Goethe, pp. 254-343.

Helmholtz, H.—Populäre Wissen-
schaftliche Vorträge. Braun-
schweig, 1865, 8vo.
  Uber Goethe's naturwissenschaft-
  liche Arbeiten, Hft. i., pp. 33-53.
——Popular Lectures on Scientific
Subjects. Translated by E.
Atkinson. London, 1873, 8vo.
  On Goethe's Scientific Researches.
  Translated by H. W. Eve, pp. 33-59.

Hillard, George Stillman.—Six
Months in Italy. 2 vols. Lon-
don, 1853, 8vo.
  Goethe, vol, ii., pp. 302-310.

Holloway, Laura C.—The Mothers
of Great Men and Women, etc.
New York, 1884, 8vo.
  The Mother of Goethe, pp. 266-
  283.

Hosmer, James K.—Short History
of German Literature. St.
Louis, 1879, 8vo.
  Goethe, pp. 330-414.

Hutton, Richard Holt.—Essays,
theological and literary. 2 vols.
London, 1871, 8vo.
  Goethe and his Influence, vol. ii.,
  pp. 3-100.
——Second edition. 2 vols.
London, 1877, 8vo.
  Goethe and his Influence, vol. ii.,
  pp. 1-79.

Japp, Alexander Hay.—German
Life and Literature, in a series
of biographical studies. London
[1880], 8vo.
  Goethe, pp. 269-379.

Jeffrey, Francis. — Contributions
to the *Edinburgh Review*. London, 1853, 8vo.
  "Wilhelm Meister's Apprenticeship," Aug. 1825, pp. 120-142.

Lazarus, Emma.—Alide: an epi-
sode of Goethe's Life. Philadelphia, 1874, 8vo.

Lewes, George Henry.—The life
and works of Goethe: with
sketches of his Age and Contemporaries from published and
unpublished sources. 2 vols.
London, 1855, 8vo.
——Second edition. Partly re-
written. London, 1864 [1863],
8vo.
——Third edition, revised according to the latest documents.
London, 1875, 8vo.
——Third edition. Copyright
edition. 2 vols. Leipzig, 1882,
8vo.
—— ——The Story of Goethe's
Life. Abridged from his "Life
and Works of Goethe." London, 1873, 8vo.
——Female Characters of Goethe.
From the original drawings of
W. Kaulbach. With explana-
tory text by G. H. Lewes.
London [1874], fol.

Lindau, W. A.—Heliodora, or the
Grecian Minstrel. Translated
from the German of Baron
Goethe [or rather of W. A.
Lindau]. 3 vols. London, 1804,
12mo.

Longfellow, Henry Wadsworth.
—The Poets and Poetry of
Europe. London, 1855, 8vo.
  Goethe, pp. 281-296.

McCarthy, Justin. — "Con
Amore;" or critical chapters.
London, 1868, 8vo.
  Goethe's Poems and Ballads, pp.
  35-76.

Masson, David.—Essays, bio-graphical and critical, chiefly on English Poets. Cambridge, 1856, 8vo.
  Shakespeare and Goethe, pp. 1-36; reprinted from the *British Quarterly Review*, Nov. 1852. The Three Devils: Luther's, Milton's, and Goethe's, pp. 53-87; reprinted from Fraser's Magazine, Dec. 1844.

——The Three Devils, Luther's, Milton's, and Goethe's; with other essays. London, 1874, 8vo.

Mazzini, Joseph. — Life and Writings of J. Mazzini. London, 1870, 8vo.
  Byron and Goethe, vol. vi., pp. 61-97.

Mendelssohn-Bartholdy, Carl.— Goethe und F. Mendelssohn-Bartholdy. Leipzig, 1871, 8vo.

——Goethe and Mendelssohn (1821-1831). Translated, with additions from the German of Dr. K. Mendelssohn-Bartholdy by M. E. von Glehn. With portraits and facsimile, etc. London, 1872, 8vo.

Menzel, Wolfgang. — German Literature. Translated from the German, with notes by Thomas Gordon. 4 vols. Oxford, 1840, 8vo.
  Goethe, vol. iii., pp. 298-355.

Merivale, Herman.—Historical Studies. London, 1865, 8vo.
  Voltaire, Rousseau, and Göthe, pp. 130-185.

Metcalfe, Rev. Frederick.— History of German Literature, based on the German work of Vilmar. London, 1858, 8vo.
  Goethe, pp. 431-486.

Monro, Rev. Edward.—Parochial Lectures on English Poetry, etc. London, 1856, 8vo.
  Dante, Goethe, and Shakspere, pp. 142-173.

Moschzisker, F. A.—A Guide to German Literature, etc. 2 vols. London, 1850, 8vo.
  Goethe, vol. ii., pp. 95-170.

Nevinson, Henry.—A Sketch of Herder and his times. London, 1884, 8vo.
  Numerous references to Goethe.

Notes and Queries.—General Index to Notes and Queries. Five series. London, 1856-1880, 4to.
  Numerous references to Goethe.

Oppler, Adolph.—Three Lectures on Education, with another Lecture, entitled Some of Goethe's Educational Views. Fourth edition. London, 1875, 8vo.

Pagel, L.—Doctor Faustus of the popular legend, Marlowe, the Puppet-Play, Goethe, and Lenau, treated historically and critically. A parallel between Goethe and Schiller, etc. 2pts. [Liverpool],8vo.

Phelps, Almira L.—Reviews and Essays. Philadelphia, 1873, 8vo.
  Goethe, p. 180, etc.

Pickering, Amelia.—The Sorrows of Werther; a poem [founded on Goethe's novel]. London, 1788, 4to.

Robinson, Henry Crabb.—Diary, Reminiscences, and Correspondence of H. C. R., etc. 3 vols. London, 1869, 8vo.
  Numerous references to Goethe.

Rudloff, F. W.—Shakespeare, Schiller, and Goethe relatively considered. An essay. Brighton, 1848, 12mo.

Sanborn, Frank B.—The life and genius of Goethe. Lectures. Edited by F. B. S. Boston, 1886, 8vo.

Scherer, Wilhelm.—Geschichte der deutschen Litteratur. Berlin, 1883, 8vo.

Scherer, William.—A History of German Literature, by W. Scherer. Translated by Mr. F. C. Conybeare. Edited by F. Max Müller. 2 vols. London, 1886, 8vo.
Herder and Goethe, vol. ii., pp. 82-114; Weimar, pp. 142-144; Goethe, pp. 145-170; Schiller and Goethe, pp. 170-199, etc.

Sime, James.—Lessing. (*English and Foreign Philosophical Library, Extra Series.*) 2 vols. London, 1877, 8vo.
Shows the literary connection between Goethe and Lessing.

Solling, Gustav.—Diutiska, an historical and critical survey of the literature of Germany, etc. London, 1863, 8vo.
Goethe, pp. 210-288.

Staël, Madame de.—L'Allemagne. 3 vols. Paris, 1810, 12mo.

——Germany; translated from the French. 3 vols. London, 1813, 8vo.
Goethe, vol. i., pp. 265-273, and vol. ii., pp. 138-226.

Steffens, Heinrich.—The Story of my Career, as Student at Freiburg and Jena, with personal reminiscences of Goethe, etc. Translated by W. L. Gage. Boston [Mass.], 1863, 8vo.

Stevens, A.—Madame de Staël; a study of her life and times. 2 vols. London, 1881, 8vo.
Numerous references to Goethe.

Taylor, Bayard.—Studies in German Literature. London, 1879, 8vo.
Goethe, pp. 304-336; Goethe's "Faust," pp. 337-387.

Taylor, W., *of Norwich.*—Historic Survey of German Poetry, etc. 3 vols. London, 1828, 8vo.
Review of Goethe's Works, with a translation of Iphigenia, etc., vol. iii., pp. 242-379.

Thackeray, William Makepeace.

——The Works of W. M. T. Miscellaneous Essays, etc. London, 1886, 8vo.
Goethe in his old age, vol. xxiii., pp. 402-405. This letter was written by Mr. Thackeray in answer to a request from G. H. Lewes for some account of his recollections of Goethe. It will be found in Lewes's "Life of Goethe," p. 560.

Thomas, Calvin.—Goethe and the Conduct of Life. (*Philosophical Papers. First Series.* No. 2. *University of Michigan.*) Ann Arbor, 1886, 8vo.

Ticknor, George.—Life, Letters, and Journals of G. T. 2 vols. London, 1876, 8vo.
Numerous references to Goethe.

Ulrici, Hermann.—Ueber Shakspeare's dramatische Kunst, etc. Halle, 1839, 8vo.

——Shakspeare's Dramatic Art: and his relation to Calderon and Goethe. Translated from the German. London, 1846, 8vo.
Goethe in relation to Shakspeare, pp. 512-554.

Vaughan, Rev. Robert Alfred.—Essays and Remains of the Rev. R. A. Vaughan. 2 vols. London, 1858, 8vo.
Lewes's Life and Works of Goethe, vol. ii., pp. 114-163.

W., E.—A letter to a friend, with a poem called the Ghost of Werter. By Lady E. W. [*i.e.,* Lady Wallace]. London, 1787, 4to.

Werther.—Werter to Charlotte. A poem [founded on Goethe's novel "Die Leiden des jungen Werther's." By E. Taylor]. London, 1784, 4to.

——Charlotte and Werter. At Mrs. Salmon's Royal Historical Wax-Work, No. 189 Fleet Street. [A handbill, June 3,

1785.] [London, 1785], s. sh,
4to.

Werther.—The Letters of Charlotte, during her connexion with
Werter. [In allusion to "Die
Leiden des jungen Werthers."]
2 vols. New York, 1797, 12mo.

——Another edition, London,
1813, 12mo.

——Werter and Charlotte. A
German story, [founded on
Goethe's novel "Die Leiden
des jungen Werther's," etc.]
London [1800], 8vo.

Wilson, H. S.—Count Egmont ;
as depicted in painting, poetry,
and history, by Gallait,
Goethe, and Schiller. London,
1863, 8vo.

FAUST.

Berlioz, Hector.—"Faust," a
dramatic legend in four parts,
by Berlioz [or rather abridged
from Goethe, by H. B. Gérard
and Gandonnière]. English
translation by Miss M. Hallé.
Manchester [1880], 4to.

Bernard, Bayle.—Faust ; or, the
fate of Margaret. A romantic
play, in four acts. Adapted
from the poem of Goethe.
(*Lacy's Acting Edition of Plays*,
vol. lxxxiii.) London [1869],
12mo.

Boileau, D.—A few remarks on
Mr. Hayward's English prose
translation of Goethe's Faust,
etc. London, 1834, 8vo.

Burnand, F. C.—Faust and
Marguerite. An entirely new
original travestie in one act.
By F. C. Burnand. (*Lacy's
Acting Edition of Plays*, etc.,
vol. lxiii.) London [1864],
12mo.

Burnand, F. C.—Faust and Loose,
written by F. C. Burnand.
London [1886], 8vo.

Coupland, William C. The
Spirit of Goethe's Faust. London, 1885, 8vo.

Crowquill, Alfred. *i.e.*, Alfred
Forrester.—Faust, a serio-comic
poem, with twelve outline
illustrations by A. Crowquill
[*i.e.*, Alfred Forrester. A
travesty of Goethe's Faust].
London, 1834, 8vo.

Edwards, H. Sutherland.—The
Faust Legend : its origin and
development : from the living
Faustus of the first century to
the Faust of Goethe. London,
1886, 8vo.

Faust: a drama in six acts. By
Goethe. As represented at the
St. James's Theatre, London,
under the direction of Mr.
Mitchell, Jan. 22, 1852.
London, 1852.

Gounod, Charles F.—The Opera
Libretto. Gounod's grand opera
of Faust [in five acts. The
words by P. J. Barbier and M.
Carré, founded on Goethe's
poem, and translated into
English]. Melbourne [1865],
12mo.

Grattan, H. P.—Faust ; or the
demon of the Drachenfels. A
romantic drama, in two acts.
By H. P. Grattan. First
produced at Sadler's Wells,
September 5, 1842. London
[1886], 8vo.
    One of "Dick's Standard Plays."

Halford, J. — Faust and
Marguerite ; or, the Devil's
Draught. A grand operatic
extravaganza. A free and
easy adaptation of Göthe's

"Faust." (*Lacy's Acting Edition of Plays*, etc., vol. lxxiii.) London [1867], 12mo.

Hatton, Joseph.—The Lyceum "Faust." [A critique of the performance of Goethe's play "Faust" at the Lyceum Theatre.] With illustrations. London [1886], obl. 8vo.

Hittell, Theodore H.—Goethe's Faust. San Francisco [1872], 8vo.

Koller, W. H.—Faust Papers, containing remarks on Faust and it translations, with some observations upon Goethe. London, 1835, 8vo.

Konewka, P.—Illustrations to Goethe's Faust. By Paul Konewka. The English text from Bayard Taylor's Translation. London, 1871, 4to.

Kyle, William.—I. An Exposition of the symbolic terms of the second part of Faust. II. How this part thus proves itself to be a dramatic treatment of the modern history of Germany worthy of the genius of Goethe, etc. Nuremberg, 1870, 8vo.

Phillips, Alfred R.—Faust: a weird story. Based on Goethe's famous play. New York [1886], 8vo.

Reichlin-Meldegg, C. A. von.—Faust: an exposition of Goethe's Faust, from the German of C. A. von Reichlin-Meldegg, by R. H. Chittenden. New York, 1864, 8vo.

Robertson, William.—Faust and Marguerite. A romantic drama, in three acts. Translated from the French of Michel Carré, by William Robertson. (*Lacy's Acting Edition of Plays*, etc.,

vol. xv.) London [1854], 12mo.

Snider, Denton J.—Goethe's Faust. First (second) part. A commentary on the literary Bibles of the Occident. 2 pts. By Denton J. Snider. Boston, 1886, 8vo.

Soane, George.—Faustus; a romantic drama, in three acts, by George Soane. (*Cumberland's British Theatre*, vol. xxx.) London [1825], 12mo.

Wills, W. G.—Faust, in a prologue, and five acts. Adapted and arranged for the Lyceum Theatre, by W. G. Wills, from the first part of Goethe's Tragedy. London [1886], 8vo.

Wysard, Alexander.—The intellectual and moral problem of Goethe's Faust, parts I. and II. London, 1883, 8vo.

SONGS, ETC., SET TO MUSIC.

Music zu Goethe's Werken. By J. F. Reichardt, 1780.

Erwin und Elmire. Ein Singspiel in zwey Acten, 1793.

Goethe's Lieder, Oden, Balladen und Romanzen, mit musik, etc. By J. F. Reichardt, 1809.

Sechs deutsche Lieder von Goethe, etc. By C. F. Rungenhagen, 1810.

Rastlose Liebe. Gedichte von Goethe, in musik gesetzt. By F. Schubert, 1810.

Drei deutsche Lieder. By G. B. Bierey, 1820.

Zwölf Lieder von Goethe. By G. E. Fischer, 1820.

Sechs Lieder von Goethe. By F. W. Grund, 1820.

Lieder von Goethe. By G. Weber, 1820.

Wilhelm Meister's Lehrjahren. By F. A. Weppen (*Sieben Lieder aus Wilhelm Meister's Lehrjahren*), 1820.

Vier Gedichte von Goethe, etc. By B. Klein, 1825.

Zwölf Lieder von Goethe. By W. von Schwertzell, 1825.

Vier Lieder von Goethe, etc. By F. A. Weppen, 1825.

V. Gedichte von Goethe. By C. F. Curschmann, 1830.

VI. Gedichte von Goethe, etc. By R. von Hertzberg, 1830.

VIII. Gedichte von Goethe, etc. By B. Klein, 1830.

Neun Gesänge zu Goethe's Faust. By J. A. Lecerf, 1830.

Sechs Lieder von Goethe, etc. By F. Reis, 1830.

Gedichte von Goethe, etc. Heft 6, 7, 8. By W. J. Tomaschek, 1830.

Drey Gesänge von Goethe, etc. By L. van Beethoven, 1835.

Vier Gesänge. By L. van Beethoven, 1835.

Drei Balladen. By J. C. G. Loewe, 1835.

Compositionen zu Goethe's Faust. By Prince Radziwill, 1835.

Faustus. A musical romance. By Sir H. R. Bishop, 1840.

Sechs Gedichte von Goethe. By C. F. Curschmann, 1840.

Gesänge und Lieder aus der Tragödie (Faust). By L. Lenz, 1840.

Deutsche Lieder von Goethe, etc. By C. G. Reissiger, 1840.

Tafelgesäng. Sechs Gedichte von Goethe. By X. Schnyder von Wartensee, 1840.

Gesäng der Geister über den Wassern. Cantata. By F. Hiller, 1850.

La Damnation de Faust. Légende dramatique en quatre parties. By Hector Berlioz, 1854.

Fünf Terzette über Worte von Goethe, Klopstock, etc. By C. Geissler, 1854.

Scherz, List und Rache. Komische Oper. By M. Bruch, 1855.

Musik zu Goethe's Faust. By H. H. Pierson, 1856.

Faust. Opera en cinq actes. By C. F. Gounod, 1859.

Claudine, Opera. By J. H. Franz, 1865.

Scenen aus Göthe's Faust für Solostimmen. By R. Schumann, 1865.

Rinaldo, Cantate. By J. Brahms, 1869.

Rinaldo, Gedicht von Goethe. By G. Hermann, 1870.

Drei Gedichte von Goethe, etc. By P. Ruefer, 1870.

Die Gedichte aus "Wilhelm Meister's Lehrjähre," etc. By A. Rubenstein, 1873.

Gesellige Lieder von Göthe. By L. Grill, 1874.

Zwei Terzette. Gedichte von Goethe. By K. J. Bischoff, 1875.

Sechs Lieder, Op. 14 (Nos. 2-5 written by Goethe). By H. von Sahr, 1877.

Drei Gesänge, Op. 72 (Nos. 2, 3 written by Goethe). By R. Wuerst, 1878.

10 Goethe 'schen Dichtungen, etc. By L. Schlottmann, 1878.

Fünf Lieder. Op. 44 (Nos. 3, 4 written by Goethe). By B. Scholz, 1879.

Sechs Lieder, etc. Op. 60 (Nos. 2, 5 written by Goethe). By F. Siebmann, 1880.

Vier Gesänge, etc. (Nos. 1, 2,

4 written by Goethe). By J. Holter, 1881.

Mahomet's Gesang. By E. Fluegel, 1882.

Sechs Duette, etc. (Nos. 2, 4 written by Goethe). By A. Glück, 1882.

Mignon's Requiem, Cantata. By R. Schumann, 1882.

Pandora. By H. Huber, 1883.

Sechs Lieder von Goethe. By K. Hübner, 1883.

Neun Lieder, etc. (Nos. 5, 6 written by Goethe). By S. Jadassohn, 1883.

Idylle von Goethe, für Soli, Chor und Orchester. By F. Kiel, 1883.

Vier Gedichte von Goethe, etc. By T. Kerchner, 1883.

Sechs Gedichte, etc. By S. Bagge, 1885.

Musik zu Goethe's Festspiel Pandora. By E. Lassen, 1886.

Faust. Musikdrama nach Goethe's Faust, I. Theil. By H. Zoellner, 1887.

———

"Ach neige du Schmerzens reiche." — *Marguerite*. By C. Huener, 1877.

"Ach, um deine feuchten Schwingen." By Mendelssohn, 1852.

"Ach! wer bringt die schönen Tage." By H. Bellermann (*Sechs Lieder* No. 2), 1860 ; E. Drobisch (*Sechs Lieder*, No. 4), 1870 ; J. Krall, 1840 ; H. Krigar (*Vier Gesänge*, No. 3), 1860 ; H. Panopka, 1830 ; F. Stockhausen, 1835 ; C. F. Zelter (*Zelter's Sämmtliche Lieder*, Heft 4), 1820.

"All my peace is gone." (*Gretchen am Spinnrade. Marguerite.*) By F. Schubert, 1861.

"Aller Berge Gipfel ruh'n in dunkler Nacht." By A. Rubinstein (*Song and Duets*, No. 10), 1869.

"An dem reinsten Fruhling-morgen." By L. Heritte-Viardot (*Sechs Lieder*. Op. 8, No. 6), 1884.

"And is it true that I have lost thee?"—*Absence*. By C. A. Dance, 1861.

"And shall I then regain thee never?"—*Absence*. By Sir J. Benedict, 1864.

"And wilt thou then no more be mine." By C. A. Lidgey, 1887.

"Aussöhnung." By H. Hüber, 1879.

"Ein Blick von deinem Augen," By J. Brahms (*Lieder*, Op. 47, No. 5,) 1869 ; A. Bungert (*Junge Lieder*, Op. 2, No. 6), 1872.

"Ein Blumenglöckchen vom Boden hervor." By J. Kniese (*Acht Duette*, Op. 6, No. 2), 1884.

"A boy a little rose espied." By M. W. Balfe, 1860.

"A boy espied in morning light." —*The Wild Rose-bud*. By J. Williams, 1870.

"Die Braut von Korinth." By J. F. Christman, 1800 ; B. Klein, 1835 ; J. C. G. Loewe, 1735.

"Brightly was the sunset glowing." By J. Thomas, 1876.

"Una calma profonda." By L. Mancinelli, 1878.

"Chi mi rende i di felici." By L. Mancinelli, 1878.

"Colma, ein Gesang Ossians." By J. R. Zumsteeg, 1825.

"Da droben an jenem Berge," By C. Fink (*Fünf Lieder*, Op.

3, No. 3), 1857 ; E. H. Goer-
ner, 1864 ; A. Levinsohn (*Drei
Lieder*, Op. 1, No. 1), 1886 ;
E. Naumann (6 *Lieder*, Op. 2,
No. 2), 1866 ; W. J. Tomaschek,
1851.

"Dämm'rung senkte sich von
oben." By J. Brahms (*Lieder
und Gesänge*, Op. 59, No. 1),
1874 ; J. O. Grimm (*Sechs
Lieder*, Op. 18, No. 3), 1873.

"Darthula's Grabgesang." By
B. Hopffer, 1878.

"Der du von dem Himmel bist."
By F. E. Bache, 1859 ; H.
Bellermann (*Sechs Lieder*, Op.
10, No. 3), 1860 ; H. Goertz
(*Sechs Lieder*, Op. 19, No. 16),
1879 ; A. Von Goldschmidt,
1880 ; C. Heymann-Rheineck
(*Fünf Lieder*, Op. 4, No. 2),
1883 ; G. King (*Vier Gesänge*,
No. 3), 1886 ; H. Krigar
(*Fünf Lieder*, Op. 1, No. 2),
1860 ; B. Scholz (*Vier Gesänge*,
No. 3, 1879 : A. Winterberger
(12 *Gesänge*, Op. 12, No. 8),
1865 ; C. F. Zelter (*Zelter's
Sämmtliche Lieder*, Heft. 4),
1820.

"Du Bächlein silber-hell und
klar." By O. Sondermann,
1882.

"Durch Feld und Wald zu
schweifen." By C. F. Zelter
(*Zelter's Sämmtliche Lieder*,
Heft, 4), 1820.

"Einst ging ich meinen Mädchen
nach." By A. Von Gold-
schmidt (2 *Lieder*, No. 2), 1880.

"Die erste Walpurgisnacht." By
Mendelssohn, 1843.

"Es fürchte die Götter das
Menschengeschlecht." By F.
Hiller, 1881.

"Es ist ein Schnee gefallen."—By
G. Hasse (*Acht Gesänge*, Op.

26, No. 8), 1877 ; J. Kniese
Acht Duette, Op. 6, No. 5),
1884.

"Es klingt in den gewohnten
Ohren," 1861.

"Es war ein Kind." By R.
Schumann, 1873.

"Es war ein König in Thule."—
By E. Duerer (*Drei Lieder*, Op.
11, No. 2), 1871 ; F. H. Himmel,
1810 ; M. V. White, 1878.

"Es war ein Ratt' im Kellernest,"
1840.

"Est ist doch meine Nachbarin
ein allerliebstes Mädchen."—
By H. von Herzogenberg
(*Gesänge*, Op. 44, No. 1), 1885.

"Füllest wieder, Busch und
Thal" By A. Amadei (*Fünf
Gesänge*, Op. 8, No. 5), 1885 ;
F. Hiller (*Sechs Lieder*, Op.
204, No. 1), 1885 ; A. Hoffmann
(*Zehn Lieder*, Op. 5, No. 1),
1884 ; G. King (*Vier Gesänge*,
No. 4), 1886 ; J. Mathieux
(*Sechs Lieder*, No. 5), 1840 ; C.
Reinthaler (*Fünf Gedichte*, Op.
3, No. 3), 1860 ; L. Schlott-
mann, 1867 ; W. J. Tomas-
chek, 1851.

"Für Männer uns zu plagen." By
B. Klein (*Fünf Lieder*, Op.
46, No. 5), 1850.

"Gesäng der Parzen." By J.
Brahms, 1883.

"Gestern liebt'ich." By C. F.
Rungenhagen (*Sechs deutsche
Lieder*, No. 5), 1810.

"Gottes ist der Orient." By J.
Stern. (*Deutsche Gesänge*, etc.,
Op. 13, No. 4), 1865.

"Der Gott und die Bajadere."
By B. Klein, 1830.

"Die Grenzen der Menschheit."
By A. Wallnoefer, 1879.

"Hab'ich tausendmal ge-
schworen." By J. Brahms.

(*Lieder,* etc., .Op. 72, No. 5), 1876.

"Harzreise im Winter." By J. Brahms, 1876.

"Heart, my heart, what means this feeling?"—*New Love, New Life.* By D. Hume, 1881.

"Herz, Mein Herz, was soll das geben?" By F. Ries (*Drei Zweistimmige* Gesänge, Op. 14, No. 2), 1869; C. F. Zelter (*Zelter's Sämmtliche Lieder,* Heft 4), 1820.

"Hier sind wir versammelt" By A. Neithardt (*Sechs Lieder,* Op. 126, No. 3), 1850.

"Hoch auf dem alten Thurme steht." By E. Naumann (*Sechs Lieder,* Op. 6, No. 6), 1860; M. Renner (*Vier Gesänge,* No. 4), 1883.

"Ich bin der wohlbekannte Sänger." By E. Naumann (*Sechs Lieder,* Op. 6, No. 5), 1860; L. Schlottmann, 1880.

"Ich dacht' ich habe keinen Schmerz." By H. von Herzogenberg (*Deutte, etc.,* Op. 38, No. 2), 1883.

"Ich denke Dein." By A. G. Barham, 1874; J. Milchert (*Drei Lieder,* Op. 27, No. 1), 1855; E. Denner (*Drei Lieder,* Op. 11, No. 3), 1862; H. Fielding (*Six Songs,* No. 3), 1860; W. H. Gratton, 1847; J. Hine, 1848; T. Kirchner, 1883; E. Lassen (*Sechs Lieder,* Op. 62, No. 1), 1878; C Macleane, 1861; C. Ritter (*Zwölf Lieder,* Op. 4, No. 3), 1857; R. Schumann (4 *Duos,* etc., Op. 78, No. 3), 1869; D. F. E. Wilsing (*Fünf Lieder,* Op. 5, No. 1), 1850.

"Ich ging im Walde so für mich

hin." By J. J. Haakman (*Zwölf Lieder,* Op. 1, No. 2), 1885; F. J. von der Heijden, (*Fünf Lieder,* No. 1), 1883; T. Leschetizky (*Sechs Gesänge,* Op. 26, No. 2), 1861; A Lewinsohn (*Drei Lieder,* Op. 2, No. 1), 1886; C. F. Rungenhagen (*Sechs deutsche Lieder*), 1810.

"Ich hab'ihn gesehen." By O. Nicolai, 1835.

"Ich hab'mein Sach auf Nichts gestellt." By F. Huenten (*Sechs Lieder,* No. 6), 1840.

"Ihr verblühet süsse Rosen." By W. Fink (*Vier Lieder,* Op. 4, No. 3), 1865; H. von Herzogenberg (*Sieben Lieder,* Op. 41, No. 5), 1883; B. Hopffer (*Zwölf Lieder,* Op. 5, No. 5), 1870; L. Schlottmann, 1880.

"Im Felde schleich' ich still und wild." By L. Heritte-Viardot (*Sechs Lieder,* Op. 8, No. 2), 1884; F. H. Himmel, 1810; H. Michelis (*Sechs Lieder,* No. 3), 1880; C. Reinthaler (*Sechs Gesänge,* Op. 17, No. 5), 1866.

"In allen guten Stunden erhört." By L. van Beethoven, 1830.

"In the blush of evening mute." —*The Convent.* By R. Taylor, 1880.

"I think of thee." — *Thy name shall bloom,* By C. Guynemer, 1840; R. H. Waithman, 1870.

"Kam' der liebe Wohlbekannte." By P. Unlauf (*Fünf Lieder,* Op. 26, No. 3), 1886.

"Kannst du nicht besänftigt werden?" By F. Gladstanes, 1835.

"Kennst du das Land?"—*Mignon's Song.* By L. van Beethoven, 1843; C. Blum, 1840; E. Clare, 1845; E. Deurer (*Drei*

Lieder, Op. 11, No. 1), 1871; E. Haensler, 1810; U. K. Hartree (*Three Songs*, No. 3), 1881; Hauptmann, 1848; A. Klughardt (*Zwei Gesänge*, Op. 14, No. 1), 1870; H. Monpon, 1850; J. F. Reichardt, 1820; H. Riese, 1820; A. Romberg, 1820; F. Schubert, 1858; L. G. P. Spontini, 1830; C. F. Zelter, 1830.

"A King of ancient Thule." By W. Hay, 1875.

"Kleine Blumen, kleine Blätter." By F. Gernsheim (6 *Lieder*, Op. 29, No. 3), 1874.

"Know'st thou the land?" By Adrian, 1862; L. van Beethoven, 1856.

"Lass mein Aug 'den Abschied sagen." By F. W. Grund, 1845.

"Lasset euch im edlen Kreis." By W. Schreiber, 1820.

"Die Leidenschaft bringt Leiden." By F. Hegar (*Drei Gesänge*, Op. 10, No. 1), 1878; W. Sturm, 1883.

"Let mine eye the farewell make thee."—*The Parting.* By B. Smith, 1863.

"Liebchen, kommen diese Lieder." By H. Wichmann (10 *Liederschen*, No. 10), 1850.

"Liebliches Kind, kannst du mir sagen." By J. Brahms (*Lieder*, Op. 70, No. 3), 1876; M. Bruch, (*Lieder*, Op. 49, No. 1), 1882.

"Eine Lilie möcht'ich pflück en. By G. Gutkind, 1860.

"Meeresstille und glückliche Fahrt." By L. van Beethoven, 1820 and 1876.

"Meine Ruh'ist hin." By F. Schubert; L. Spohr (*Sechs deutsche Lieder*, No. 3), 1815; C. Weitzmann, 1835.

"Des Menschen Seele gleicht dem Wasser." By F. Hiller, 1847 and 1860; B. Klein, 1840; J. C. G. Loewe, 1850.

"Mit vollem Athemzügen sang ich Natur aus dir." By H. Verazi (*Mannheimer Monatschrift*, iii. Jahrgang) 1780.

"My rest is gone."—*Margaret's song in Faust.* By F. Steers, 1837.

"Nun verlass ich diese Hütte." By K. Danysz (*Zwei Lieder*, No. 1), 1881.

"Nur wer die Sehnsucht kennt." By L. van Beethoven, 1825 and 1835; B. Dersen (*Sechs Lieder*, Op. 2, No. 1), 1884. E. Jonas (*Zwei Lieder*, Op. 29, No. 2), 1879; W. Speier, 1835; P. Tschaikowsky, 1881; D. F. E. Wilsing (*Fünf Lieder*, Op. 5, No. 5), 1850.

"O'er the meadows." By B. Smith, 1863.

"O gieb vom weichen Pfühle." By M. Blummer (*Sechs Lieder*, Op. 10, No. 1), 1860; A. Levinsohn (*Drei Lieder*, Op. 6, No. 3), 1886; J. Mathieux (*Drei Duetten*, etc., No. 3), 1850; C. Reinecke (*Sechs Lieder*, Op. 178, No. 3); C. Reinthaler (*Fünf Gedichte*, Op. 3, No. 1), 1860; G. Rheinberger (7 *Lieder*, etc., Op. 3, No. 7), 1863.

"O' Mädchen, Mädchen." By E. Philp, 1868.

"On the brow of yonder mountain"—*The Shepherd's Lament.* By H. Smart, 1872.

"O schönes Mädchen du." By M. P. Viardot (*Vier Lieder*, No. 1), 1880.

"Quella terra conosci"—*Canzone di Mignon.* By P. M. Costa, 1881.

"Der Ruf des Herrn, des Vaters tönt." By A. Blomberg, 1875.

"Sah ein Knab' ein Röslein stehen." By A. Compton, 1874 ; M. Ernemann (*Sechs Lieder*, Op. 13, No. 4), 1850 ; N. W. Gade (*Eight duettinos*, Op. 9, No. 5), 1849 ; A. Hollaender (*Sechs Lieder*, Op. 28, No. 1), 1882 ; S. Jadassohn (*Sechs Chor Lieder*, Op. 67, No. 2), 1882 ; A. Kleffel (*Zehn Zweistimmige Lieder*, No. 6), 1875 ; J. Milder, 1830 ; R. Philipp (*Sechs Lieder*, No. 3), 1880 ; B. Ramann (*Drei Lieder*, Op. 50, No. 1), 1878 ; W. F. Scherer, 1876.

"Dem Schnee, dem Regen, dem Wind entgegen " — *Rastlose Liebe*. By B. Hopffer (*Zwölf Lieder*, Op. 9, No. 1), 1870 ; B. Klein (*Fünf Lieder*, Op. 46, No. 4), 1850 ; J. Kniese (*Acht Duette*, etc., Op. 6, No. 8), 1884 ; C. Kreutzer, 1830 ; E. Naumann (*Sechs Lieder*, Op. 6 No. 4), 1860 ; O. Nicolai, 1840 ; G. Weber (*Fünf Zweistimmige Lieder*, No. 5), 1878 ; C. F. Zelter (*Zelter's Sämmtliche Lieder*, Heft 4), 1820.

"Seht der Felsenquell freudehell." By J. C. G. Loewe, 1850.

"So hab ich wirklich dich verloren ?" By W. H. Callcott (*Vocal Gems of Germany*, vol. iii.) 1844.

"The soul of man is like the waters." By F. Schubert, 1880.

"Der Strauss den ich gepflücket." By C. J. Curschmann, 1840, 1848, 1851 ; J. J. Haakman (*Zwölf Lieder*, Op. 1, No. 4), 1885 ; A. Levinsohn (*Drei Lieder*, Op. 1, No. 2), 1886 ;

H. Wichmann (*Sechs Lieder*, Op. 3, No. 5), 1845.

"Tage der Wonne kommt ihr so bald." By L. Dahmen, 1868 ; H. von Herzogenberg, Op. 41, No. 4, 1883.

"There was a King in Thule." By F. Hueffer (*Seven Songs*, No. 7), 1873 ; S. B. Mason, 1873.

"Through the turf, through pebbles flowing." *From Faust.* J. Hine, 1857.

"Der Thürmer der schaut zu Mitten der Nacht." By W. H. Veit, 1840.

"Tiefe Stille herrscht im Wasser." By C. J. Brambach (2 *Chöre*, No. 1), 1881 ; C. Gollmick, 1840 ; M. Roeder (*Sechs Lieder*, No. 5), 1878 ; E. H. Seyffardt (*Vier Lieder*, Op. 5, No. 3), 1883.

"'Tis I am the Gipsy King." By E. Ransford, 1861 ; W. West, 1862.

"Trocknet nicht Thränen der ewige Liebe "—" Der du von dem Himmel bist "—" Ueber allen Gipfeln ist Ruh ?" By A. J. Becher (Acht Gedichte, No. 2, 4, 5), 1840.

"Trocknet nicht, trocknet nicht Thränen der ewige Liebe." By L. Hoffmann, 1840 ; S. Warteresiewicz (*Sechs Gesänge*, No. 2), 1874.

"Ueber allen Gipfeln ist Ruh." By L. Ehlert (*Fünf Lieder*, No. 5), 1860 ; A. Hollaender (*Sechs Lieder*, No. 6), 1878 ; F. Kempe (*Drei deutsche Lieder*, No. 3), 1863 ; E. Naumann (Sechsvierstimmige Lieder, Op. 7, No. 5), 1850 ; E. Naumann (*Loschwitzer Liederbuch*, No. 2), 1868 ; V.

E. Nessler (*Sechs Lieder*, Op. 76, No. 5), 1875 ; R. Radecke (*Vier Terzette*, Op. 27, No. 2), 1850 ; B. Ramann (*Dreistimmige Lieder*, Op. 58, No. 1), 1882 ; F. Ries (*Sechs Lieder*, Op. 8, No. 5), 1869 ; C. Stoer (*Lieder*, No. 10), 1883 ; D. F. E. Wilsing (*Fünf Lieder*, Op. 5, No. 3), 1850.

" Uber Thal und Fluss getragen." By A. Levinsohn (*Drei Lieder*, Op. 1, No. 3), 1886.

" Uľ'm Bergli bin i gesässe." By L. Gill (*Neun Lieder*, No. 9), 1874 ; A. Jensen (*Sechs Lieder*, Op. 57, No. 6), 1877.

" Und frische Nahrung, neues Blut." By R. Emmerich (*Sechs Gesänge*, Op. 45, No. 6), 1875 ; W. Taubert. 1882.

" Unter allen Gipfeln ist Ruh'." By F. Reichel (*Vier Terzetten*, Op. 6, No. 1), 1874.

" Up yonder on the Mountains." By C. M. Hewke, 1870.

" Ein Veilchen auf der Weise stand." By A. H. Dendy, 1856 ; J. C. W. A. Mozart, 1850 ; A. Staeger (*Sechs Lieder*, No. 4), 1884 ; D. F. E. Wilsing (*Fünf Lieder*, Op. 5, No. 4), 1850.

" Verfliesset, vielgeliebte Lieder." By B. Hopffer, (*Zwölf Lieder*, Op. 6, No. 12). 1870.

" Viele Gäste wünsch ich heut." By C. F. Zelter, 1832.

" A violet on the mead." By H. Glover, 1861.

" Von dem Berge zu den Flügeln." By C. Reinthaler (*Fünf Gedichte*, Op. 3, No. 5), 1860.

" Die Walpurgisnacht." By J. C. G. Loewe, 1830.

" Warum doch erschallen." By J. Brahms (*Quartette*, Op. 92, No. 4), 1884 : A. von Goldschmidt, 1881.

" Was hilft euch Schönheit junges Blut." By W. S. Rockstro (*Lyra Anglo-Germanica*, No. 9), 1852.

" Das Wasser rauscht." By C. F. Curschmann, 1845 ; E. Degele, 1873 ; H. W. Ernst, 1852 ; L. Steinmann, 1840 ; F. H. Fruhn, 1840.

" Wenn zu der Regenwand." By J. Brahms (*Duette*, Op. 61, No. 3), 1874.

" Wer nie sein Brod mit Thränen ass." By A. Diabelli, 1830 ; F. Vanderstucken (*Drei Gesänge*, No. 2), 1879.

" Wer reitet so spät"—*Erlkönig* By L. Berger, 1830 ; S. Mend heim, 1830 ; C. G. Reissiger, 1840 ; W. S. Rockstro (*Lyra Anglo-Germanica*, No. 16), 1853; C. H. Zoellner, 1825.

" West-oestliche Divan."—By C. Eberwein, (*Lieder*, etc.), 1836.

" Where the Rose is fresh and blooming." By H. G. Deacon, 1865.

" Who longs in solitude to live." The Harper's Song (*Wilhelm Meister*). By H. P. Greenwood, 1884.

" Wie Feld und Au." By A. von Goldschmidt (22 *Lieden*, No. 22), 1883 ; F. Hegar (*Vier Lieder*, Op. 7, No. 3), 1875.

" Wie herrlich leuchtet mir die Natur." By E. F. C. Albert (*Zehn Lieder*, Op. 3, No. 5), 1886 ; L. van Beethoven (VIII. *Lieder*, Op. 52, No. 4), 1835 ; G. Huberti, 1886 ; W. Jacoby (*Ein-und Zweistimmige Lieder*, No. 2), 1882 ; E. Lassen (*Sechs Lieder*, Op. 85, No. 6), 1886 ;

E. Naumann (*Sechs vierstimmige Lieder*, Op. 7, No. 6), 1850.
" Wie Kommt's dass du so traurig bist." By J. Brahms, (*Lieder*, Op. 48, No. 5), 1869 ; O. Tiehsen (*Sieben Gedichte*, Op. 6, No. 5), 1860 ; H. Wichmann (10, *Liederchen* No. 6), 1850.
" Wie mit innigem Behagen."— *Suleika.* By G. Meyerbeer, 1840.
" Wie stehet von schönen Blumen." By F. von Holstein (*Acht Lieder*, Op. 48, No. 1), 1882.
" Wir singen und sagen von Grafen so gern." C. Schneider, 1875.
" Zwischen Weizen und Korn." By A. Bungert, 1884 ; C. P. L. Delibes, 1883 ; B. Hopffer, (*Zwölf Lieder*, Op. 9, No. 2), 1870 ; B. Klein (*Fünf Lieder*, Op. 46, No. 1), 1850.

Magazine Articles.

Goethe, J. W. von.—Edinburgh Review, vol. 26, 1816, pp. 304-337 ; vol. 28, pp. 83-103.— North American Review, by E. Everett, vol. 4, 1817, pp. 217-262.—Blackwood's Edinburgh Magazine, vol.16, 1824, pp. 369-385 ; vol. 46, 1839, pp. 476-493, 597-613; vol. 47, 1840, pp. 31-45, 607-620 ; vol. 56, 1844, pp. 54-68, 417-432 ; vol. 57, 1845, pp. 165-180.—Westminster Review, vol. 1, 1824, pp. 370-383.—North American Review, by G. Bancroft, vol 19, 1824, pp. 303-325. —United States Literary Gazette, vol. 2, 1825, pp. 81-90. —Foreign Review, vol. 2, 1828, pp. 80-127.—Christian Examiner, by C. C. Felton, vol.

Goethe, J. W. von.
8, 1830, pp. 187-200.—Fraser's Magazine, by Thomas Carlyle, vol 5, 1832, p. 206. — Foreign Quarterly Review, by Thomas Carlyle, vol. 10, 1832, pp. 1-44 ; vol. 12, pp. 81-109 ; vol. 14, pp. 131-162 ; vol. 16, pp. 328-360. — Tait's Edinburgh Magazine, vol. 1, 1832, pp. 314-320.—Dial, by Margaret Fuller, vol. 2, 1841, pp. 1-41.—Democratic Review, vol. 10, N.S. 1842, pp. 581-594 ; vol. 19, pp. 443-446; vol. 20, pp. 14-21; vol. 24, pp. 66-69. — British and Foreign Review, vol. 14, 1843, pp. 78-135.—Southern Quarterly Review, vol. 11, 1847, p. 441, etc. —Eclectic Review, vol. 12 N.S. 1856, pp. 447-472.—Edinburgh Review, vol. 106, 1857, pp. 194-226 ; same article, Littell's Living Age, vol. 54, pp. 769-787.—Littell's Living Age, vol. 61, 1859, pp. 181-187.—Radical, by A. E. Kroeger, vol. 2, 1867, pp. 273, etc., 332, etc.—Blackwood's Edinburgh Magazine, vol. 112, 1872, pp. 675-697 ; same article, Littell's Living Age, vol. 116, pp. 3-19 ; and Eclectic Magazine, vol. 17 N.S., pp. 172-188.—Every Saturday, vol. 1, 1872, p. 1, etc.—Le Correspondant, by Léo Quesnel, tom. 109, 1877, pp. 492-520.— Contemporary Review, by Prof. J. R. Seeley, vol. 46, 1884, pp. 161-177, 488-506, 653-672.— Catholic World, by Rev. J. Gmeiner, vol. 45, 1887, pp. 145-151.
——*and Bettina.* National Quarterly Review, by C. White, vol. 41, 1879, p. 74, etc.
—— ——*Few Words for Bettina.*

Goethe, J. W. von.

Blackwood's Edinburgh Magazine, vol. 58, 1845, pp. 357-365.

——*and Carlyle.* Contemporary Review, by Prof. Max Müller, vol. 49, 1886, pp. 772-793.— Atlantic Monthly, June, 1887, pp. 849-852.

——*and Dumas.* Nation, by H. James, Jun., vol. 17, 1873, pp. 292-294.

——*and Eckermann.* Dublin University Magazine, vol. 37, 1851, pp. 732-749.—Canadian Monthly, by A. M. Machar, vol. 3, 1879, pp. 230-241 and 386-395.

——*and Frederika Brion.* Once a Week, vol. 11, 1864, pp. 358-364.

——*and the Germans.* Blackwood's Edinburgh Magazine, vol. 45, 1839, pp. 247-256.

——*and German Fiction.* Journal of Speculative Philosophy, by F. G. Fairfield, vol. 9, 1875, pp. 303-311.

——*and the Grand Duke of Weimar.* Revue Contemporaine, by A. Buchner, tom. 41, 1864, pp. 699-734.

——*and his Contemporaries.* Westminster Review, vol. 24, 1836, pp. 197-231.—Dublin University Magazine, vol. 8, 1836, pp. 350-366.

——*and his Critics.* Fraser's Magazine, vol. 36, 1847, pp. 481-493.

——*and his Works.* Monthly Repository, by H. Crabb Robinson, vol. 6, N.S., 1832, pp. 289-308, 361-371, 460-469, 505-520, 595-603, 681-689, 742-756.

——*and Mendelssohn.* Bentley's Miscellany, vol. 49, 1861, pp.

Goethe, J. W. von.

68-71.—Every Saturday, vol. 9, 1870, p. 247, etc.; vol. 17, 1874, p. 365, etc.—Temple Bar, vol. 42, 1874, pp. 165-176.

——*and Mill; a Contrast.* Westminster Review, vol. 46, N.S., 1874, pp. 38-70.

——*and Minna Herzlieb.* Contemporary Review, by A. Hamilton, vol. 27, 1876, pp. 199-221; same article, Littell's Living Age, vol. 128, pp. 554-567.

——*and Music.* Le Correspondant, by C. Pautrier, tom. 122, 1881, pp. 1117-1129.

——*and Religion.* Theological Review, by J. F. Smith, vol. 6, 1869, pp. 76-98.

——*and Schiller, Characteristics of.* Dublin University Magazine, vol. 87, 1876, pp. 684-688.

—— ——*Dwight's Versions from Goethe and Schiller.* North American Review, by G. S. Hillard, vol. 48, 1839, pp. 505-514.—Christian Examiner, by G. Bancroft, vol. 26, 1839, pp. 360-378.—Boston Quarterly Review, vol. 2, 1839, pp. 187-205.

—— ——*Friendship of Goethe and Schiller.* New Englander, by W. H. Wynn, vol. 32, 1873, pp. 718-737.

—— ——*Weimar under Schiller and Goethe.* Contemporary Review, by H. Schütz Wilson, vol. 29, 1877, pp. 271-288; same article, Littell's Living Age, vol. 132, pp. 550-560.

——*and Shakespeare.* British Quarterly Review, by David Masson, vol. 16, 1852, pp. 512-543; same article, Littell's

Goethe, J. W. von.
Living Age, vol. 36, pp. 605-617.
—— ——*Female Characters of Goethe and Shakespeare.* North British Review, vol. 8, 1848, pp. 265-296 ; same article, Eclectic Magazine, vol. 14, pp. 1-18.
——*and Suleika.* Western, by L. F. Soldau, vol. 1, 1875, pp. 621-626.
——*and Washington.* Christian Examiner, by C. A. Bartol, vol. 60, 1856, pp. 317-326.
——*and Werther.* Littell's Living Age, vol. 43, 1854, pp. 334-336. — National Review, vol. 1, 1855, pp. 197-209.— Revue Contemporaine, by A. Baschet, tom. 16, 1854, pp. 441-464.—Revue Contemporaine, by Sainte-Beuve, tom. 20, 1855, pp. 148-165.
—— *Aphorisms of.* American Monthly Magazine, vol. 1, N.S., 1836, pp. 448-452.
——*as a Man of Science.* Westminster Review, by G. H. Lewes, vol. 2, N.S., 1852, pp. 479-506 ; same article, Eclectic Magazine, vol. 27, pp. 460-475.
——*as a Naturalist.* Revue Contemporaine, by Ernest Faivre, tom. 4, 1858, pp. 837-856 ; tom. 5, pp. 326-343, 681-698 ; vol. 7, pp. 39-68 ; vol. 8, pp. 263-278 ; vol. 9, pp. 464-480.—La Critique Française, by M. Hemerdinger, 1862, pp. 125-131.
—— *Autobiographical Sketches.* London Magazine, vol. 7, 1823, pp. 68-73.
——*Character and Moral Influence of.* Edinburgh Review, vol. 106, 1857, pp. 194-226.
——*Characteristics of.* National

Goethe, J. W. von.
Review, vol. 2, 1856, pp. 241-296 ; same article, Littell's Living Age, vol. 50, pp. 1-31.
—— ——*Mrs. Austin's Characteristics of.* Edinburgh Review, vol. 57, 1833, pp. 371-403.— Monthly Review, vol. 2, N.S., 1833, pp. 307-317.—Littell's Museum of Foreign Literature, vol. 23, p. 500, etc.
——*Carus on.* Foreign Quarterly Review, vol. 32, 1844, pp. 182-189.
——*Conversations of.* New Monthly Magazine, vol. 91, 1851, pp. 256-259.
——*Conversations with.* Foreign Quarterly Review, vol. 18, 1837, pp. 1-30. — Boston Quarterly Review, vol. 3, 1840, pp. 20-57. —Westminster Review, vol. 50, 1849, pp. 555-568 ; same article, Eclectic Magazine, vol. 16, pp. 460-468. — Dublin University Magazine, vol. 37, 1851, pp. 732-749.
——*Cornelia, the Sister of.* Victoria Magazine, by P. P. André, vol. 6, 1866, pp. 97-105.
——*Correspondence with a Child.* Monthly Review, vol. 3, N.S., 1837, pp. 386-392.—Dial, vol. 2, 1842, pp. 313-356.—Tait's Edinburgh Magazine, vol. 9, N.S., 1842, pp. 157-167.
——*Correspondence with the Duke of Saxe Weimar.* National Review, vol. 18, 1864, pp. 1-19.
——*Das Märchen* (from *The German Emigrants*). Journal of Speculative Philosophy, by Gertrude Garrigues, Oct. 1883, pp. 383-400.
——*Death of.* New Monthly Magazine, vol. 34, 1832, pp. 508-512.

Goethe, J. W. von.

—— —*Poem on Death of.* Dublin University Magazine, by T. Irwin, vol. 50, 1857, pp. 333-337.

——*Edinburgh Review on.* Blackwood's Edinburgh Magazine, vol. 4, 1818, pp. 211-213.

——*Egmont.* American Review, by D. P. Noyes, vol. 1, 1845, pp. 183-194.

——*Elective Affinities.* American Review, vol. 3, 1812, pp. 51-69.

——*Falk's Character of.* New Monthly Magazine, vol. 38, 1833, pp. 302-304.

——*Faust.* London Magazine, vol. 2, 1820, pp. 125-142.—Blackwood's Edinburgh Magazine, by R. P. Gillies, vol. 7, 1820, pp. 236-258.—New Edinburgh Review, by Thomas Carlyle, vol. 2, 1822, pp. 316-334.—Quarterly Review, vol. 34, 1826, pp. 136-153.—Dublin University Magazine, vol. 2, 1833, pp. 361-385. — Westminster Review, vol. 25, 1836, pp. 366-390.—Foreign Quarterly Review, vol. 25, 1840, pp. 90-113. — Dublin University Magazine, vol. 64, 1864, pp. 537-542 ; same article, Eclectic Magazine, vol. 1, N.S., pp. 97-102.—Baptist Quarterly, by J. L. Lincoln, vol. 3, 1869, pp. 278-309.—Old and New, vol. 4, 1871, pp. 471-480.—Journal of Speculative Philosophy, by Anna C. Brackett (from the German of Rosenkranz), vol. 9, 1875, pp. 48-61, 225-239, 401-406. — Canadian Monthly, vol. 9, 1876, pp. 123-129.

—— *And Marlowe's Faust.* Contemporary Review, by Chas. Grant, vol. 40, 1881, pp. 1-24.

Goethe, J. W. von.

—— —*Anster's Translation of Faust.* Edinburgh Review, vol. 62, 1835, pp. 36-45.—Dublin University Magazine, vol. 6, 1835, pp. 96-118.

—— —*Blackie's Translation of Faust.* St. James's Magazine, vol. 9, 4th Series, 1881, pp. 98-103.

—— —*Blackie and Syme's Translations of Faust.* Fraser's Magazine, vol. 10, 1834, pp. 88-96.

—— —*Brooks's Translation of Faust.* New Englander, by Mrs. C. R. Corson, vol. 22, 1863, pp. 1-21.—Christian Examiner, by F. H. Hedge, vol. 63, 1857, pp. 1-18.

—— —*Decline and Fall of Dr. Faustus.* Contemporary Review, by Elizabeth R. Pennell, vol. 51, 1887, pp. 394-407.

—— —*English Translations of Faust.* Cornhill Magazine, vol. 26, 1872, pp. 279-294.— Littell's Living Age, vol. 115, 1872, pp. 412-421.

—— —*Facts and Fancies about Faust.* Modern Review, by H. S. Wilson, vol. 1, 1880, pp. 771-791 ; vol. 2, pp. 148-171.

—— —*Faust and the Devil.* Fraser's Magazine, vol. 23, 1841, pp. 269-283, 464-477.

—— —*Faust and its English Critics.* London Quarterly Review, vol. 55, 1880, pp. 118-148.

—— —*Faust and Margaret.* Journal of Speculative Philosophy, by Anna C. Brackett (from the German of K. Rosenkranz) vol. 10, 1876, pp. 37-43.

—— —*Faust and Minor Poems.* Dublin University Magazine, vol. 7, 1836, pp. 278-302.

Goethe, J. W. von.

—— ——*Faust for English Readers.* St. Paul's Magazine, by E. J. Hasell, vol. 11, 1872, pp. 694-714 ; vol. 12, pp. 403-429.

—— ——*Faust in the German Puppet Shows.* Fraser's Magazine, vol. 37, 1848, pp. 32-40.

—— ——*Faust set to Music.* All the Year Round, vol. 9, 1863, pp. 439-443. — Contemporary Review, by Frank Sewall, vol. 52, 1887, pp. 370-380.

—— ——*Gower's Faust.* London Magazine, vol. 6, N.S., 1826, pp. 164-173.

—— ——*Hayward's Translation of Faust.* Fraser's Magazine, vol. 7, 1833, pp. 532-554.— Edinburgh Review, vol. 57, 1833, pp. 137-143.

—— ——*Klingemann's Faust.* Blackwood's Edinburgh Magazine, by R. P. Gillies, vol. 13, 1823, pp. 649-660.

—— ——*Letters on Faust.* Journal of Speculative Philosophy, by H. C. Brockmeyer, vol. 1, 1867, pp. 178-187 ; vol 2, pp. 114-120.

—— ——*Martin's Translation of Faust.* North British Review, vol. 44, 1866, pp. 95-123.

—— ——*Poetical Translations of Faust.* Blackwood's Edinburgh Magazine, vol. 47, 1840, pp. 223-240.

—— ——*Sacred Poetry of Faust.* Dublin Review, vol. 9, 1840, pp. 477-506.

—— ——*Second Part of Faust.* Dublin University Magazine, vol. 2, 1833, pp. 361-385 ; vol. 64, 1864, pp. 537-542.—Foreign Quarterly Review, vol. 12, 1833, pp. 81-109.—Fraser's Magazine, vol. 68, 1863, pp. 497-512.— Journal of Speculative Philo-

Goethe, J. W. von.

sophy, by K. Rosenkrantz, vol. 1, 1867, pp. 65-79 ; vol. 11, pp. 113-122. — Lippincott's Magazine, by W. H. Goodyear, vol. 19, 1877, pp. 223-229.—Westminster Review, vol. 69, N.S., 1886, pp. 313-354.

—— ——*Taylor's Translation of Faust.* Nation, by J. R. Dennett, vol. 12, 1871, pp. 201-203. —Broadway, vol. 4, 3rd Series, 1872, pp. 159-166.

—— ——*Translations of Faust.* Westminster Review, vol. 25, 1863, pp. 366-390.

——*Female Characters of.* North British Review, vol. 8, 1848, pp. 265-296.

——*French Critic on (Scherer.)* Quarterly Review, by M. Arnold, vol. 145, 1878, pp. 143-163 ; same article, Littell's Living Age, vol. 136, pp. 451-461.

——*Funeral of; a Poem translated from the German of Harring.* Democratic Review, by A. H. Everett, vol. 2, 1842, pp. 471-474.

——*Genius and Influence of.* Edinburgh Review, by H. Merivale, vol. 92, 1850, pp. 188-220 ; same article, Eclectic Magazine, vol. 21, 1856, pp. 98-115, and Littell's Living Age, vol. 26, pp. 365-379.

——*Genius, Theories, and Works.* Dublin University Magazine, vol. 60, 1862, pp. 671-681 ; same article, Eclectic Magazine, vol. 58, 1863, pp. 295-304.

——*Goetz von Berlichingen.* Blackwood's Edinburgh Magazine, vol. 16, 1824, pp. 369-385.

——*Gossip about, in Frankfort.* Littell's Living Age (from the Spectator), vol. 143, 1879, pp.

Goethe, J. W. von.

  vol. 56, 1844, pp 54-68, 417-432.—Fraser's Magazine, by A. H. Clough, vol. 59, 1859, pp. 710-717 ; same article, Eclectic Magazine, vol. 49, 1860, pp. 53-59.—Bentley's Miscellany, vol. 45, 1859, pp. 401-405.—London Magazine, vol. 12, 1859, pp. 121-145.—Littell's Living Age, vol. 61, 1859, pp.181-187.

——*Posthumous Works.* Dublin University Magazine, vol. 2, 1833, pp. 361-385.

——*Prometheus.* Dublin University Magazine, vol. 36, 1850, pp. 520-530.

——*Recent Works on.* Nation, by T. W. Higginson, vol. 32, 1881, pp. 408-410.

——*Relation of, to Christianity.* National Magazine, vol. 1, p. 468, etc.

——*Religion of.* Macmillan's Magazine, by A. Schwartz, vol. 29, 1873, pp. 128-137.

——*Scherer on.* Quarterly Review, by Matthew Arnold, vol. 145, 1878, pp. 143-163 ; reprinted in *Mixed Essays*, 1879.

——*Scientific Biography of (Faivre's).* North British Review, by Sir D. Brewster, vol. 38, 1863, pp. 107-133.

——*Social Romances.* Journal of Speculative Philosophy, by C. Rosenkrantz, vol. 2, 1868, pp. 120-128, 215-225 ; vol. 4. pp. 145-152, 268-273.

——*Sorrows of Werter.* Western, vol. 5 N.S., 1879, pp. 345-352.

—— ——*French Criticism on the Sorrows of Werter.* London Magazine, vol. 1, 1820, pp. 49-52.

—— ——*Originals of Werther.* Temple Bar, by C. E. Meetkerke,

Goethe, J. W. von.

  vol. 47, 1876, pp. 244-250 ; same article, Littell's Living Age, vol. 130, pp. 172-176.

——*Story of the Snake.* Journal of Speculative Philosophy, by Anna C. Brackett (from the German of C. Rosenkrantz), vol. 5, 1871, pp. 219-226.

——*The Tale; translated.* Fraser's Magazine, by Thomas Carlyle, vol. 6, 1832, pp. 257-278.

——*Torquato Tasso.* Monthly Review, vol. 6, N.S., 1827, pp. 182-197. — Fraser's Magazine, vol. 13, 1836, pp. 526-539.—Blackwood's Edinburgh Magazine, vol. 58, 1845, pp. 87-95. —Chambers's Edinburgh Journal, vol. 16, 1852, pp. 87, 88.

—— ——*Scenes and Passages from the Tasso.* New Monthly Magazine, vol. 40, 1834, pp. 1-8.

——*Theory of Colours.* Quarterly Review, vol. 10, 1814, pp. 427-441.— Edinburgh Review, vol. 72, 1840, pp. 99-131. — Fortnightly Review, by John Tyndall, vol. 27, N.S., 1880, pp. 471-490; the same appeared also in the Popular Science Monthly, vol. 17, 1880, pp. 215-224, 312-321.

——*Visit to, in Weimar.* Hours at Home, vol. 1, 1865, pp. 145-151.

——*Visit to the Home of.* New Monthly Magazine, vol. 104, 1855, pp. 203-206 ; same article, Littell's Living Age, vol. 46, pp. 39-41.

——*Weimar under Schiller and Goethe.* Contemporary Review, by H. S. Wilson, vol. 29, 1877, pp. 271-288.

——*West-Eastern Divan.* Black-

Goethe, J. W. von.
wood's Edinburgh Magazine,
vol 132, pp. 742-756.
——*Wilhelm Meister.* Blackwood's Edinburgh Magazine,
vol. 15, 1824, pp. 619-632.—
London Magazine, vol. 10, 1824,
pp. 189-197, 291-307.—Edinburgh Review, by F. Jeffrey,
vol. 42, 1825, pp. 409-449.—
Southern Review, vol. 3, 1829,
pp. 353-385.—Southern Literary
Messenger, vol. 17, 1851, pp.
431-443. — North American
Review, by Henry James, Jun.,
vol. 101, 1865, pp. 281-285.—
Atlantic Monthly, by D. A.
Wasson, vol. 16, 1865, pp. 273-
282, 448-457.

Goethe, J. W. von.
——*Wisdom of.* Temple Bar, vol.
70, 1884, pp. 262-272.
——*Words of Wisdom from.*
Blackwood's Edinburgh Maga-
zine, vol. 130, 1881, pp. 785-792.
——*Works.* Le Correspondant,
by V. de Laprade, tom. 71,
1867, pp. 122-140.
——*Works of, explained by his
Life.* Le Correspondant, by A.
Mézières, tom. 81, 1870, pp.
629-653; 1011-1040; tom. 82,
pp. 599-626; tom. 83, pp. 35-62.
——*Youth of.* Sharpe's London
Magazine, vol. 8, 1849, pp. 155-
162, 237-240.—Western, by
Ellen M. Mitchell, vol. 2, 1876,
pp. 347-352.

X. CHRONOLOGICAL LIST OF WORKS.

Winkelmann und sein Jahr-
hundert . . . 1805
Faust [Theil I.] . . 1808
Die Wahlverwandtschaften 1809
Pandora 1810
Zur Farbenlehre . . 1810
Aus meinem Leben, Dicht-
ung und Wahrheit 1811-22
Philipp Hackert. Bio-
graphische Skizze . 1811
Gedichte 1812
Willkommen ! . . . 1814
Des Epimenides Erwachen 1815
Italiänische Reise (Aus
meinem Leben) . 1816-17
Ueber Kunst und Alter-
thum . . . 1816-32
Zur Natur - Wissenschaft
überhaupt, besonders
zur Morphologie . 1817-23
West-Oestlicher Divan . 1819
Wilhelm Meisters Wander-
jahre, Th. 1 . . 1821
(Completed and published in 1830.)
Die Campagne in Frank-
reich. (Aus meinem
Leben.) . . 1822
Wilhelm Meisters Wander-
jahre 1830
(Vol. 1 originally appeared
in 1821.)

Faust [Theil II.] . . 1833
Das Tagebuch, 1810 . . 1879

Briefwechsel zwischen
Schiller und Goethe 1828-9
Kurzer Briefwechsel zwisch-
en Klopstock und
Goethe . . . 1833
Briefe von Goethe an Lavater 1833
Briefwechsel zwischen
Goethe und Zelter . 1833-4
Briefwechsel mit einem
Kinde . . . 1835
Briefwechsel zwischen
Goethe und Schultz . 1836

Goethe's Briefe in den Jahren
1768-1832 . . . 1837
Briefe an die Gräfin Auguste
zu Stolberg. . . 1839
Briefe Schillers und Goethes
an A. W. Schlegel . 1846
Briefe von Goethe und dessen
Mutter an Friedrich
Freiherrn von Stein . 1846
Briefe von Goethe, 1766-
1786 1846
Briefwechsel zwischen
Goethe und F. H.
Jacob. . . . 1846
Goethes Briefe an Leipziger
Freunde . . . 1849
Briefwechsel zwischen
Goethe und Reinhard . 1850
Briefwechsel zwischen
Goethe und Knebel . 1851
Briefwechsel zwischen
Goethe und Grüner . 1853
Briefe des Grossherzogs
Carl August und
Goethe an Döbereiner. 1856
Briefe an Herder . . 1856
Briefe von Goethe und
seiner Frau an N. Meyer 1856
Briefwechsel des Grossher-
zogs Carl August von
Sachsen - Weimar-
Eisenbach mit Goethe 1863
Briefwechsel zwischen
Goethe und Kasper
Graf von Sternberg . 1866
Briefe an F. A. Wolf . 1868
Briefe an C. G. von Voigt 1868
Briefe an Eichstädt . . 1872
Briefe an Johanna Fahlmer 1875
Briefe an Soret . . . 1877
Briefwechsel zwischen
Goethe und Marianne
von Willemer (Suleika) 1877
Briefwechsel zwischen
Goethe und K. Göttling 1880
Correspondence between
Goethe and Carlyle . 1887